FABRICE SAMYN

TO SEE WITH ELLIPSE

HATJE CANTZ

PREFACE

The Royal Museums of Fine Arts of Belgium are very pleased to host this wide-ranging exhibition devoted to the multidisciplinary artist Fabrice Samyn. This event is part of an ongoing program aiming to promote modern Belgian and international culture by establishing a dialogue between contemporary creation, the Old Masters collection, and the Magritte Museum. In doing so, the institution wants to allow the widest possible public to become acquainted with contemporary art in order to show how it can encourage a fresh understanding of works from the past, but also to underline how contemporary artists are today still fascinated by them.

Fabrice Samyn's approach is very much part of this process: firmly embedded in the present, it encourages a rereading and a reinterpretation of art from the past. His work, however, is in no way dated or backward looking, and the artist approaches his different subjects from a resolutely modern perspective, drawing on a wide-ranging repertoire of styles and techniques. The sculptures, paintings, and installations that are interspersed throughout the rooms of the Old Masters Museum, encourage us to look at the works of Memling, Cranach, Jordaens, and Rubens, among others, in a brand-new way.

Many other aspects of Fabrice Samyn's work resonate with the collection from the Royal Museums of Fine Arts of Belgium. For example, the artist draws particular attention to the visual qualities of language, which naturally steers him in the direction of René Magritte. Many works on display at the Magritte Museum are evidence of the continuing influence of the master from Lessines on contemporary creativity.

We would like to warmly thank the many people who, in agreeing to lend works, have made this exhibition possible, and thanks to whom the public will be able to discover a complete overview of Fabrice Samyn's work. Our sincere appreciation also goes to the Wallonia-Brussels Federation for their significant support, without which this exhibition would not have been possible. Finally, the Royal Museums, together with the artist, dedicate this exhibition to the memory of Cédric Liénart, along with his wife Cookie, who together had the original idea for this project.

Michel Draguet
General Director of the RMFAB

THE GAZE OF THAUMAS

Donatien Grau

In a famous phrase from the late dialogue *Theaetetus*, Plato writes: "Philosophy is the child of Thaumas." That is, philosophy is the child of wonder.

It seems the same holds true for modern and contemporary art, even if it would be too long a history to retrace here. This heritage is undoubtedly what Diaghilev consciously or unconsciously had in mind when he demanded of Cocteau, "Astonish me." The principal consequence of this tradition is that, in the critical perspective that has emerged over the past two hundred years—and particularly over the past one hundred years, the past seventy years, and the past twenty years—artistic experience must be born of or follow from a state of "wonder." This wonder may be that of the artist, constantly astonished by the world; but it may also be that of the viewers, the "gazers," who might well not understand what is happening here. Fabrice Samyn's work is like an emblem of these questionings. It disconcerts us: Fabrice Samyn is a painter, and a talented one. But to be a painter is not enough for him. He also makes videos, sculptures, and carries on with the tradition of "appropriation" from the late 1970s; he also writes, albeit in secret. He never stops thwarting categorizations: as soon as one thinks one likes his art for something, it undergoes a metamorphosis, and the thing that one liked in it no longer seems to be there.

Further, he does not limit himself to a perpetual mutation of forms: he seems to confront themes—or rather, to use a Cézannian term, "motifs"—that do not immediately appear bound to each other by direct chains of meaning. At first glance, it is not obvious to see the "thematic" community of a tree, a neighbor, and the Bible. One almost gets the feeling of a shattered oeuvre that refuses to be reassembled—and that even forges a principle out of this refusal to be reassembled. As the artist says, his position has been "shattered in the will to crack Narcissus' mind-mirror and cause the river current to scintillate. What lies beyond the mirror? The river of time. And what lies at the heart of the river of time? The freshness of the instant."

His fundamental wish is to be free. He rejects categorizations and, like his predecessors from the 1970s, he rejects the brilliance of his technique to seek out other paths. Baudelaire once sought to add the right to leave to the list of human rights. For Samyn's aesthetics are also a politics: a rejection of any fixed identity whatsoever—whether of species, sex, race, society, or creative discipline—all while taking stock of the positionings that any identity imposes. For after all, the figure of the artist is no less to Samyn than what the whore was to Pierre Guyotat: an ambiguous, hybrid being where the theater of life, still human, deploys its figures upon the stage.

One feels a tension here, a progression. Samyn has integrated within himself all languages. First of all, he seized hold of painting, which he practices with true virtuosity. He might have stopped at that and continued to live solely as a painter, in the

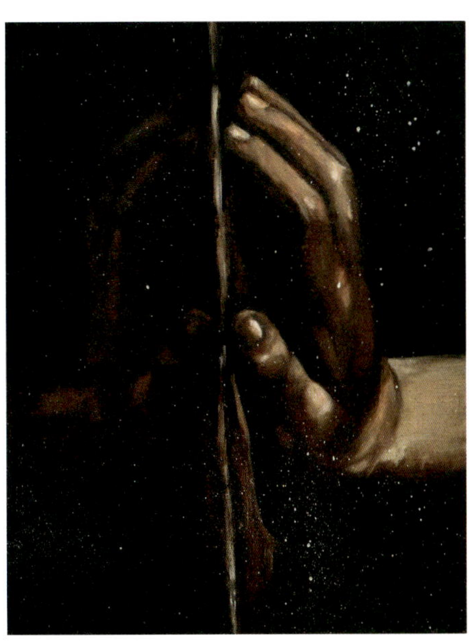

 Narcissus? (2010), oil on canvas, 30 × 24 cm, private collection

sensuous experience of his relationship to pictorial
matter. And indeed, he has never detached himself
from it: in his painted works, one still feels the
carnal relation that a painter has with the canvas,
with colors, with people. The colors are vivid,
strong. One thinks of flaming reds and trembling
blues, but also shades of ocher, violet: a vivid and
violent palette. Painting is a world unto itself where,
if one accepts the frame, it is possible to assert a
supreme liberty, dancing in chains. But Samyn does
not accept the frame. He does not accept to have
the reality of his work manifested in a window.
Art is not the contemplation of a floating world.
It is a wrestling with what is.

This is painting, but not only painting. For history is also present in this body of work so precisely
anchored in the present: the works are in dialogue
with many themes at the heart of contemporary
thought and creation; the lives of plants are in
Samyn's work. A key to this work might lie in the
group of "de-painted" paintings he has made over
the past several years: he acquires from antique
dealers old paintings whose varnish has often
obscured the image, and he withdraws the varnish
from the canvas to make another painting appear
[fig. 2]. The withdrawal of the varnish is conjoined
with the laying on of a new image. It is a painting
made without paint, an image born not by adding,
but rather by digging into material—a reality that
goes beyond the tensions between mimicry, work,
and light. And so it is also a sculpture.

Such a method is eloquent to an understanding
of Samyn's work: he plays material against itself,
with itself, for itself. His talent rests in the coincidence of these three actions. One might object
that, after all, to accept contradiction and even turn
it into a resource, a principle, is an act common to
many modern and contemporary painters. Samyn's
action is to push the acceptance of contradiction
wide open—toward what he calls "the twilight
of solipsism." One recalls the words of Conrad

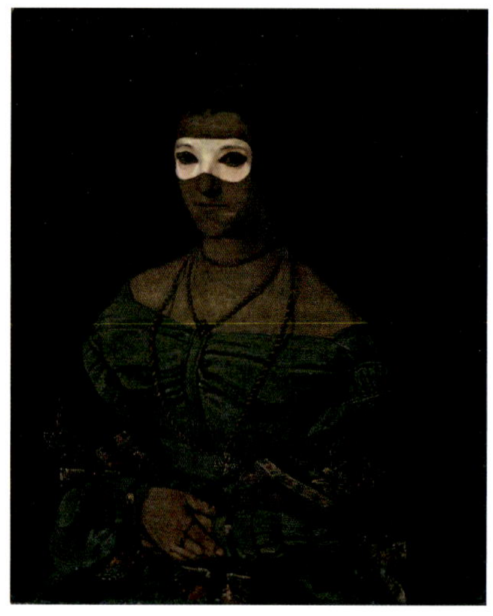

FIG. 2 *Pupil's Mask* (ca. 1850–2013),
locally devarnished antique painting,
48 × 39.5 cm, private collection

Ferdinand Meyer: "I am not an ingeniously contrived
book, I am a man with his contradictions."[1] These
words find company with those of Walt Whitman:
"Do I contradict myself? . . . I am large, I contain
multitudes."[2] In an archetypal way, Samyn's work
ties these two approaches together: he is "a man
with his contradictions," and his oeuvre is an oeuvre
with its own contradictions. But these contradictions are not merely unresolved dynamics; they are
also sources of strength. And here another key to
understanding his work emerges: while the work
sometimes feels like a landscape that one might
map—this practice here, that practice there—it is
more truly a battlefield of creation, of thought, of
life in tension. All things affront each other, confront
each other, and the works are born out of their own
impossibility and out of the question—almost in the
old sense of torture—of how to create within a life.

Samyn's twofold presence at the Royal
Museums of Fine Arts of Belgium raises a similar
issue, in hyperbolic form. He is present both in the
Oldmasters Museum, with collections from the early
Flemish masters to Rubens, and in the Magritte

Museum. If one excludes the Fin-de-Siècle Museum from the museological construction that composes the Royal Museums of Fine Arts, one realizes that the institution itself is founded upon an internal contradiction, as it weaves connections between two entities that apparently stand in opposition to each other. The Oldmasters Museum is dedicated to a historical, intellectual, and creative period when the painted image was the be-all and end-all of the oeuvre. Everything began from it; everything ended with it. The perfect image—though varying from period to period—was the painter's goal that allowed the work to enter another dimension, another stratum of reality: the sacred. Conversely, Magritte, author of *The Treachery of Images*, demonstrated—along with De Chirico and Picabia— that a work can only exist as a visual pun, and that pictorial perfection is a mere illusion. Magritte's work does not appeal to a higher meaning; rather, it affirms the foreclosure of meaning. These things are known: Magritte is the child of Platonism and advertising, two approaches to the world that are presumably contradictory, but that he managed to hold together. The cave was not an end: to live in the cave, among shadows, did not have to be a manifestation of the end of the world of belief. On the contrary, it could be an opening onto multiplicity, where forms and ideas in permanent tension do not resolve themselves, but instead cause existence to open itself to the world.

Samyn stands on both sides, and his oeuvre is the exact mirror of this association between the "fine arts" and Magritte. From the fine arts, Samyn inherited his regard for meticulous work, for toil, his taste for images that arise manifest, by deduction, and therefore open the way toward an existence that is ampler, stronger than the one religion allowed. From Magritte, he acquired the awareness of another history, a poetry that lies beyond letters and affixes a question mark to the matter of meaning. Meaning is no longer a given; it must be constructed, regained, and this construction might never come to an end, might even prove impossible. And yet we must go on. This is Fabrice Samyn's aspiration. It manifests itself in distinct and complementary ways in the project's two parts: at the Magritte Museum one finds a multitude of mediums, of works that one might qualify as more "conceptual" (some, like *Please Respect What Breaks When Spoken* [fig. 3] are in direct conversation with the 1970s avant-gardes). At the Oldmasters Museum one finds timeless questionings and a strong presence of painting: but these opposite shores are linked by bridges, notably the paintings with Magrittian titles (*The Mask of Your Image* [p. 77]).

FIG. 3 *Please Respect What Breaks When Spoken* (2013), marble, 20 × 44 × 2 cm, private collection

The work that first welcomes the visitor, in the Bernheim room, is *The Fallen Tree of Knowledge* [fig. 4 and pp. 44–45]. This is nearly a manifesto of the artist's position—a little like the Hegelian thematization of the death of art: the tree of knowledge has fallen, but it is still there. The biblical theme evokes multiple inquires: Did the tree fall on its own? Or by fact of lightning—weather conditions, divine intervention? Or was it chopped down? And in that case, by whom? This state of indeterminacy as to human or natural responsibility is symptomatic of Samyn's work. In any event, the tree of knowledge has fallen. And by the fact of falling, it has become a work of art. This mutation—from knowledge to art—is complicated by the problem of *qualunque*, the Italian term made famous by Giorgio Agamben as a summing up of his concept of "the coming community." *Qualunque* is the smallest common denominator of a shared identity; it is the commonplace made visible. The tree has been named *The Fallen Tree of Knowledge*—one might think of Thierry de Duve's reading of the naming of things in Duchamp[3]—and from a certain perspective this causes it to become what it has been named. It is the fallen tree of knowledge—or the tree of fallen knowledge, which itself evokes vast questions as to whether this tree is the tree of

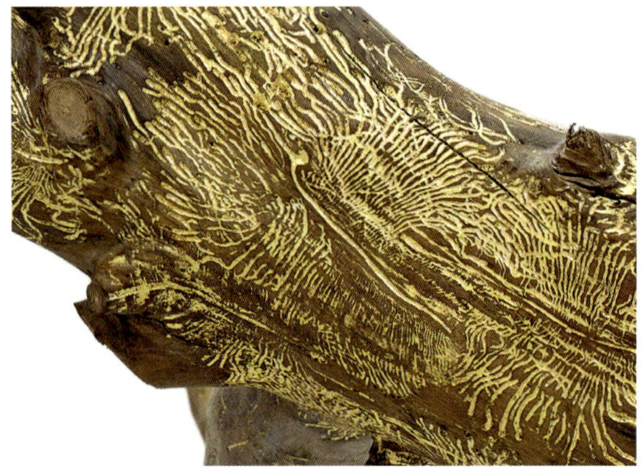

FIG. 4 *The Fallen Tree of Knowledge* (2020), wood and gold leaf, 480 × 287 × 232 cm, detail

knowledge that has fallen, or a fallen tree that has to do with knowledge. In sum: To what extent does this work invoke biblical precedents? It does so in an evident way, but the meaning remains open.

This tree of knowledge has another thing: gold. In taking up this fallen tree—which raises a further question, about the ethical and moral significance of the Fall—Samyn has gilded the vermiculation left by bark beetles, commonly known as "bookworms." It is as if the structure of the tree, the place where the worms have caused it to fall, the place where it is broken—the "cracks" as Leonard Cohen would have put it—are exactly the site where gold is necessary, is right: and this gold comes from recycled computer chips, themselves sourced from the Belgian mining union that was implicated in the colonization of the Congo. Gold is not simply an insertion of value here—gold in a tree whose value is nil, except perhaps as cords of firewood—it is also a collusion between temporalities: the time of politics, of the digital noosphere, the time of this tree that has died but might still remain a long while here before us, together with gold that has the power to open time. That was its property in alchemy. It is as if, through the time of the gold insertion—a long, measurable time—Samyn has yoked together two contradictory temporalities: the finite temporality of the dead tree, still physi-cally present, and the infinite temporality of belief, of gold. We might recall the phrase André Breton dictated to be inscribed on his tombstone: "I seek the gold of time." The question of time appears incessantly in the work of Samyn, who is the author of a *Portrait of Time* [fig. 5] and a portrait entitled *Timelessness* [p. 21], to name only two. Not to mention the works of erasure and rewriting, whose very material is time.

The Surrealists liked stones, flowers, trees—things in which they found an opening of forms as they faced an aesthetic, political, and sensuous closure in the human world. Georges Bataille and

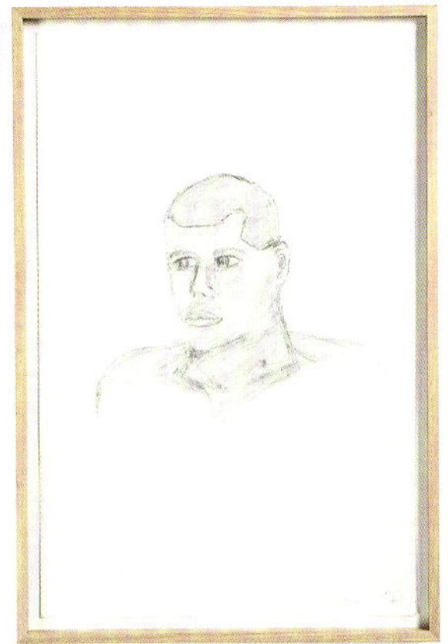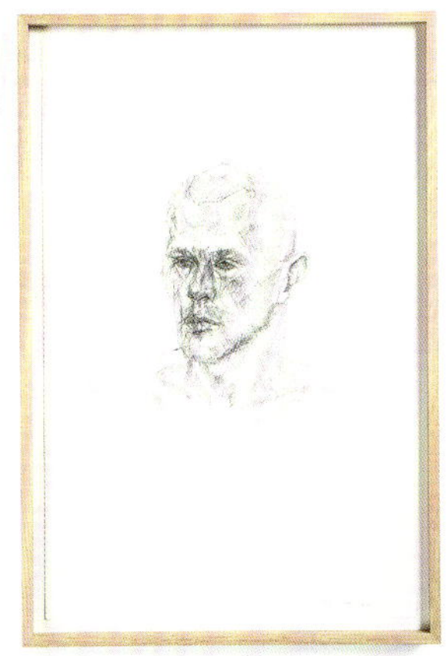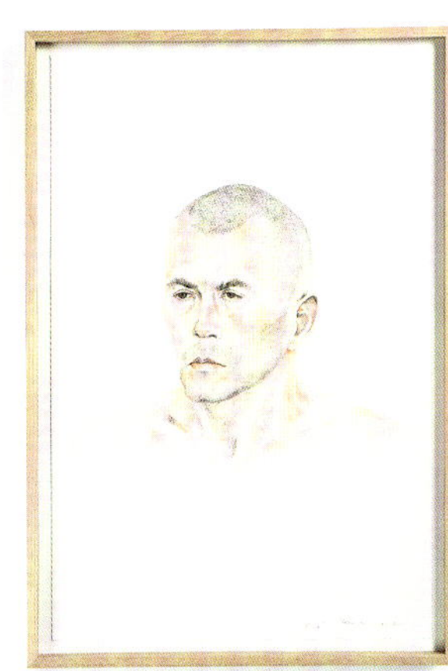

Roger Caillois's proximity to the movement is well known, even if they maintained their own lives as scholars and theorists. Samyn revives the Surrealists' spirit of openness. He pushes it wide open and inscribes it in the long temporalities of meticulous work and the history of painting. Magritte and Surrealism is another subject: this fallen tree bridges two worlds, the fine arts and Magritte. Samyn's relationship to the world is anatomical (*Stigmata*), metaphorical, sensuous, mystical, and filled with desire: to lose oneself within, beyond, before matter.

Start out again, continue along the path. One feels this preoccupation in Samyn's work. "Everything has been said, and we have come too late, now that men have been living and thinking for seven thousand years and more,"[4] La Bruyère once wrote. An expertise and broad knowledge of artistic methods are also to be found in Samyn's works: he has worked on icons and their techniques; he has undertaken a precise study of the history of representation and the forms of contemporary creation. This preoccupation appears in his work.

It serves as a foundation, but it could also have represented a risk for the artist—a possibility of slipping into a kind of commentary, the imaged marginalia of thoughts and ideas. When commentary is rooted in deep study, it endangers itself if it aims to expand its field of action. For, above all, the subject of Samyn's work is the gaze. One could of course adopt a theoretical approach to this work and speak of current reflections on the human, the nonhuman, the "natural" world and the ample belatedness of such a category. One could offer an identity-based reading, but the artist has never ceased to contradict all approaches that might pin him down one way or another. His choice of formal, aesthetic, and personal fluidity is at the heart of his work. He refuses to allow the creative force of a work to be impeded by one category or another. He is not defined by his works alone, or rather he would never allow the reality of one kind of work to obliterate the metamorphic field of his existence and his art. His works are traces, stones along a path; they have participated in a moment, but they continue on their way—just as Samyn has a penchant for salvaging

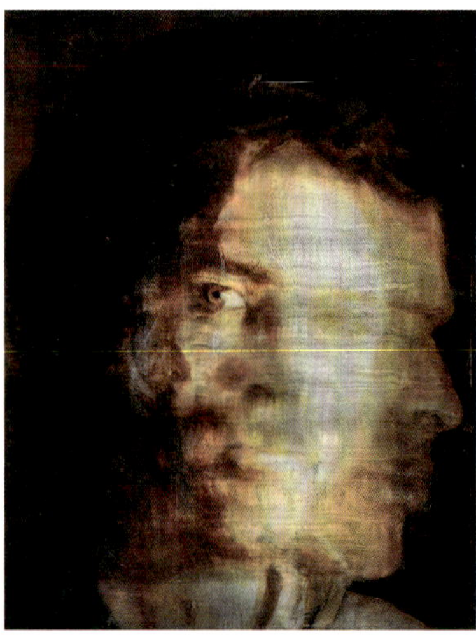

FIG. 6 *From Matter* (2009), oil on canvas,
30 × 24 cm, private collection

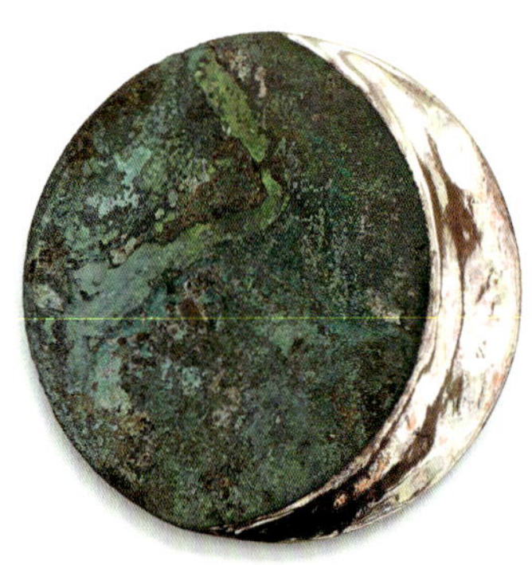

FIG. 7 *Untitled*, from the *Toward Total Eclipse* series (2014),
Chinese antique bronze mirror partially polished, ⌀ 16 cm,
private collection

preexisting objects, often in a state of disintegration or destruction, and giving life to them again. That is the case with the mirrors out of which he creates compositions, works.

Samyn has chosen to incorporate a significant number of his works into the Oldmasters Museum and the Magritte Museum. Instead of striving to impose a monumental presence upon the visitor by creating an installation that might dictate a perception, he has chosen to insert each of his works as echoes, encounters, and conversations. The works, his own and those of the two museums, speak to each other through a constant play of references. The exercise to which he has committed himself is truly a series of furtive glances in which the detail of a work from the museum collection comes to call for a contemporary response from a work of Samyn's, or, conversely, one of his own creations highlights a trait from the museum collection.

The practice of placing contemporary works in heritage collections—an established practice for fifteen years now—reveals Samyn's art: it allows for a *mise en abyme* of what his art is in itself.

The gaze is the medium of his work. He works with all the resources that we are able to mobilize in order to see, gaze at, experience the world around us. He starts from the most traditional conception of art—artworks that we see with our eyes—but only to expand it, just as our very conception of the gaze has expanded and become more distinct: one can see through one's ears and hear through one's eyes, according to the synesthesia peculiar to the opening out of contemporary artistic creation. Samyn's work operates according to the rules of a permanent synesthesia, nonetheless anchored in the gaze. One might associate this with a post-Duchampian vein that puts our physical relation to the work into perspective, through our entrance into a world where the fourth dimension, the "infrathin," dominates the principle of our inner construction of art. In this light, the gaze becomes a quintessential form of our haptic relationship to the world, where to touch and to see are two forms of a creative intensity. This dissolves the duality between the physical intelligence of touch and the superior intelligence claimed by the eye:

the gaze, after all, is what gives access to the contemplation of ideas in the Platonic tradition—a contemplation otherwise known as theory. One particularly finds traces of this in Samyn's work *Voir des nues* [pp. 116–117], where the artist writes in braille to a congenitally blind friend the description of a cloud inscribed on a plinth—and this same friend, on the basis of the description, sculpts the cloud. The piece incarnates the permanent dynamic between fixity and movement in his work: that which is given, refused, and nevertheless comes into being.

In rendering the very nature of the shifting gaze, Samyn calls into question the foundations of our experience of the world: each oscillation invites us to question the status of things, and our own status among and with these things. Often in his paintings Samyn deals directly with the matter of the gaze, now by painting an eye itself, now by painting a reflection—within an eye—now by painting a solar eclipse, an analogue of pupil and iris, now by marking the eyes of the de-painted figures that become like embers. The gaze is a living, tremulous material, whether it annihilates itself and nearly disappears, or whether it becomes an infinite mirror of metamorphoses. The gaze goes the furthest into darkness, into dazzling light, into existence itself and the opening toward vertigo. Often his paintings offer up, epitomize, incarnate, or even withhold their gaze: each portrait concedes or denies the right to this exchange (in *Timelessness* [p. 21], the model lowers his eyes).

By making the gaze the material of his work, he opens his creations up to a multitude of reflections. His work is not merely speculative, but specular: it operates according to a play of inner and outer mirrors. Each work plays with the specularity of art face-to-face with the world and that of the museum face-to-face with life, just as the Magritte Museum and the Oldmasters Museum mirror each other. This reflection is also that of the outside

faced with the inside: Samyn makes the outside enter into these two museums with his works that are part of neither of their permanent collections. In doing to, he sets the identity of the museum in play: the work that he ushers in for a day—contemporary portraits, fragments of *nature*—reinforces the status of the collection in its fixity at the same time as it lends a fluidity to the visiting experience. His works accomplish a double action of confirmation and disruption.

In the biblical passage devoted to the burning bush (Exodus 3:1-7), Moses does not dare to lay eyes on the bush, for he fears it is God. God's apparition is immediately linked to the impossibility of seeing him and therefore of measuring him. Samyn has painted many flames in his work, and many of them are incorporated in this exhibition. One cannot help thinking that each of these paintings is like a flamelet from the burning bush that has come to set itself down on the canvas: the burning bush was a means for God to manifest himself to Moses all while maintaining his invisibility, befitting the incommensurability of the divine. Fabrice Samyn's

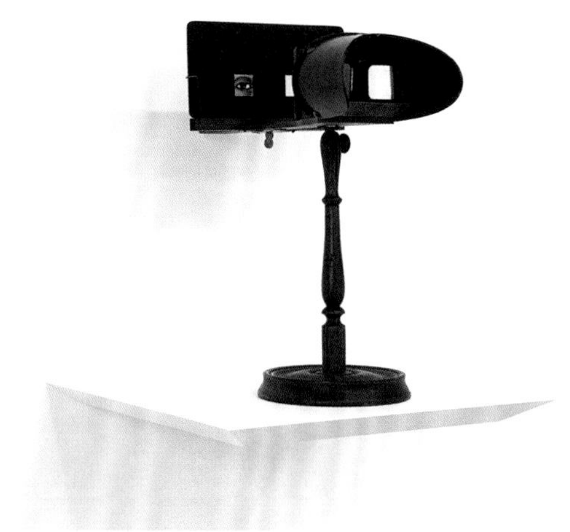

FIG. 8 *You and Eye* (2016), wood and metal, 34 × 33 × 18 cm

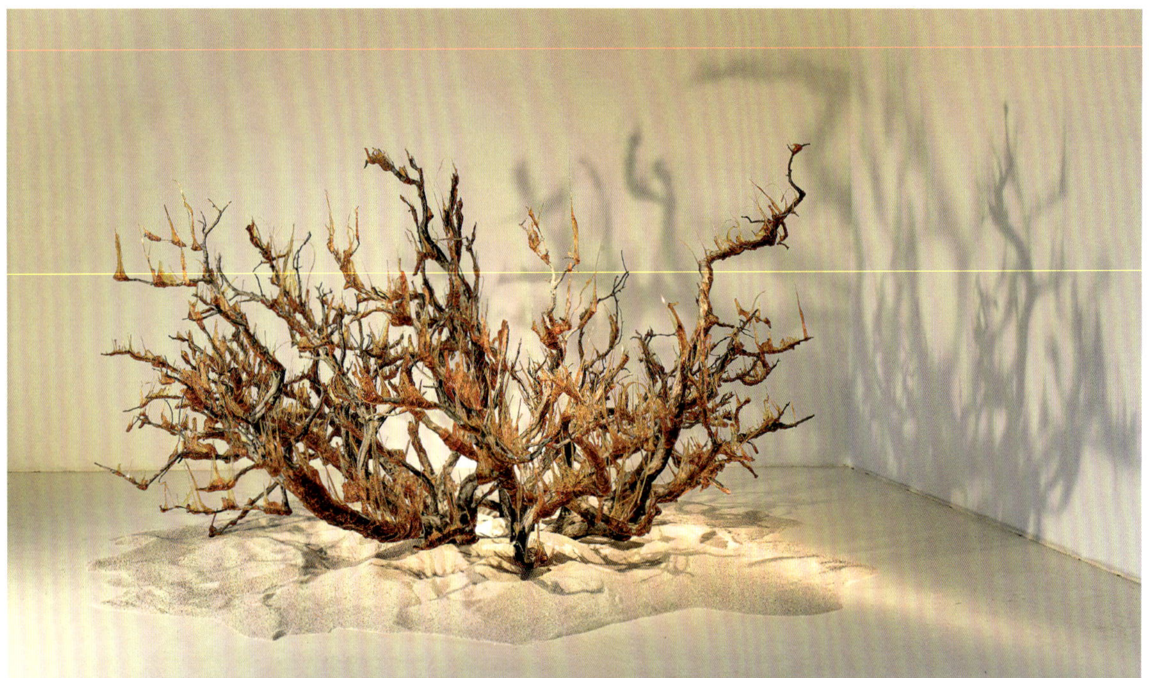

flamelets are ways of accessing the experience of the burning bush: of course, one can also see traces of the *vanitas* tradition in them—a form very present in Samyn's oeuvre. One might read them as flames of desire, of sexuality even. But each time, now and always, it is the burning bush, the divine manifestation, that returns through the poetics of the gaze. Through this series of works, Samyn multiplies the burning bush's effects and asks himself about the bush opening into flames of fire: in doing so, he reenacts the tension of the gaze between the bush's religious unity and the flames' profane multiplicity.

Here, we touch upon an inherent tension in Samyn's project: on one hand, he works within a contemporary, post-Duchampian perspective, every trope of which matters; on the other hand, and this might be the main key to his work, he is a painter. His relationship to flesh is that of a painter.

His relationship to life is that of a painter. Even his relationship to the multiplicity of his mediums is that of a painter. But to be a painter is not to limit oneself to painting: it is to accept that the world exists through waves of sensation emitted by matter and perceived in order to recreate worlds. Dürer, at the end of his work that we know, arrived at the conclusion: "Die Kunst steckt in der Natur." "Art stands embedded in nature." He recognized that his duty as a painter was not only to create semblances but to draw a conclusion from art's presence in nature, in a way that would not deny but on the contrary strengthen his creative force. Few artists are able to depict such a tension. Fabrice Samyn is fully a painter, a passionate and fertile practitioner of painting. But he is also the author of sculptures, installations, films. He does not want to be boxed in, here or elsewhere. In images, he comes to look for what is, but also for what is not. Multimedia artists call him one of their own; painters call him one of their own. But to be fully both is rare. As a painter, he constantly plays with the precision it takes to make an image and the vagueness that makes the image tremble pictorially and inlays it with a doubt, an uncertainty: images may betray us.

In this respect, he touches upon the tension in Magritte, a Platonist who made advertising the material of his art. Samyn's politics keep him at a distance from advertising, but he still lives in the world's public space. Accordingly, all material can serve as fuel to the fire whose flames inhabit his work. The images he creates are akin to a contradiction in terms: his goal, he says, is to "create physical images to destroy mental images." His works make these images into realities of the external world, and in making them into realities they undo their purely mental character: destruction is also an act of entering into the world, finding a foundation there—and, in his words, it is "the flaming twilight of the metamorphosis of the world." He also says, "An ill-seen image controls you, which is why you have to manifest it to free yourself from it." Images are political, and the gaze is an instrument of liberty. We become free through the gaze in so far as it reveals a state of attention, a presence to the world, a capacity to act rather than be acted upon: Samyn never ceases to gaze at things, and in his project at the Royal Museums of Belgium he invites us to gaze at works, to gaze at the world, and, through the synesthesia at the heart of his work, he urges us to live.

His work is alive: it refuses to allow itself to be limited, and it has the grace that arises from years of difficult work. For looking at a thing is not easy or obvious: it is an education—at once the least wearisome and the most demanding of all. It isn't necessary to be rich or powerful to know how to see. But it is necessary to be free. Through his work, Fabrice Samyn invites us to be freer, stronger, more fully present.

Art is the child of wonder. Accordingly, it shares philosophy's demand for knowledge. We have recognized that art has the potential to speak to us about the world, to change our existence. For this to happen, we must take nothing as a given, and we must ask ourselves about the potential even of monstrous things. Samyn's work is inhabited by such questions. When we talk of astonishment and wonder, we often think of the gaze: "a look of astonishment," so to speak. And this wonder is all the more powerful if the gaze is not only astonished but also knowledgeable, expert. Such is Fabrice Samyn's gaze. He comes to give us mirrors to carry along our path. He makes this path begin here in these two museums, where shadow wrestles incessantly with light . . . As a painter, Samyn likes to represent, through realism's multiple forms, people he has loved, known, or met; but he also likes nearly invisible faces. The eyes are like embers or hidden. On the path to wonder and knowledge, Fabrice Samyn's artistic contribution lies hidden in the manifold gifts and refusals of the gaze.

1. Conrad Ferdinand Meyer, "Ich bin kein ausgeklügelt Buch, Ich bin ein Mensch mit seinem Widerspruch," in *Huttens letzte Tage* (1871).
2. Walt Whitman "Do I contradict myself? . . . I contain multitude," from "Song of Myself" in *Leaves of Grass* (1892).
3. Thierry De Duve, *Nominalisme pictural: Marcel Duchamp, la peinture et la modernité*, Paris, Éd. de Minuit, 1984.
4. Jean de La Bruyère, from "Les caractères," in *Des ouvrages de l'esprit* (1688).

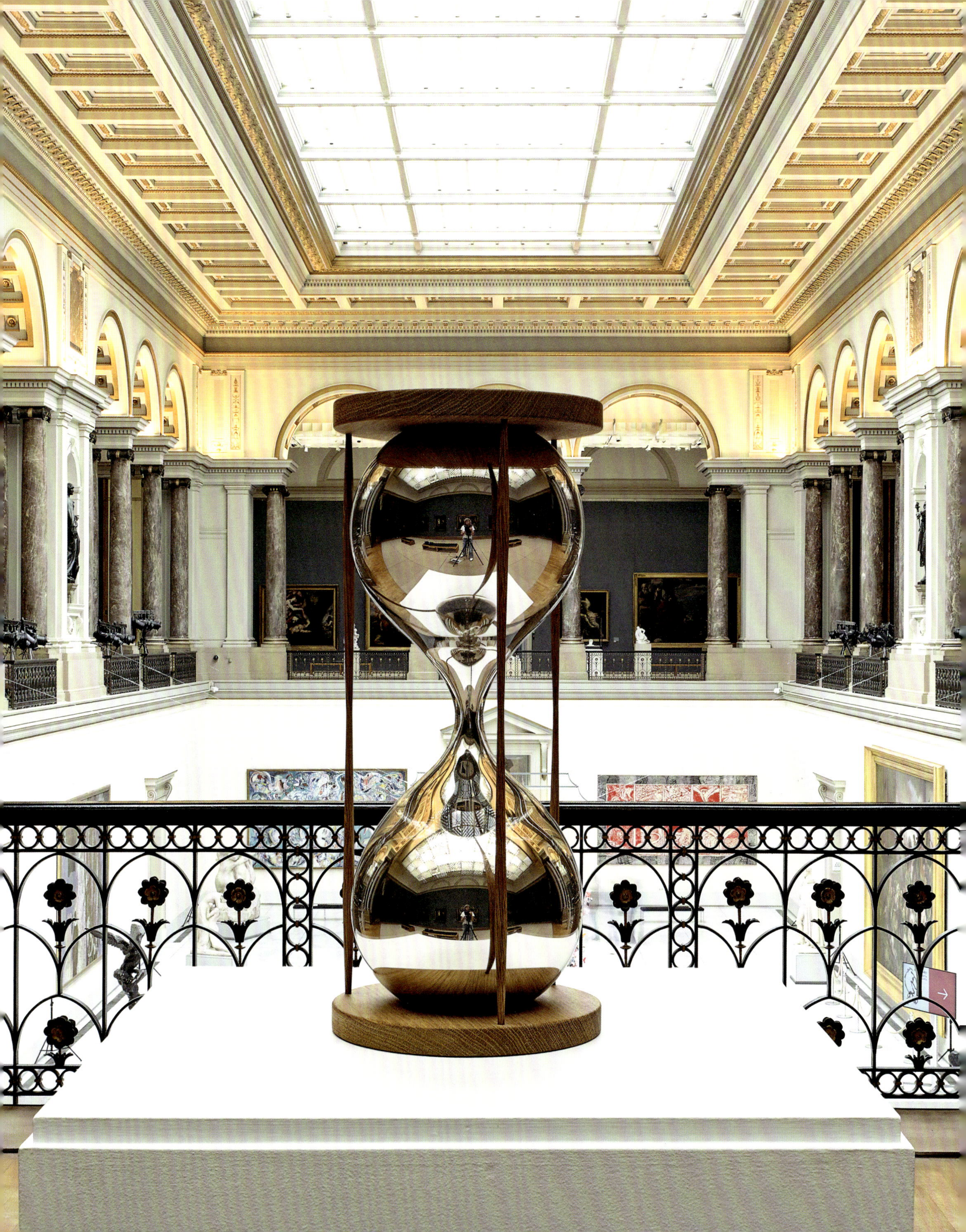

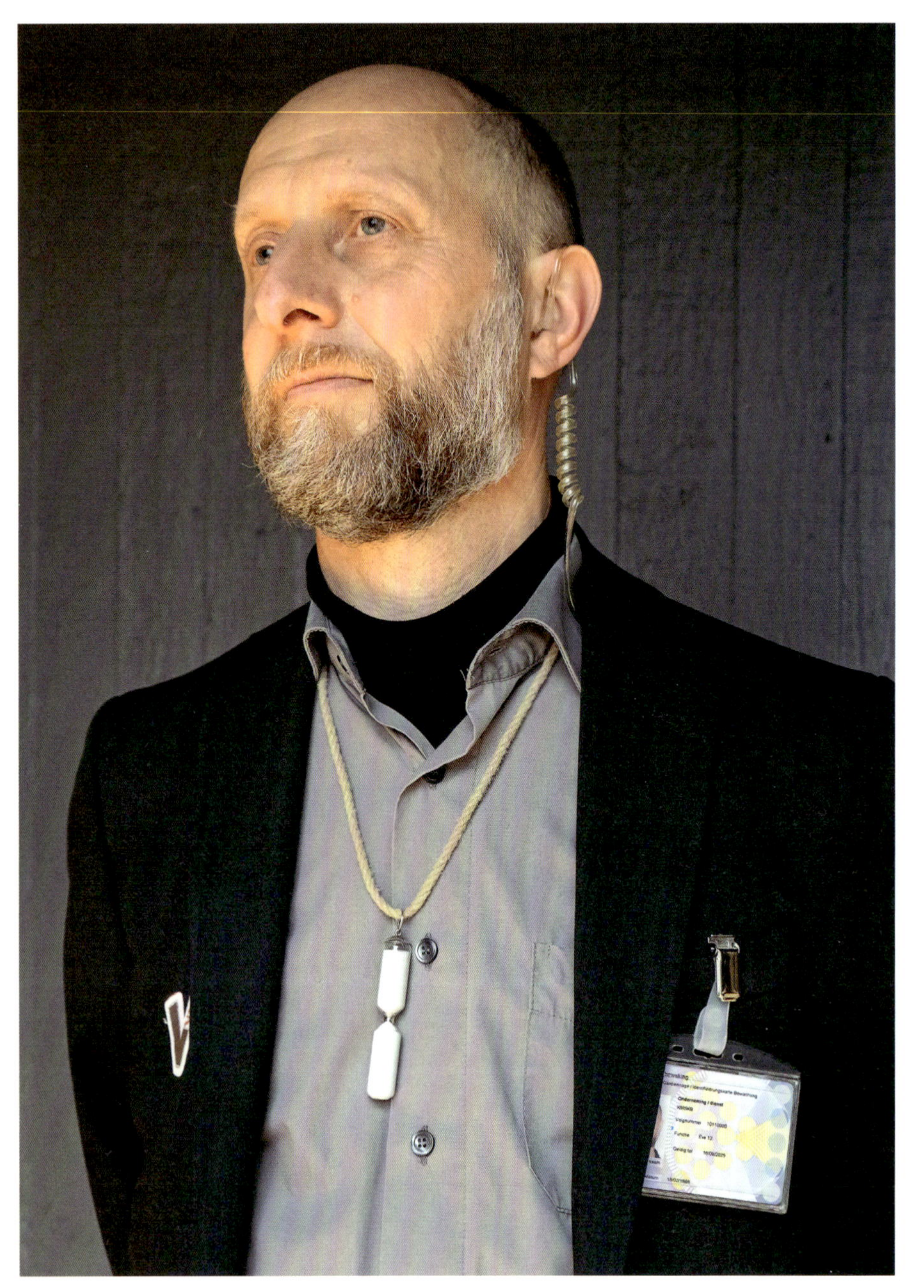

Still Flow (2018)

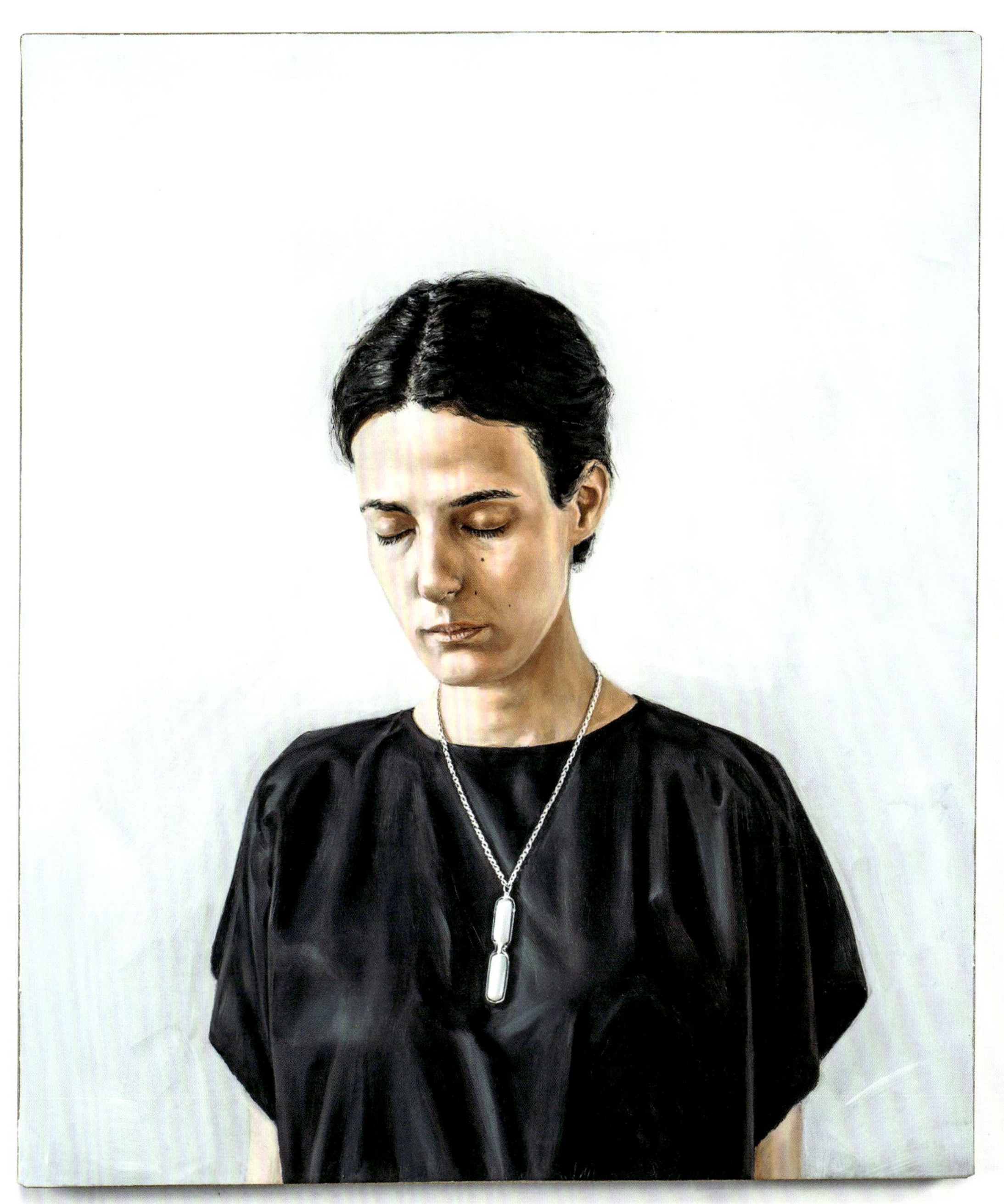

Timelessness (2018)

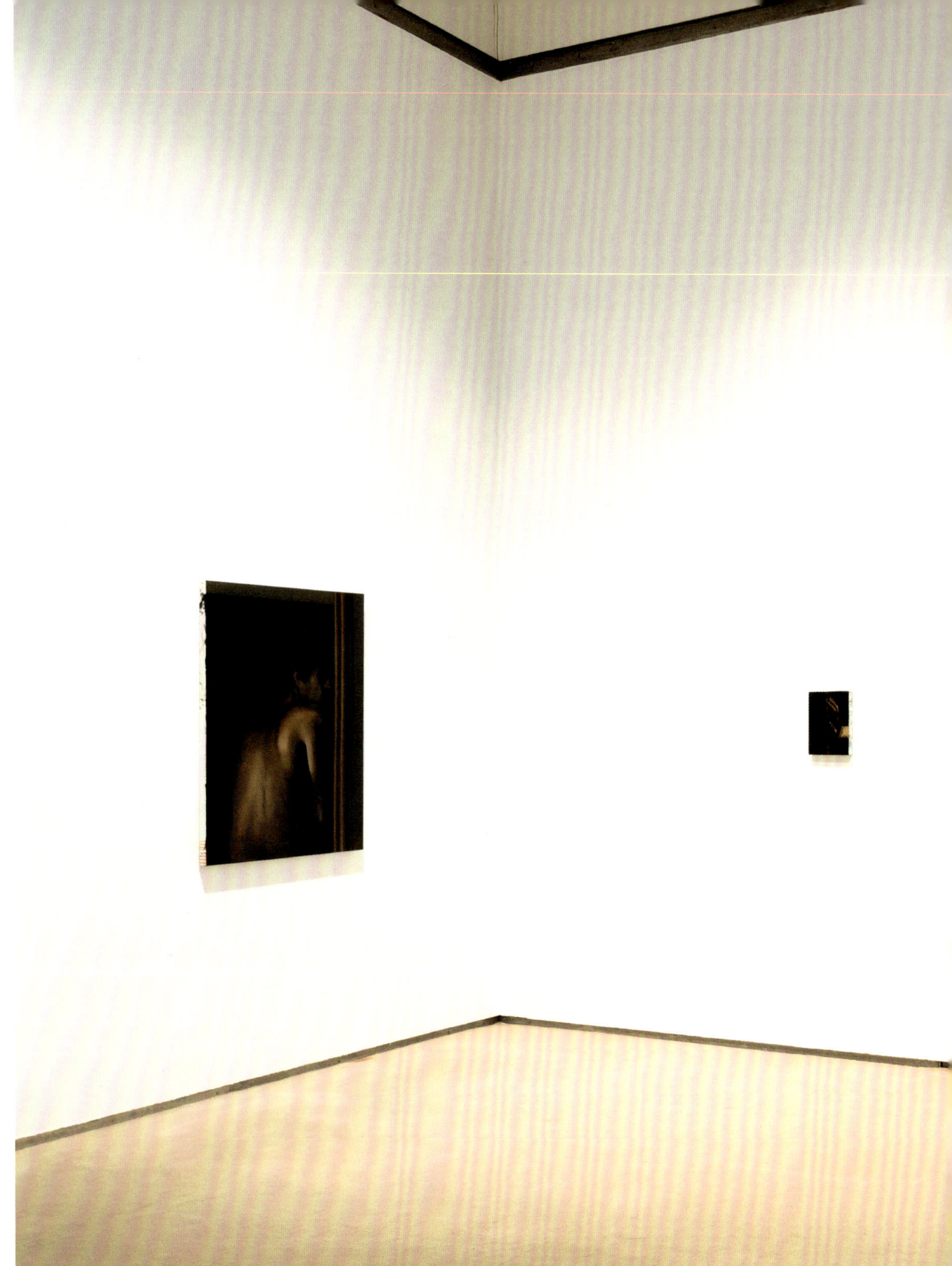

 Exhibition view in the RMFAB, October 2021 (cat. 4 to 21)

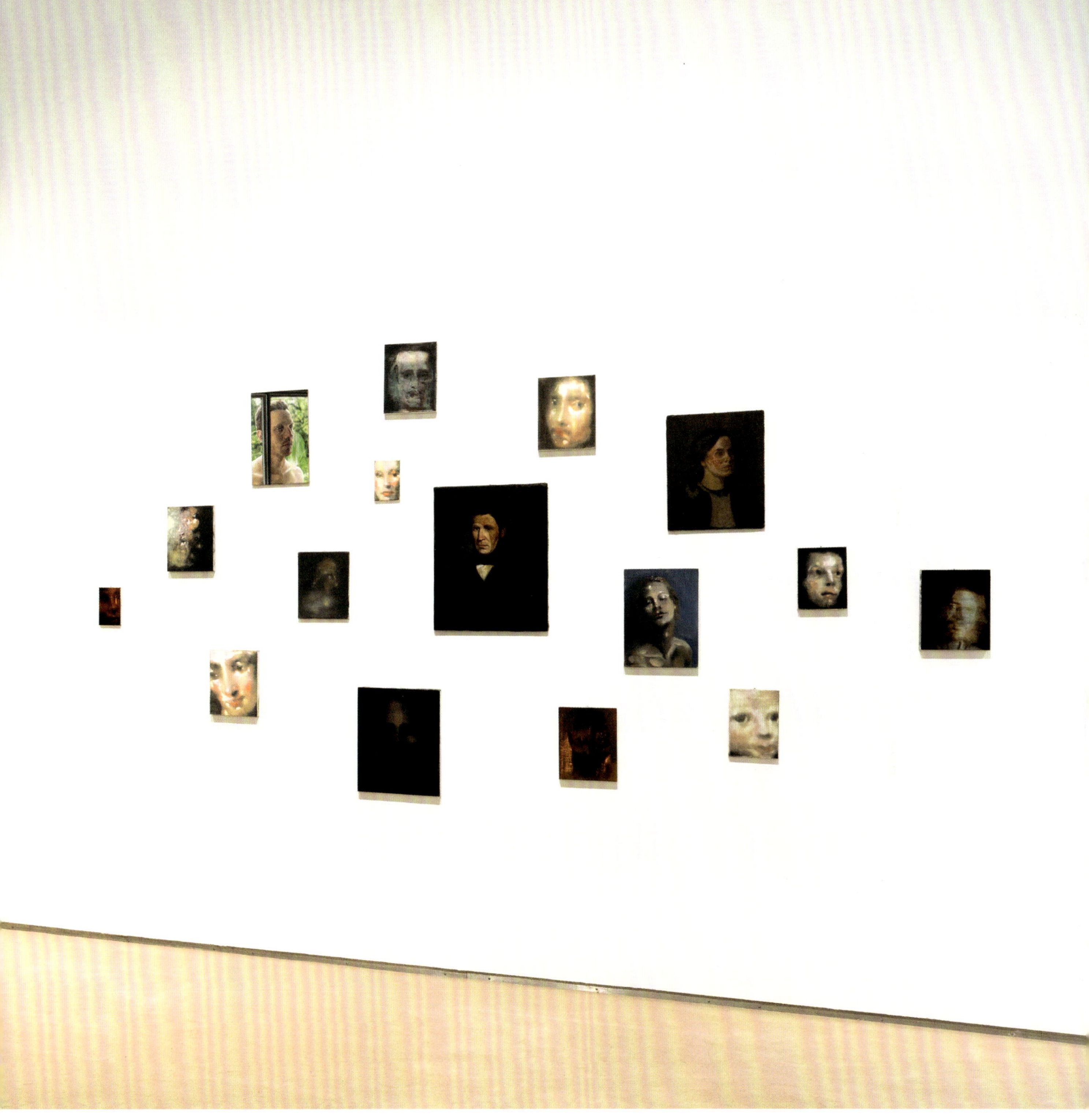

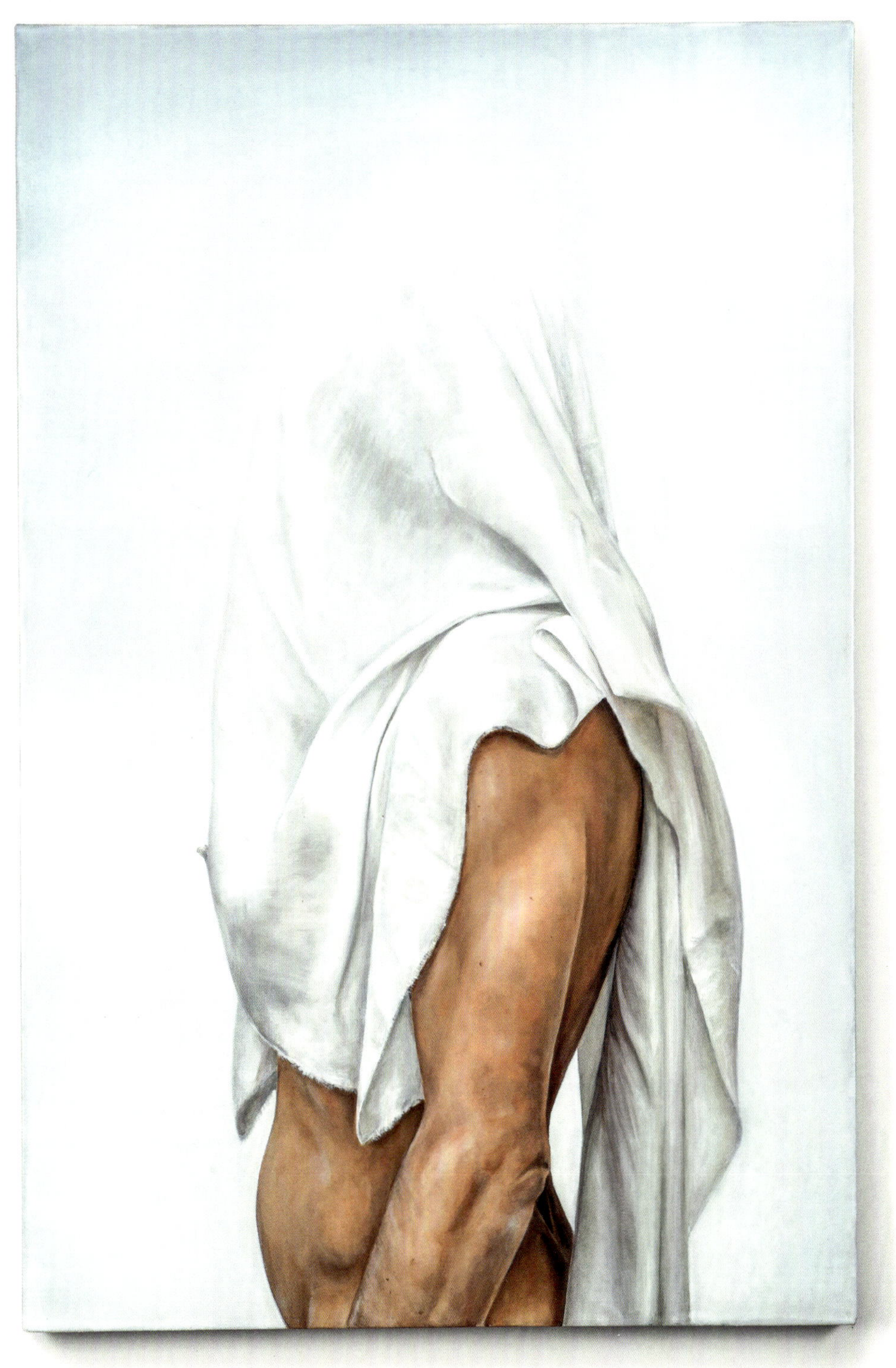

Treshold (2018)

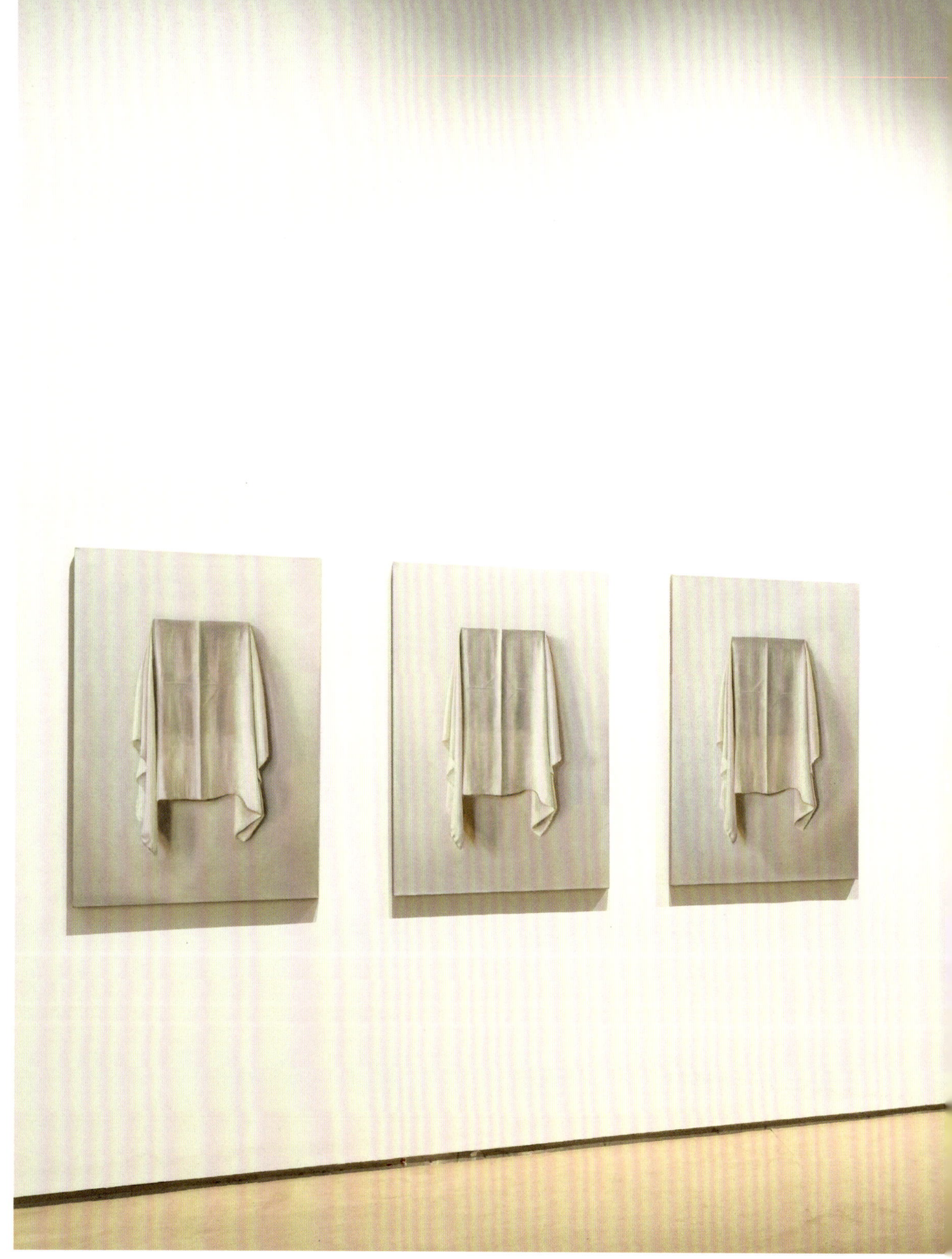

26 Exhibition view in the RMFAB, October 2021 (from left to right: cat. 23–25, 3, 26, and 22)

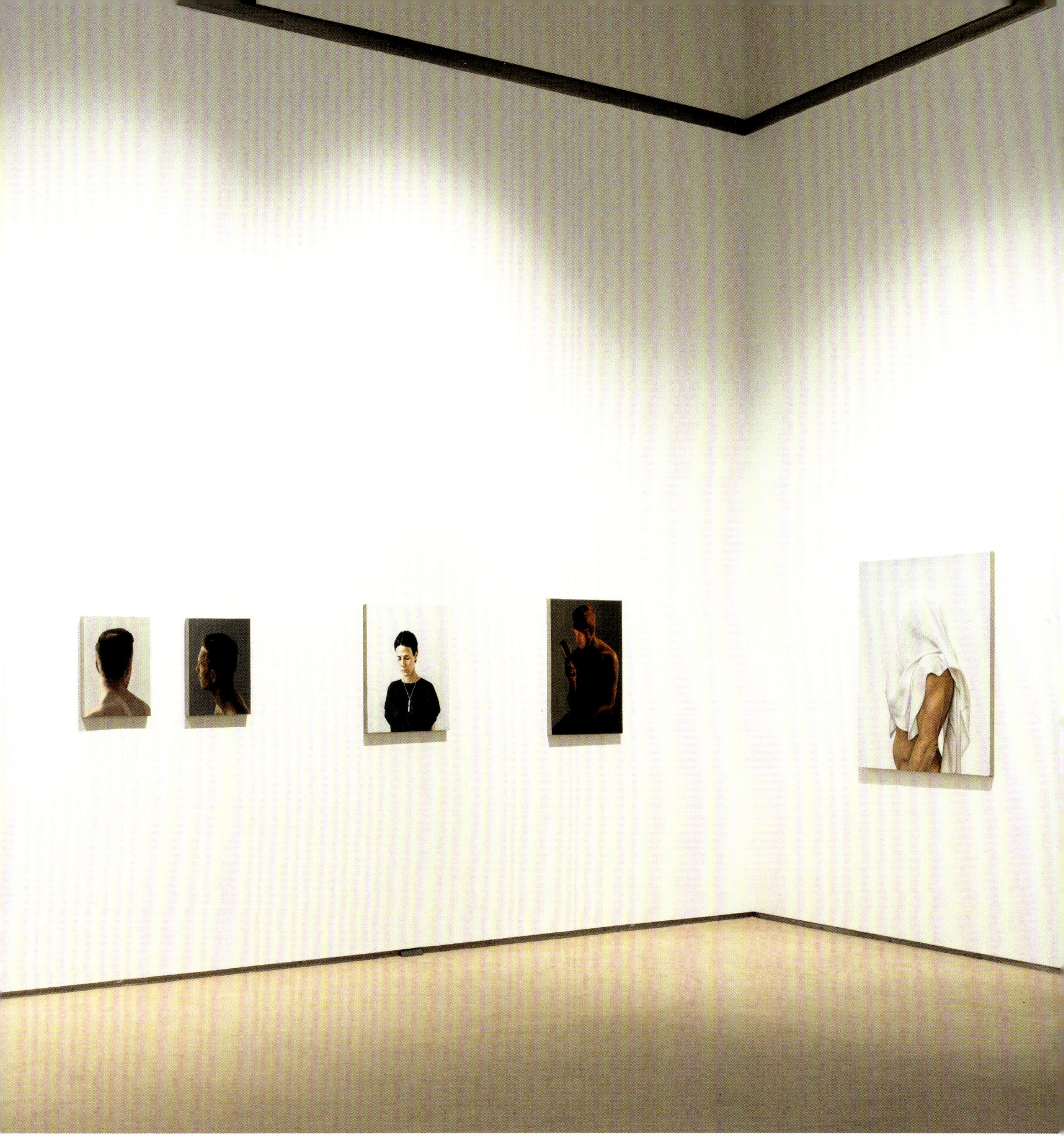

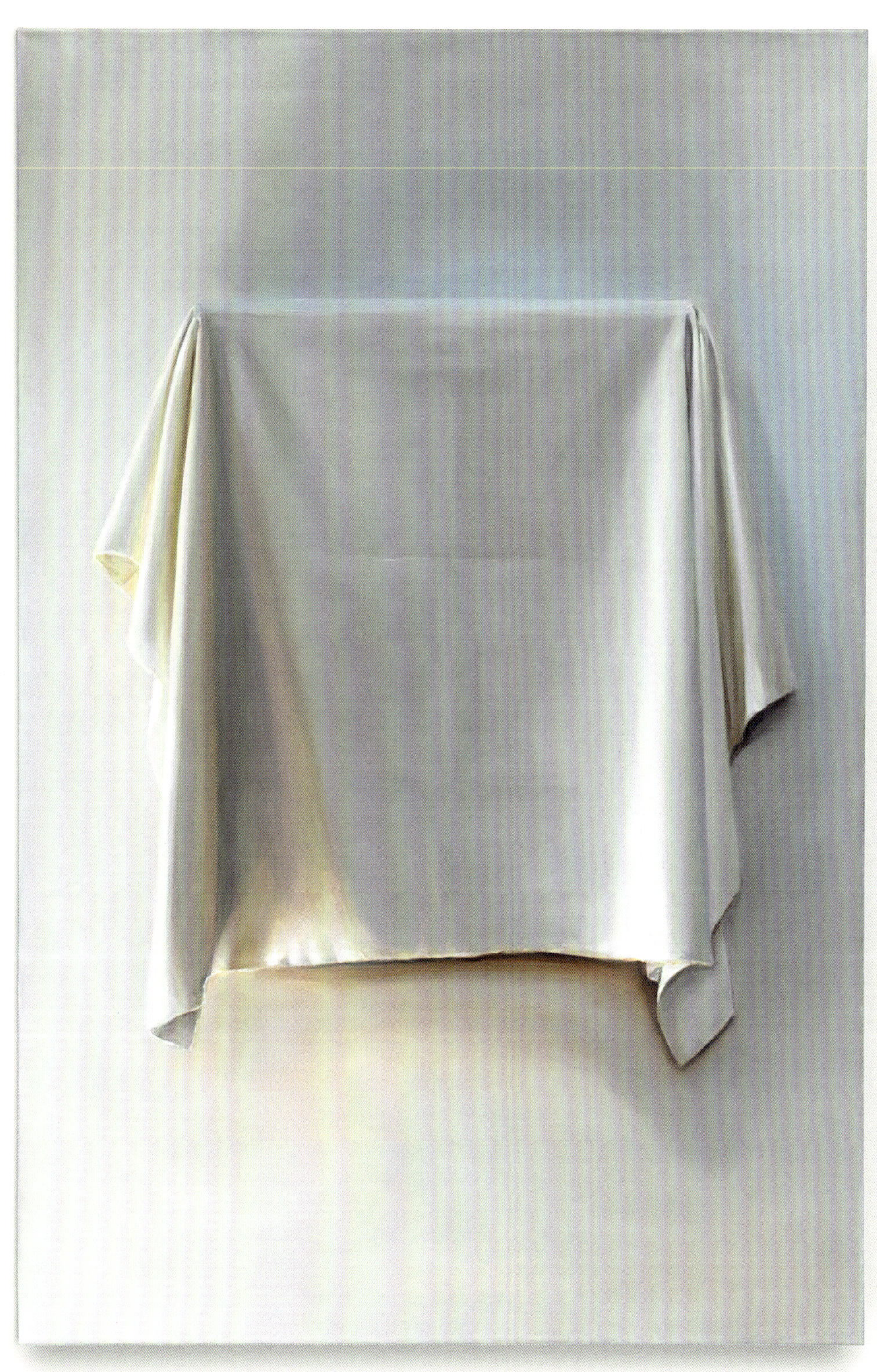

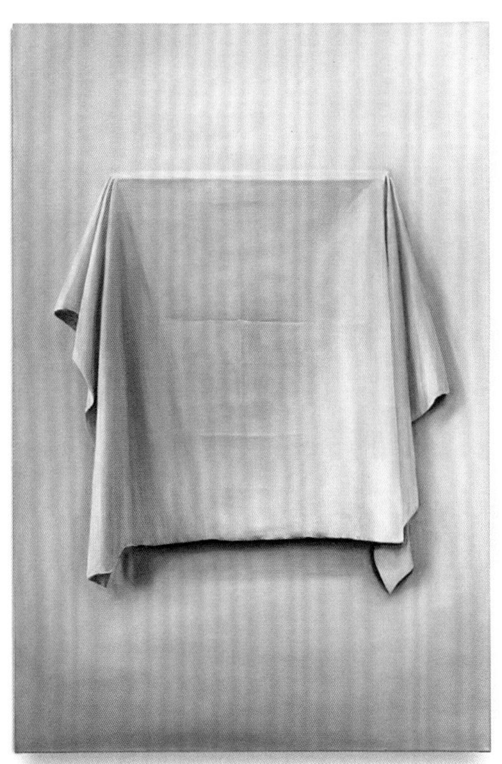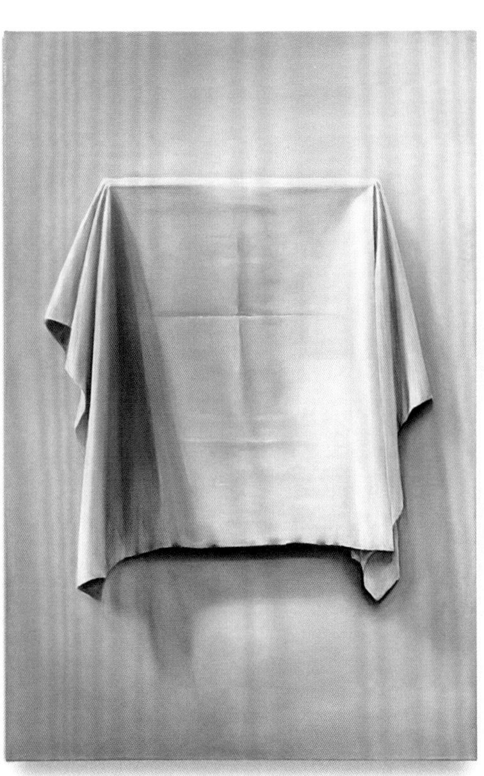

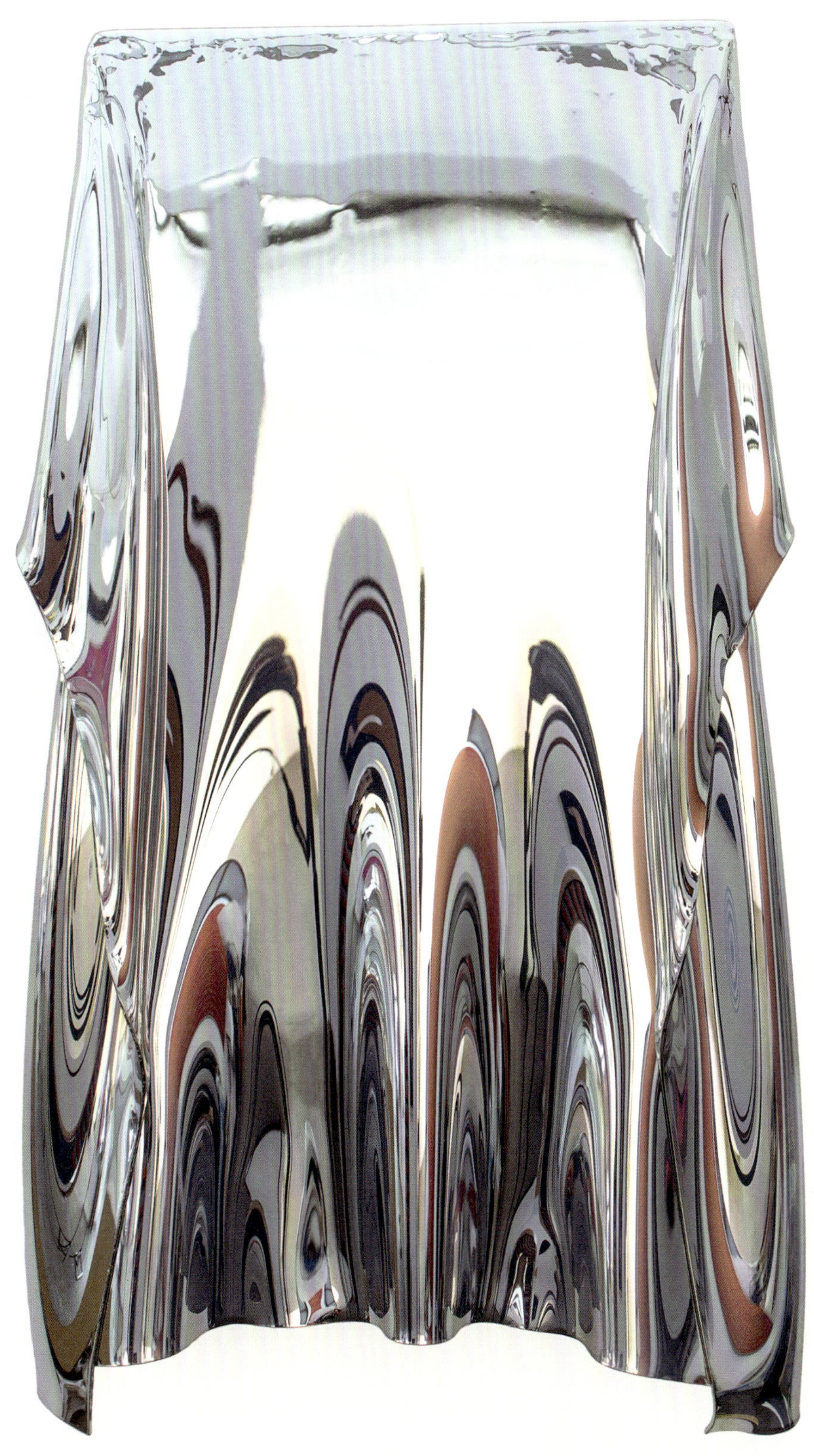

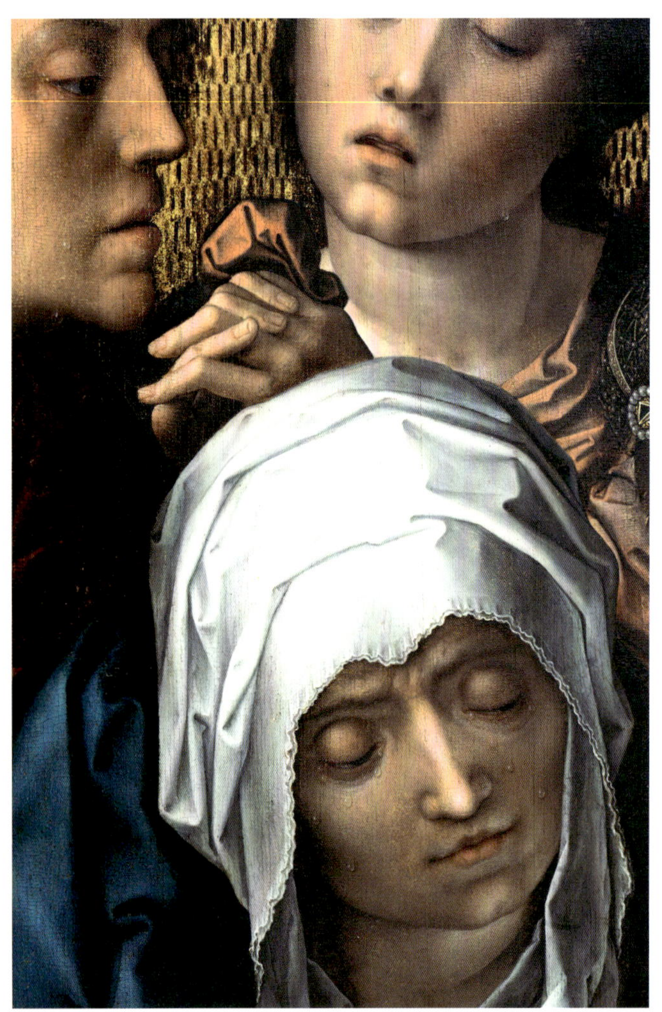

 Bernard van Orley <u>Haneton Triptych</u> (early 1520s), detail

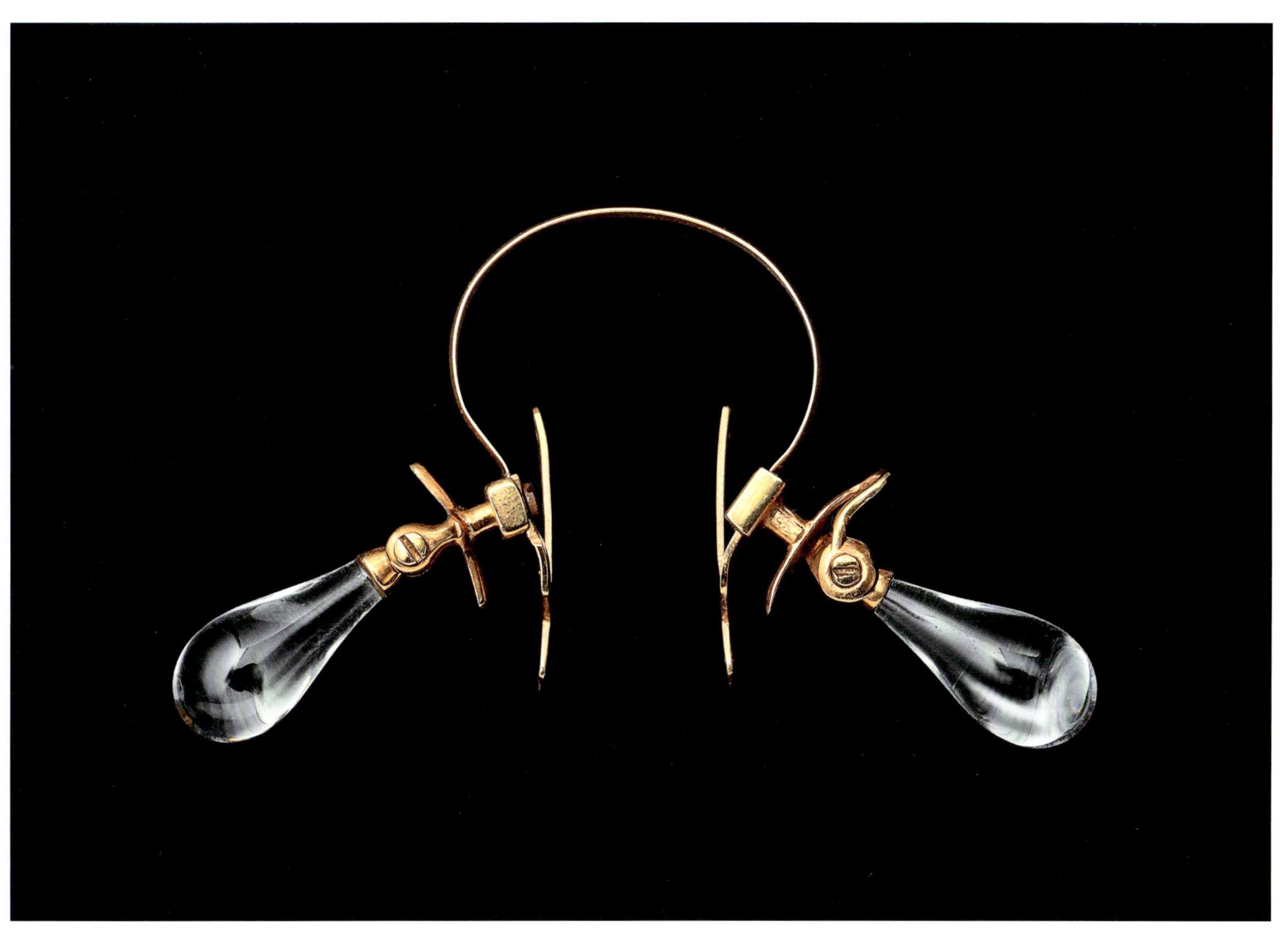

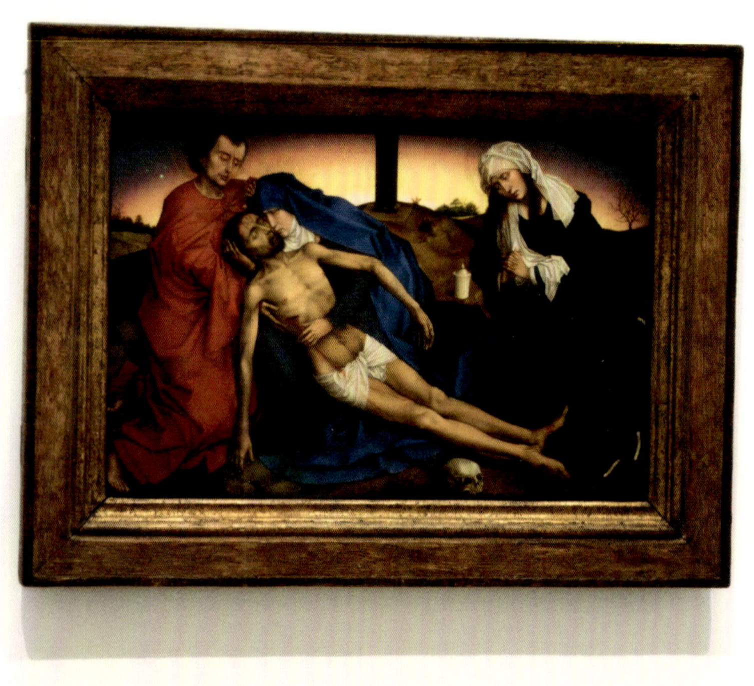

↑ Rogier van der Weyden <u>Lamentation</u> (ca. 1441)

→ <u>Untitled</u>, from the series "The Color of Time" (2014)

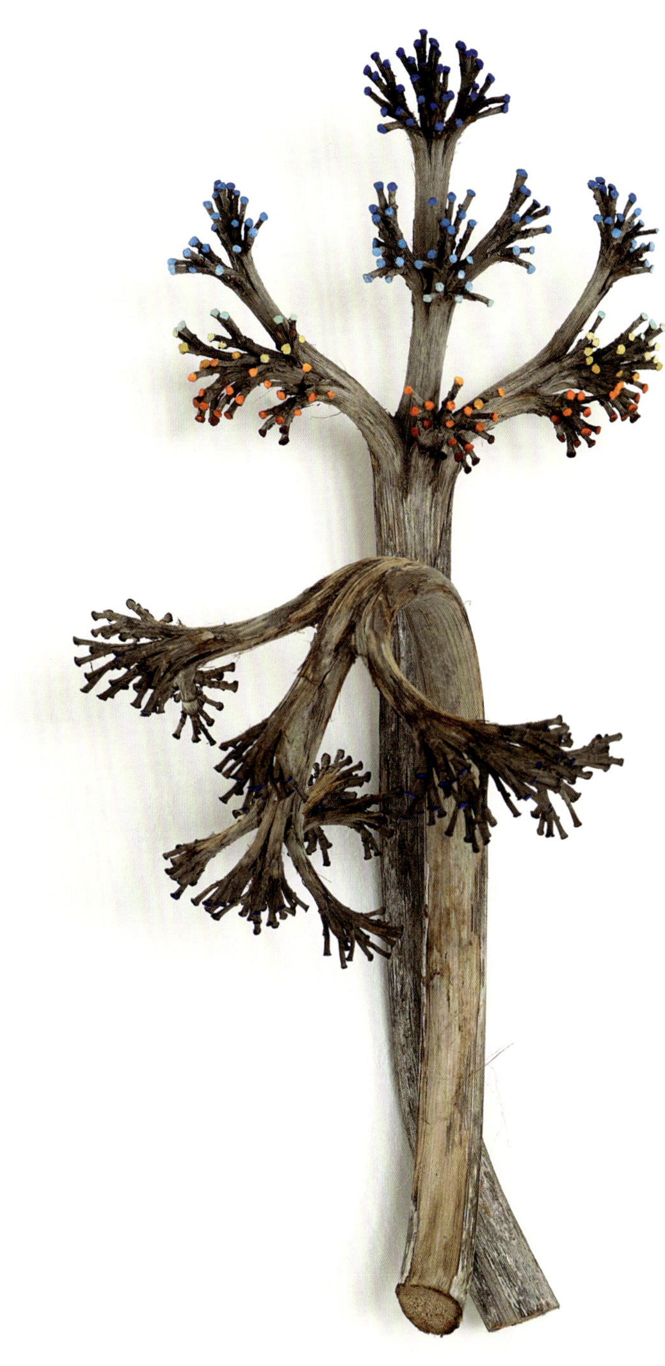

Inhaling Dawn (2020)

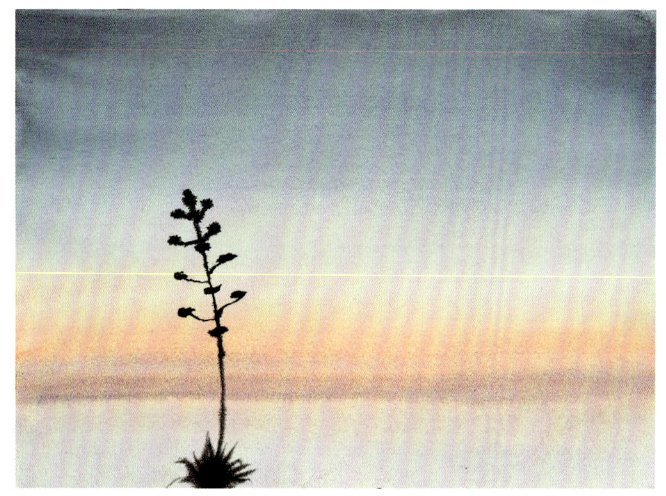

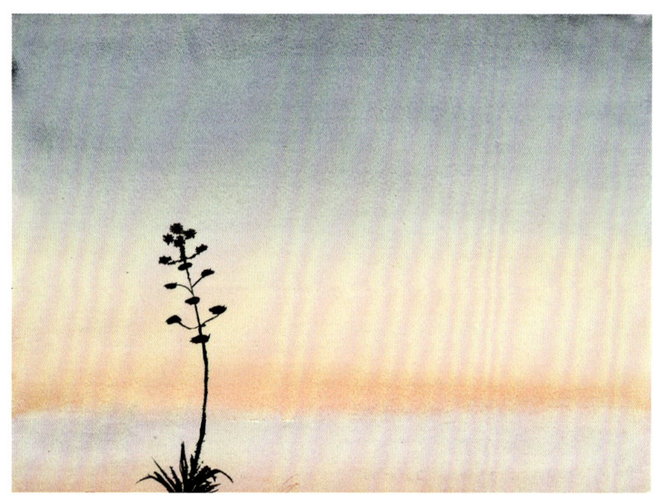

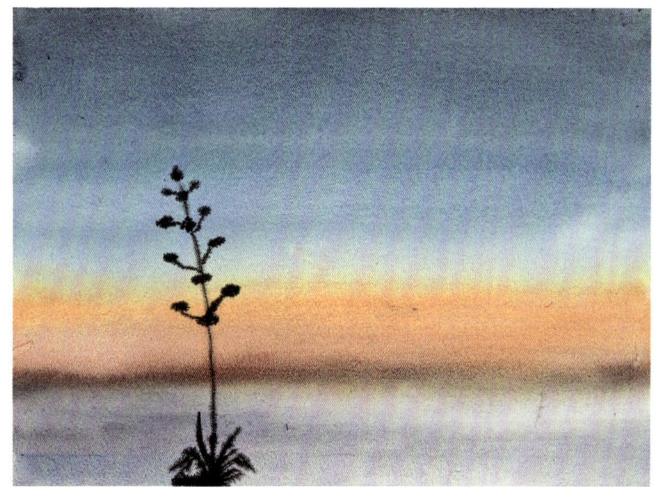

  Agave Sunset (2019)

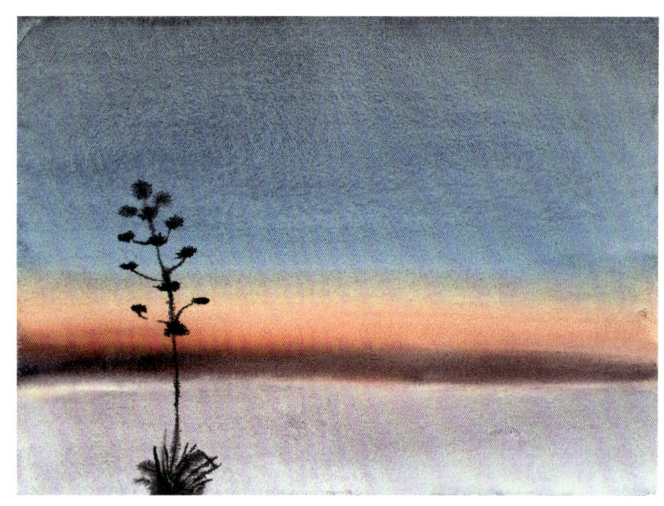

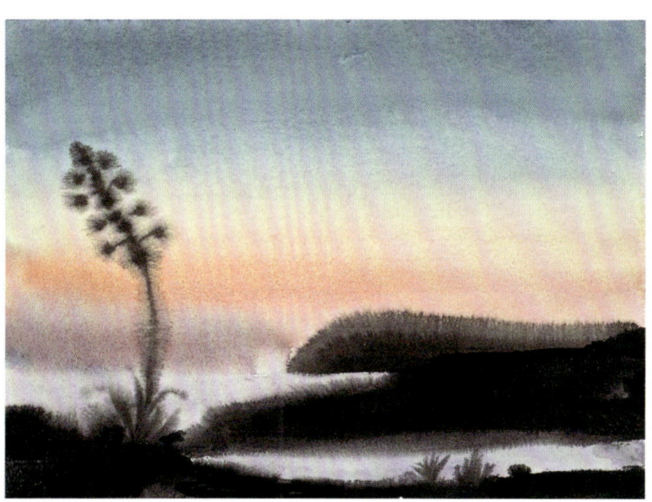

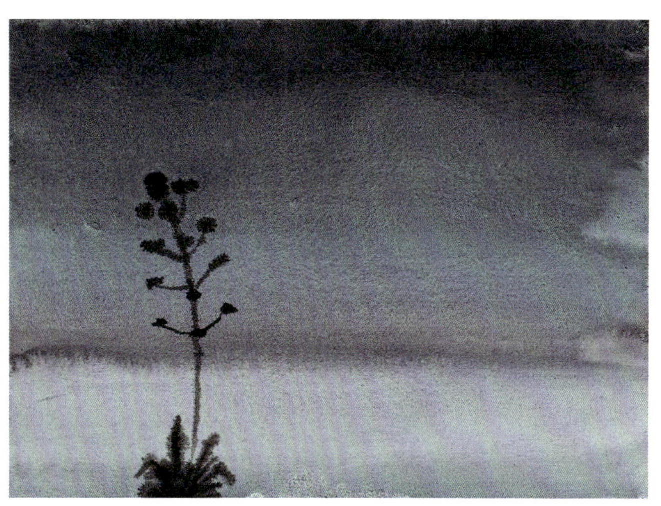

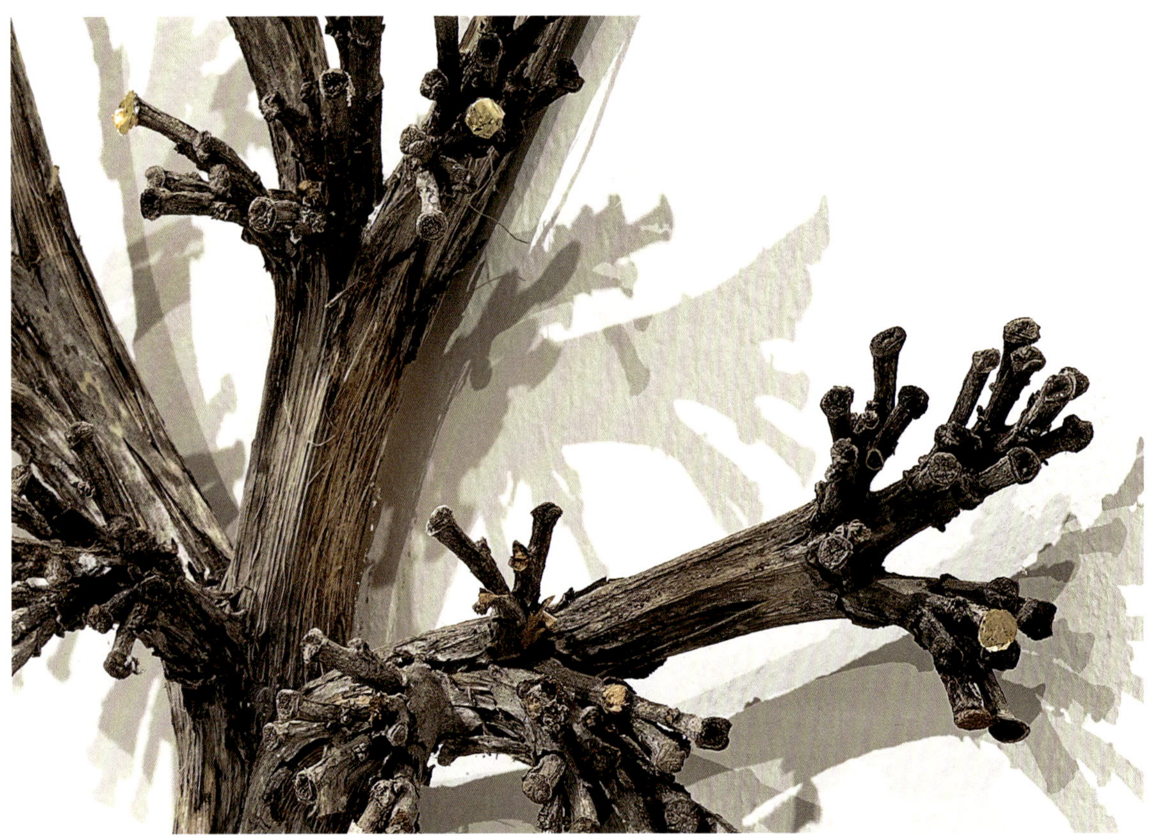

Endogène / Exogène is part of a series that uses agave flowers, a recurring material in the artist's work. The agave is a succulent monocarpic plant, which means it only blossoms once every several years and dies after flowering. The *Agave americana* is native to Central America. Toward the middle of the sixteenth century it was introduced to Europe, where it became established around the Mediterranean basin. It's large floral stem (which can be up to eight meters tall) produces tubular flowers. It is these flowers that are used in the works, as much for their symbolic value as for their beauty. "Agave" comes from the Greek ἀγαθός which means "worthy of admiration." The Mayas used it, and still do, as much for the fibers it produces as for the extraction of pulque or mescal, a source of sacred intoxication.

Simultaneously a symbol of migration, last elevation, and sacred intoxication, this flower has a particular resonance at a time in which we are faced with religious and border tensions, between the United States and Mexico, or around the Mediterranean basin.

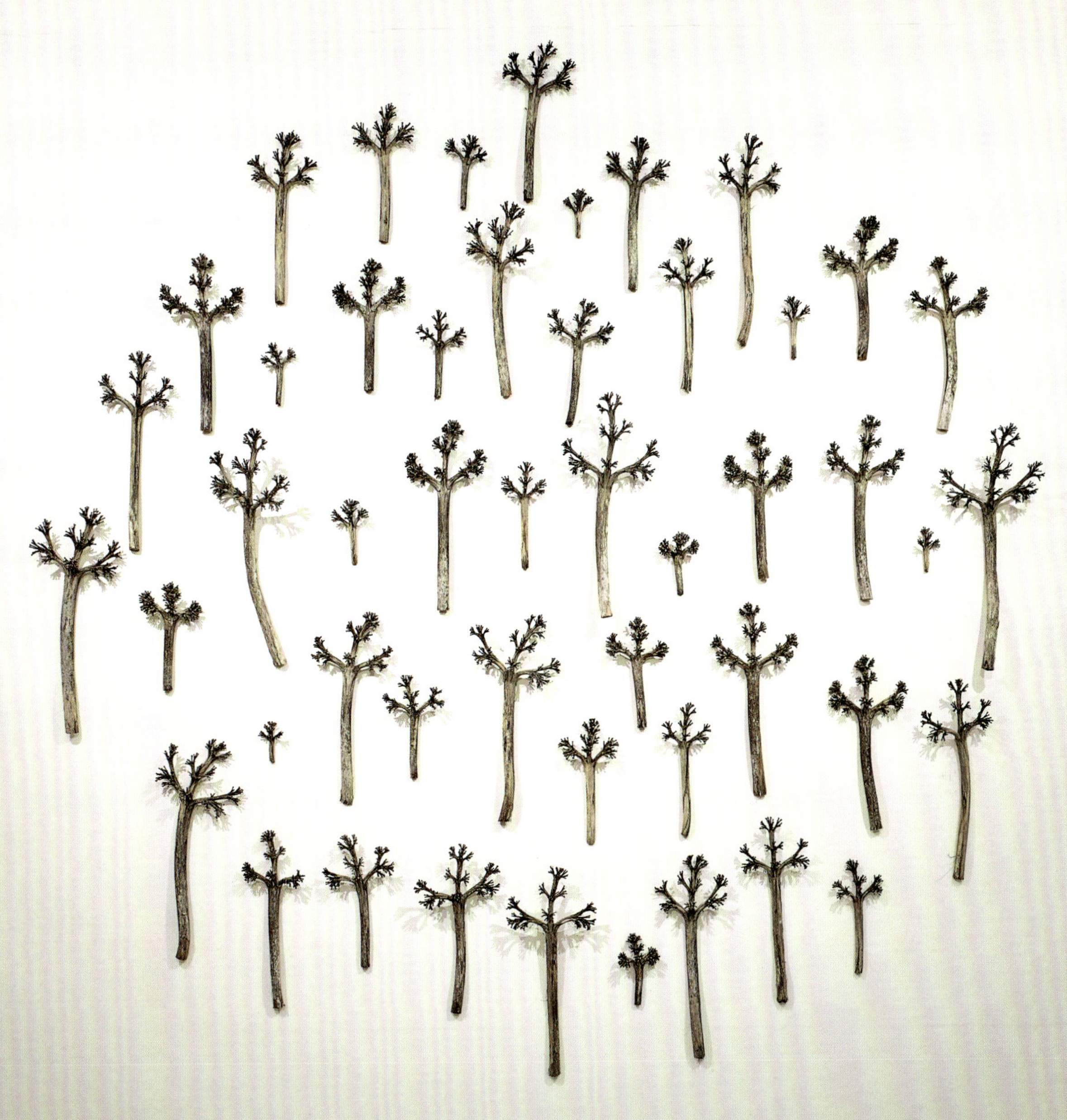

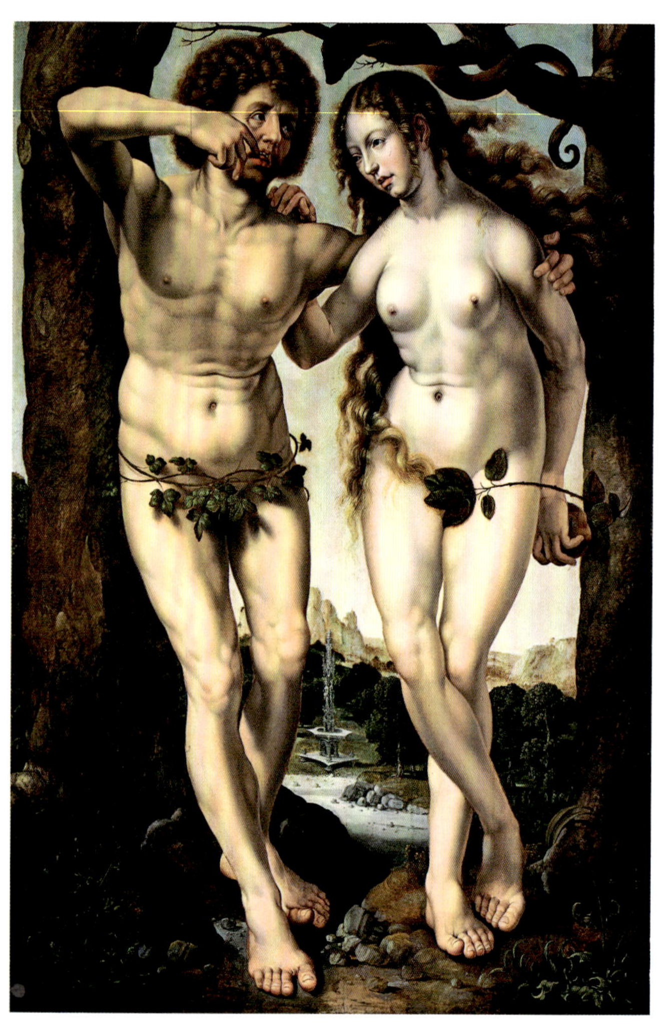

   Jan Gossaert, named Mabuse <u>Adam and Eve</u> (n.d.)

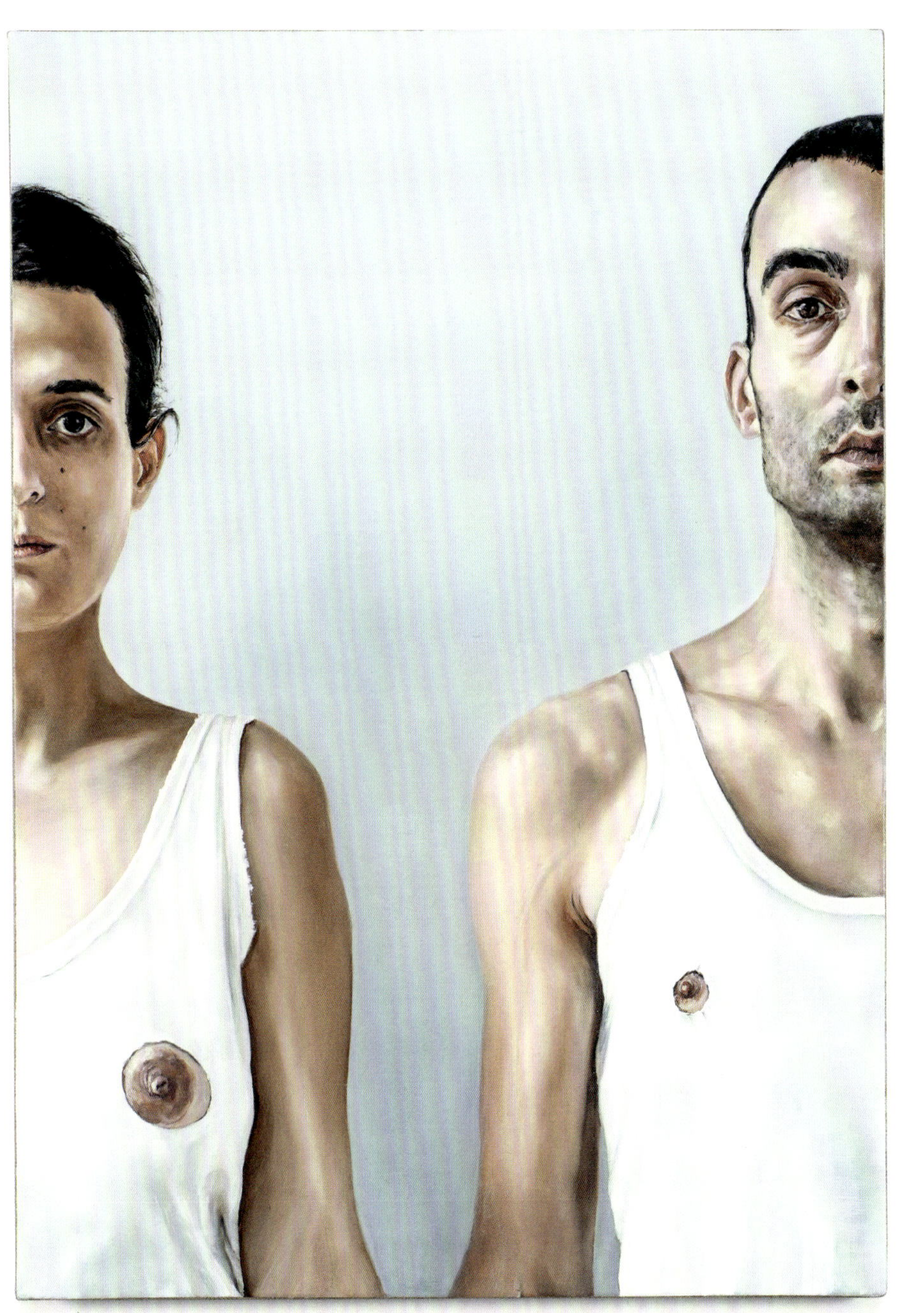

Eve & Adam (2018)

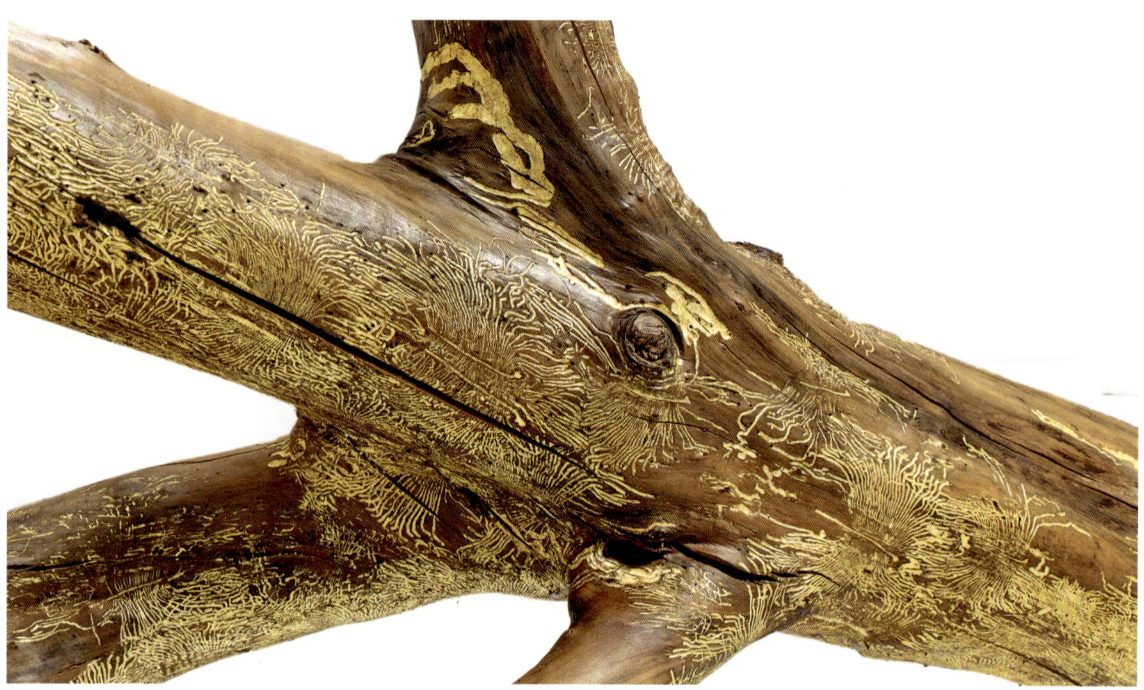

The Fallen Tree of Knowledge is a sculpture on an apple tree whose surface has been completely eaten by xylophagous insects. The engravings of astonishing precision, which transformed the aspect and texture of the tree branches, were made by different species, among which there are some called "the typographers." Each of these trajectories has been patiently gilded with golden leaves recycled from computers.

As in the majority of Fabrice Samyn's body of work, this piece seeks to evoke and transcend opposites, like a formalized oxymoron. The worms' traces allude, as a *vanitas*, to our impermanence—to the underground future of our corpses. And the gold, a noble material historically used by a variety of civilizations in sacred arts, recalls the eternity and the world above, as the metal is believed by different traditions to come from the stars. Once transformed by the artist, the labyrinthine traces remind us also of the computer chips from which the used recycled gold has been extracted.

By recalling the myth of Eden, the title of this work invites us to ask ourselves: Where has knowledge, in the ideological frame of progress, brought us? Global warming, air pollution, and intensive agricultural practices have been causing massive outbreaks of xylophagous insects. The consequences of the vertiginous spread of the species are devastating for European forests and ecosystems. The recycled gold used by the artist to highlight the paths sculpted by the insects alludes to the tragic history of gold mining, which is at the source of ecocides, the destruction of the biosphere, and of our common lungs: the forest.

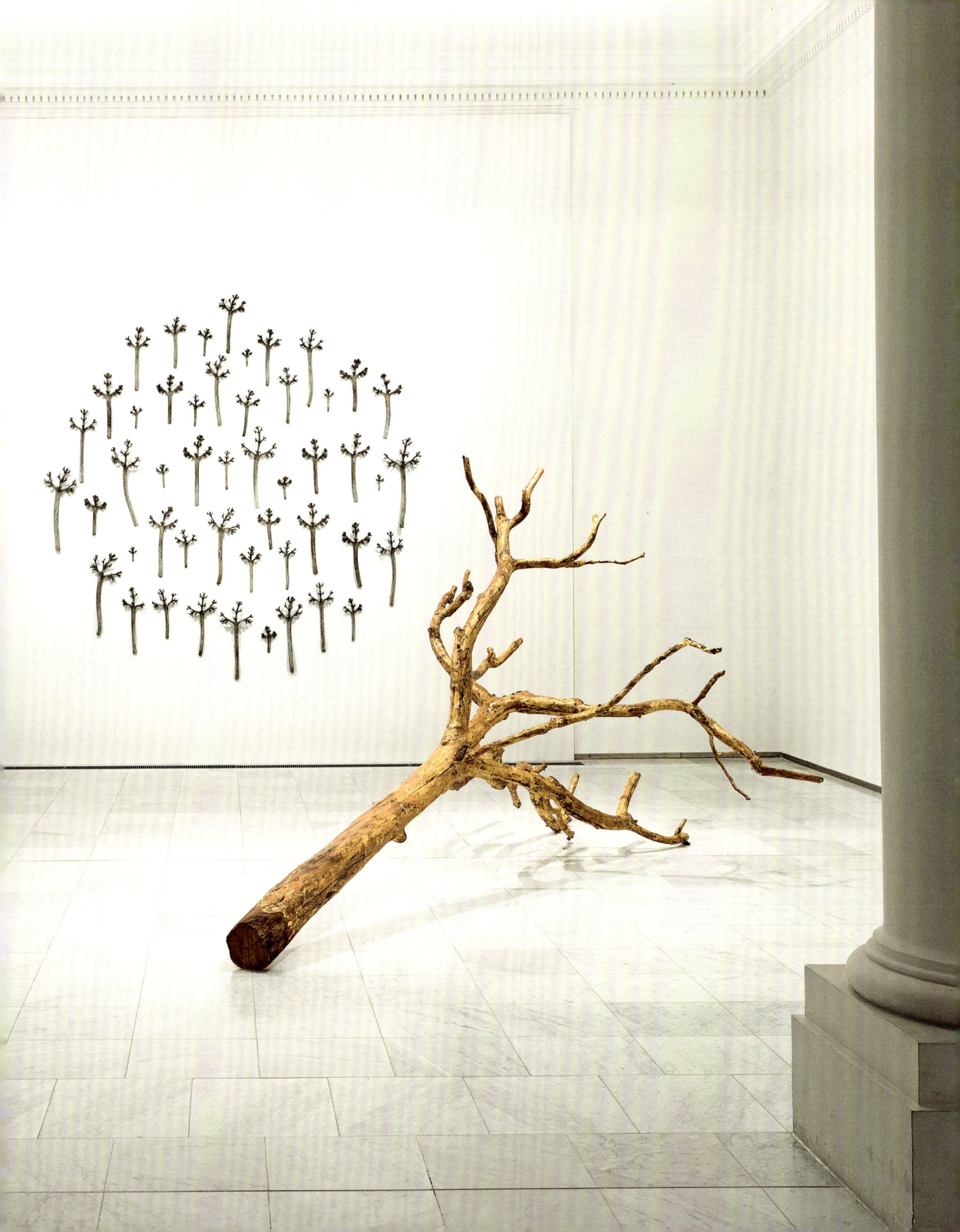

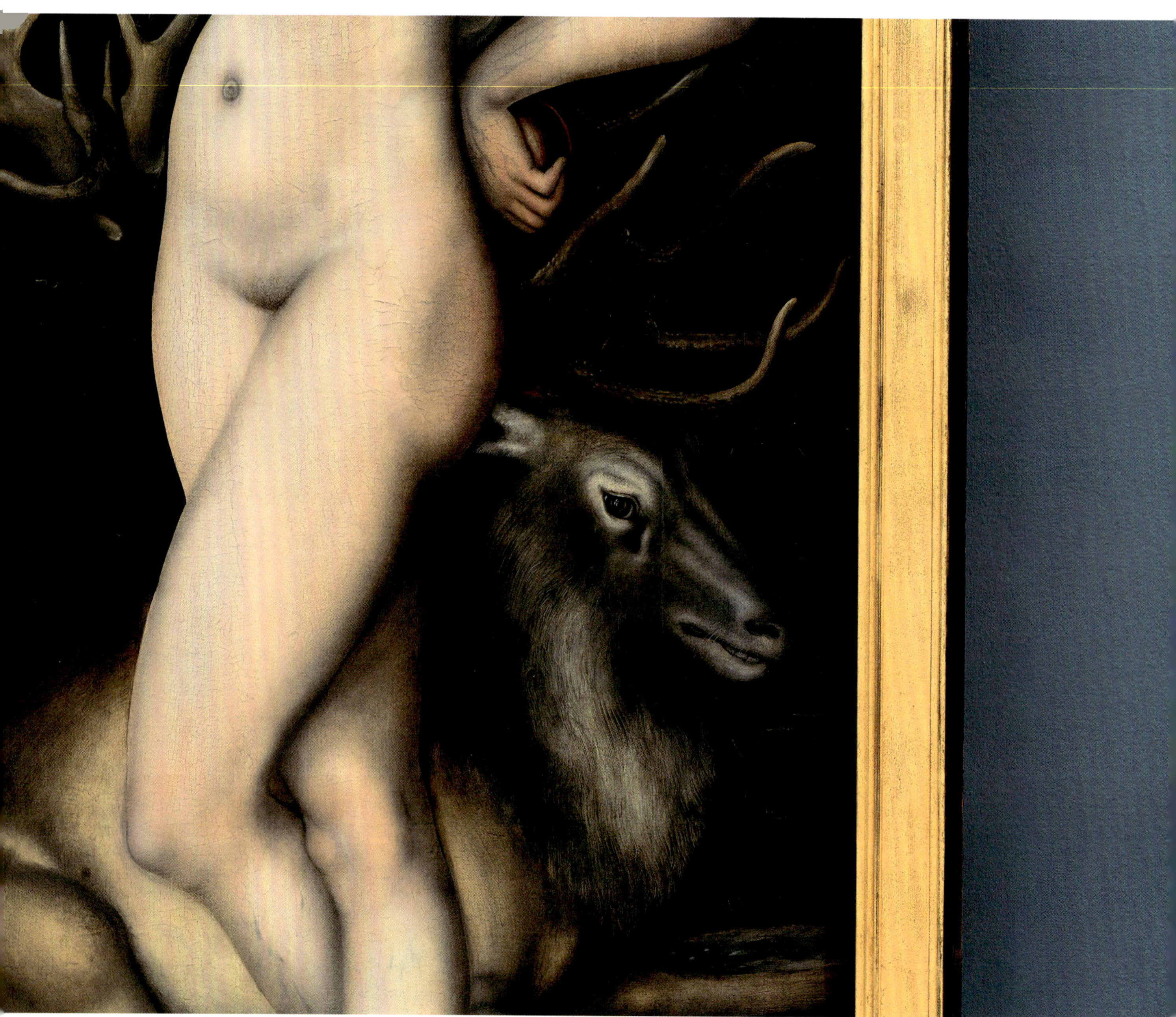

46 Lucas Cranach <u>Eve</u>, detail (n.d.)

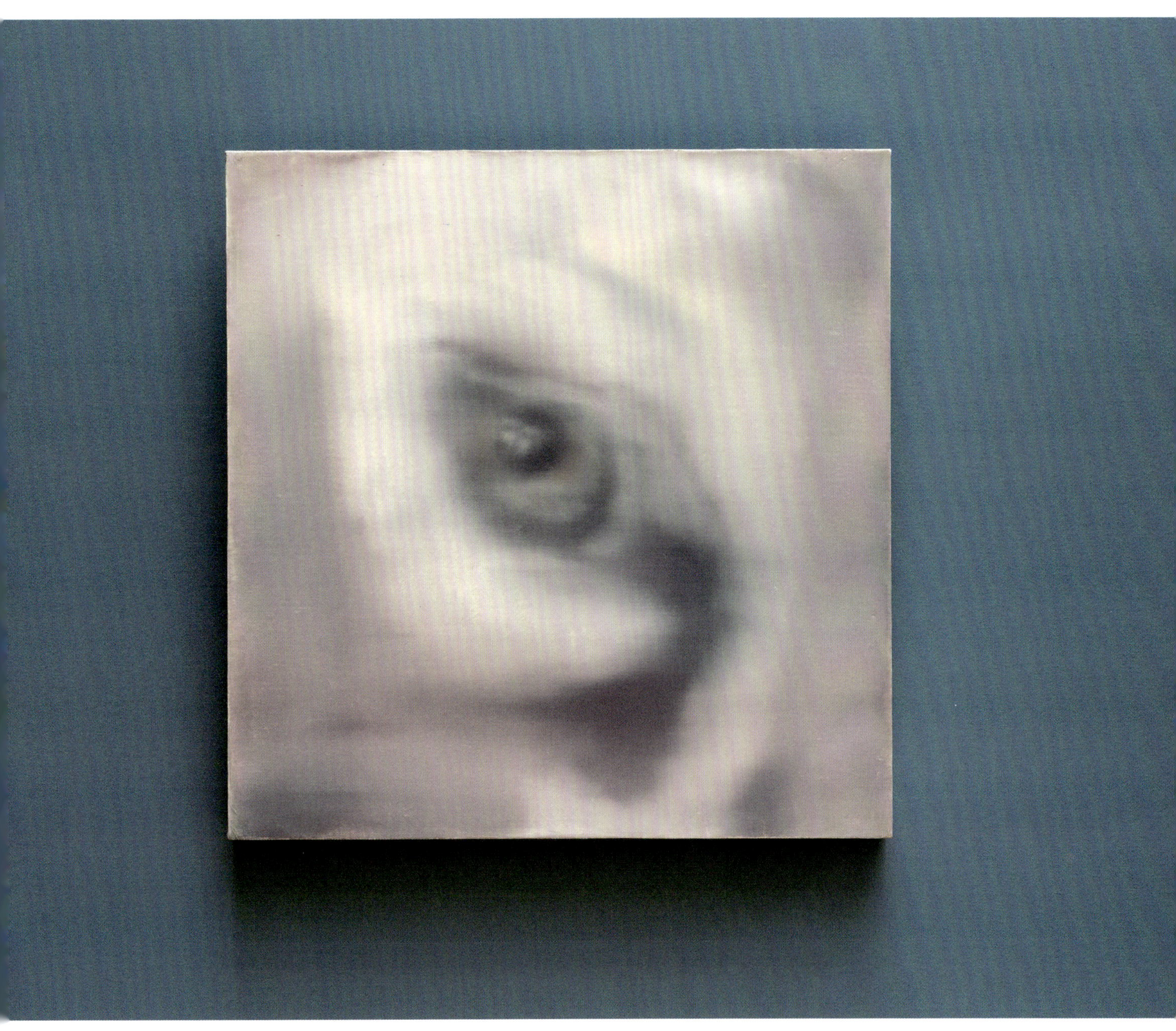

Lucas Cranach's Studio (2007)

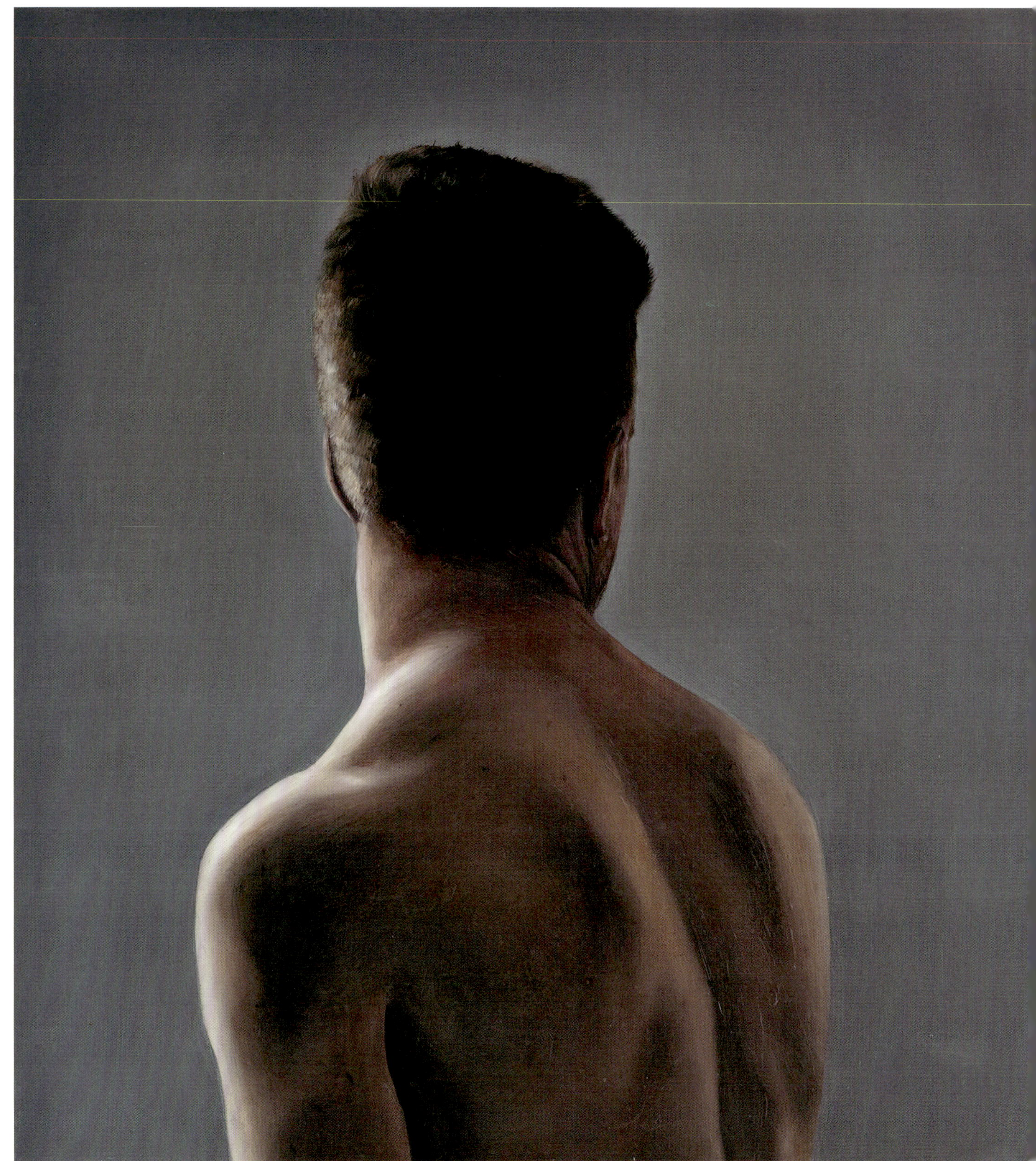

    <u>Blind Spot</u> (2016)

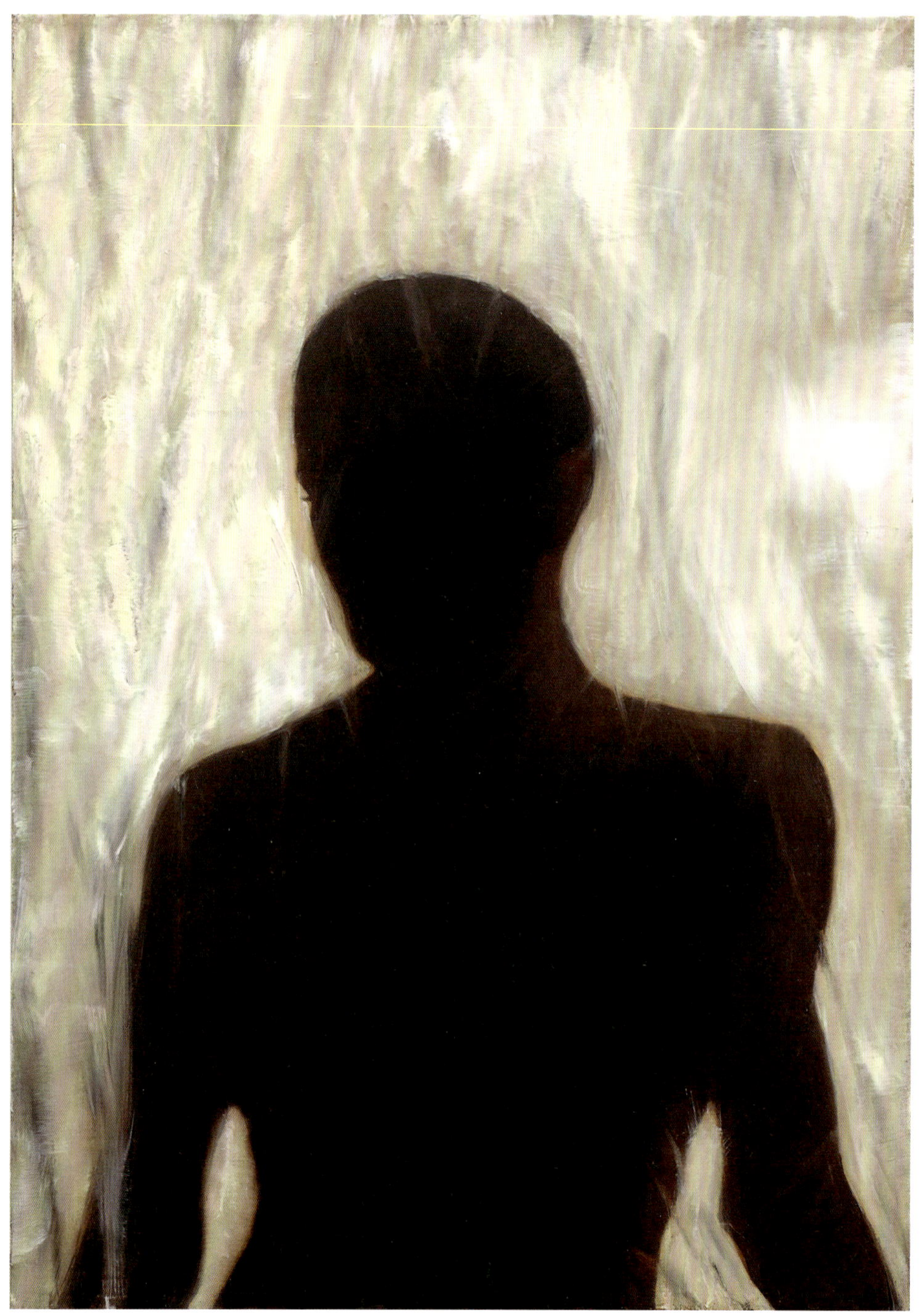

    Through (2013)

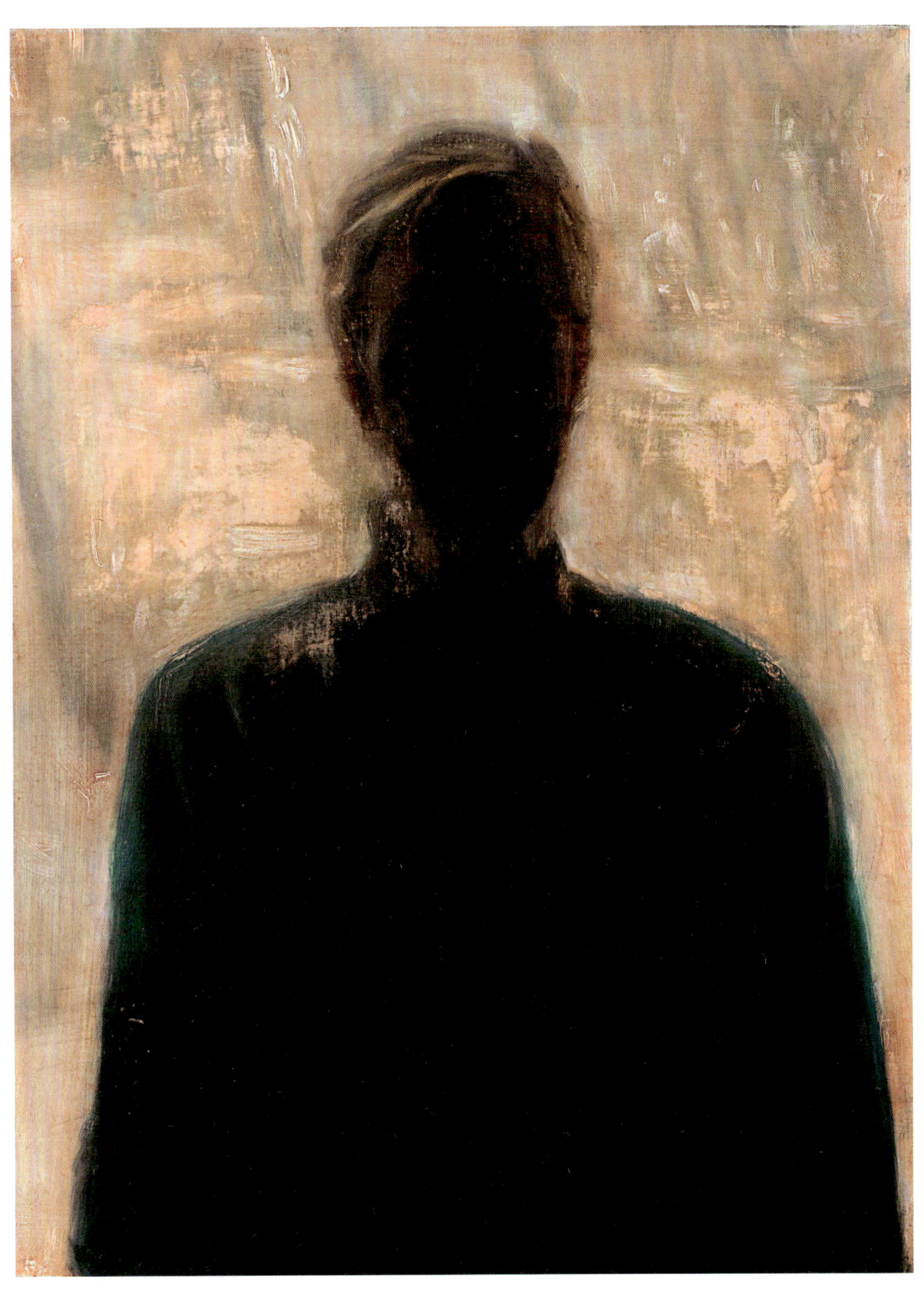

Mother (2011)

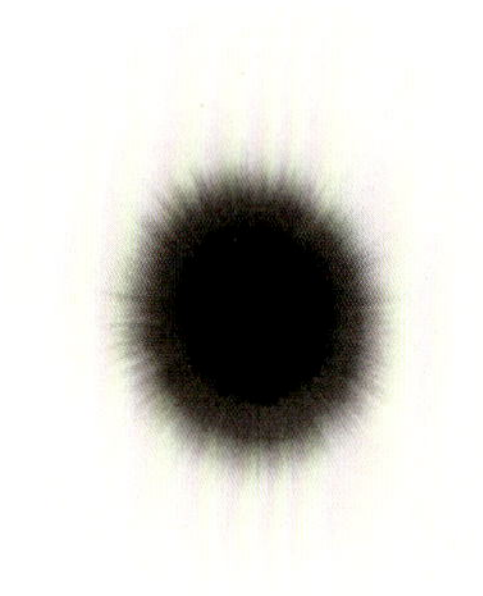

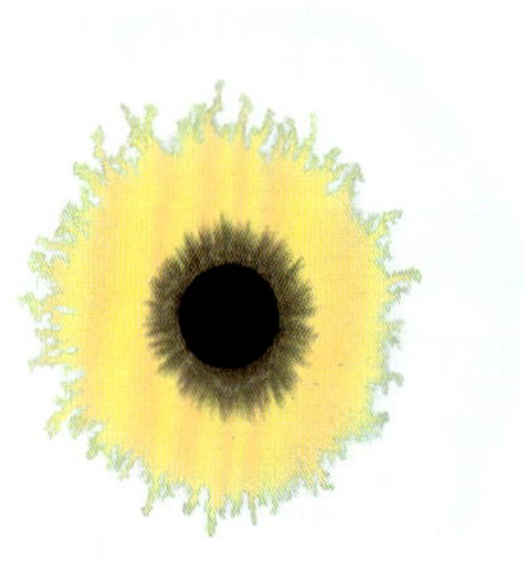

 Untitled, from the "Looking from the Black Hole" series (2015)

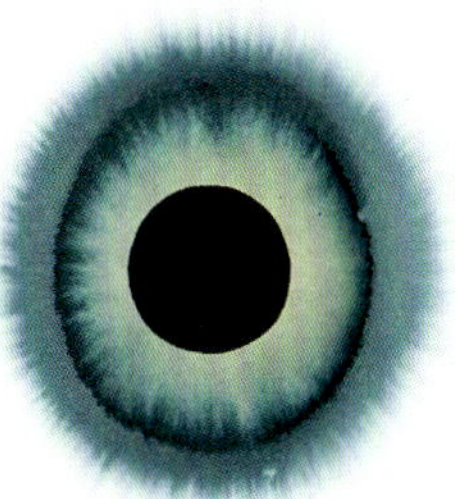

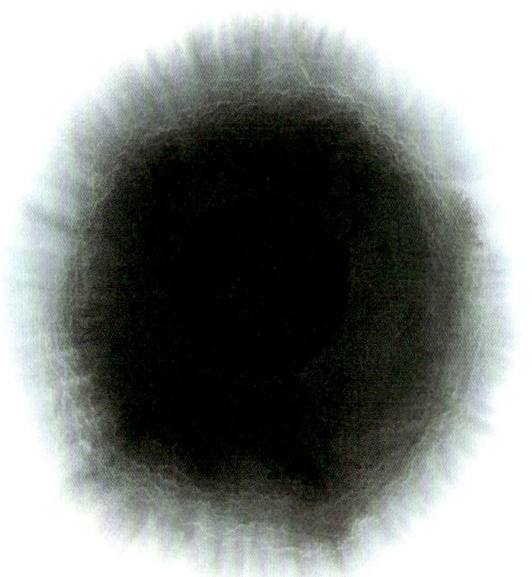

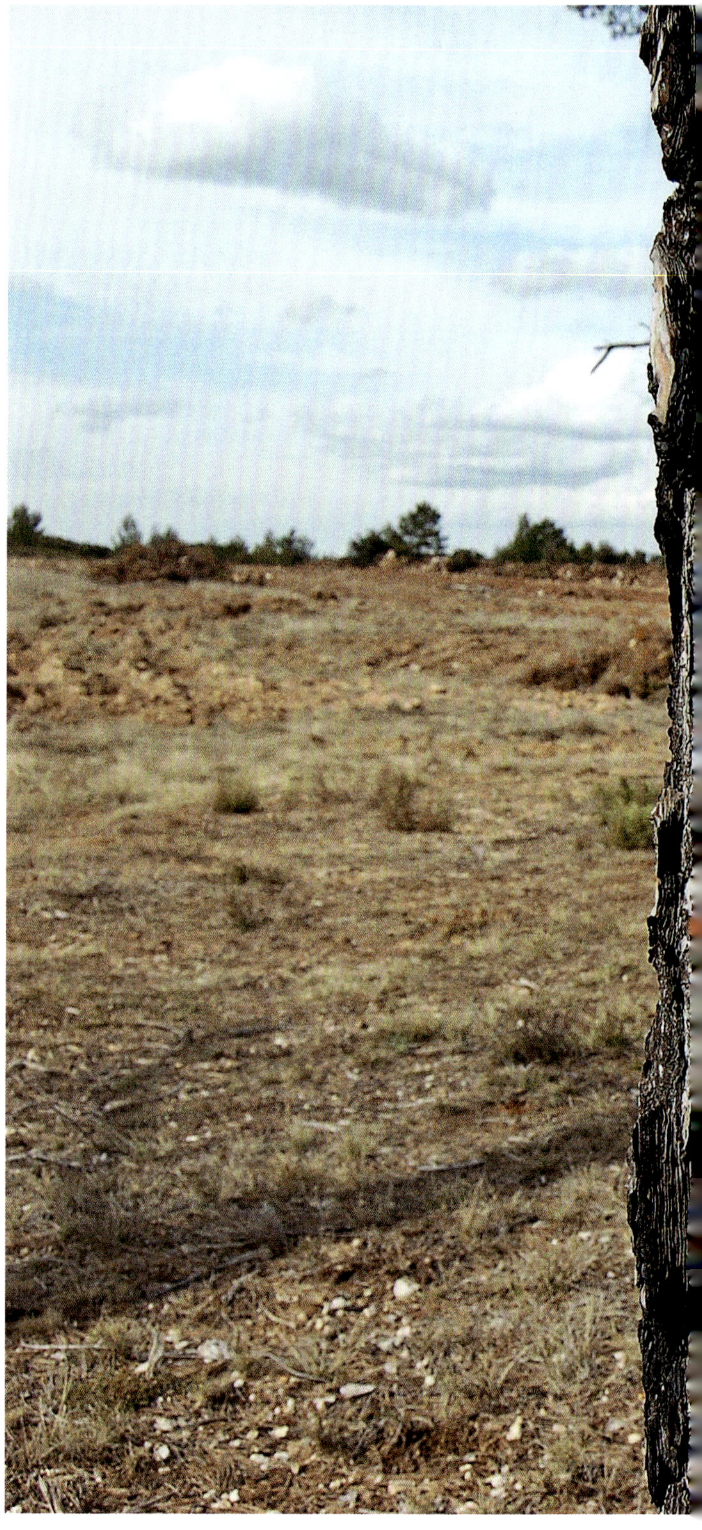

  From Fire to Fire (2011)

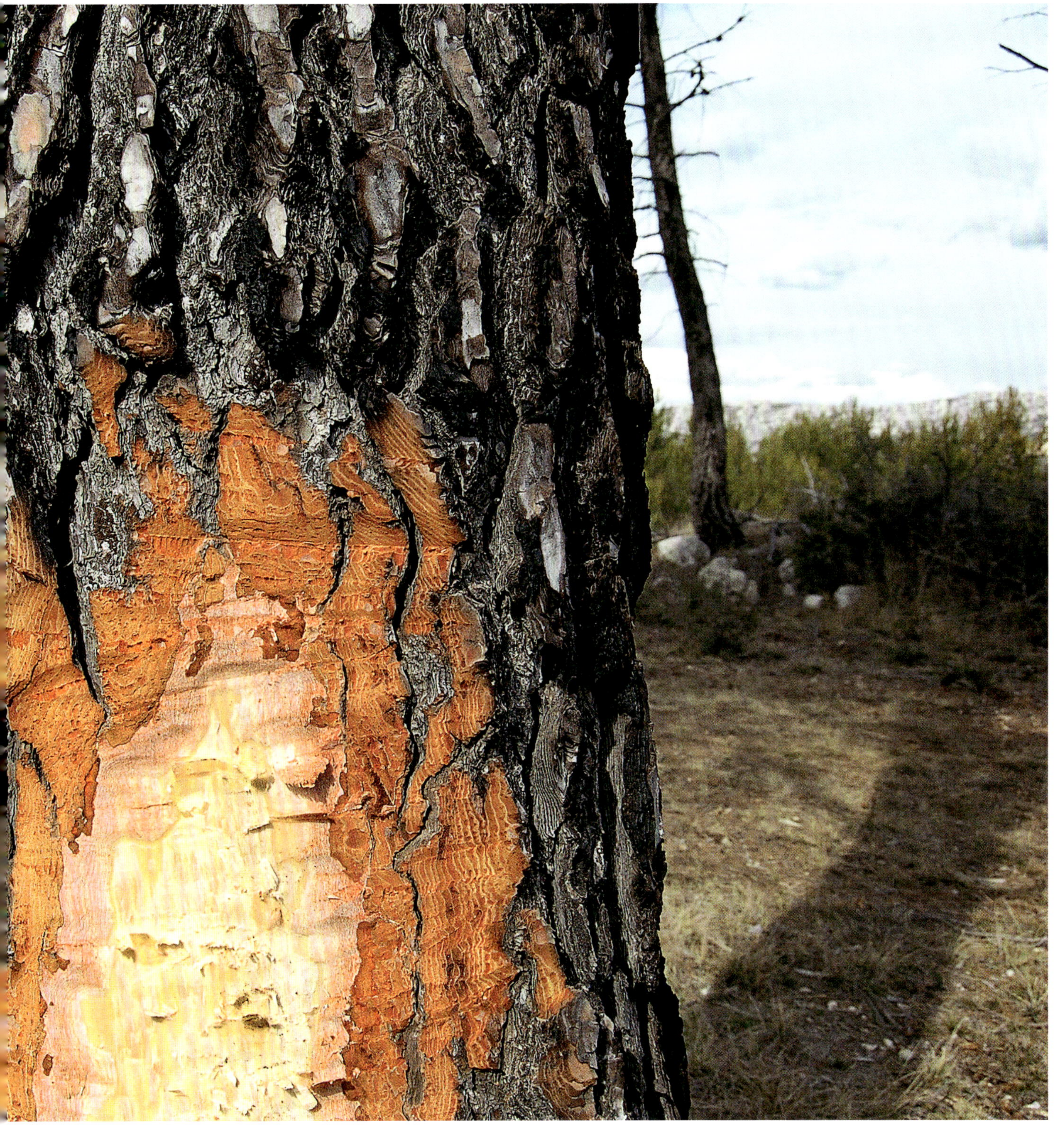

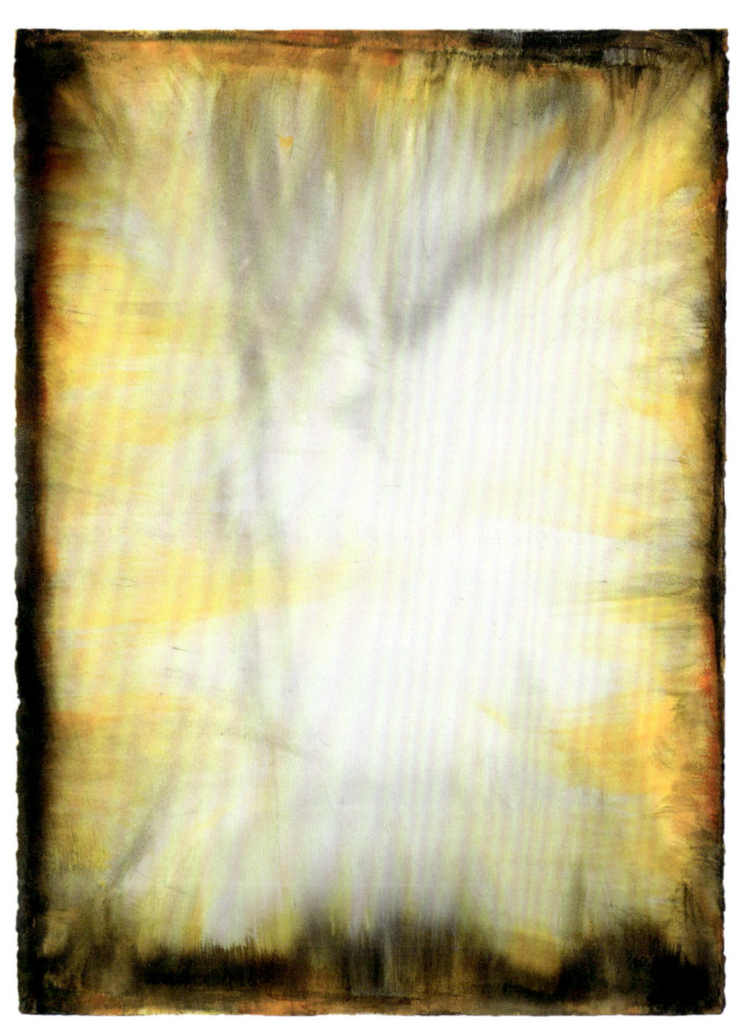

↑ <u>Untitled</u>, from the "Sacrifice Drawings" series (2016)

→ <u>Untitled</u>, from the "Treshold" series (2016)

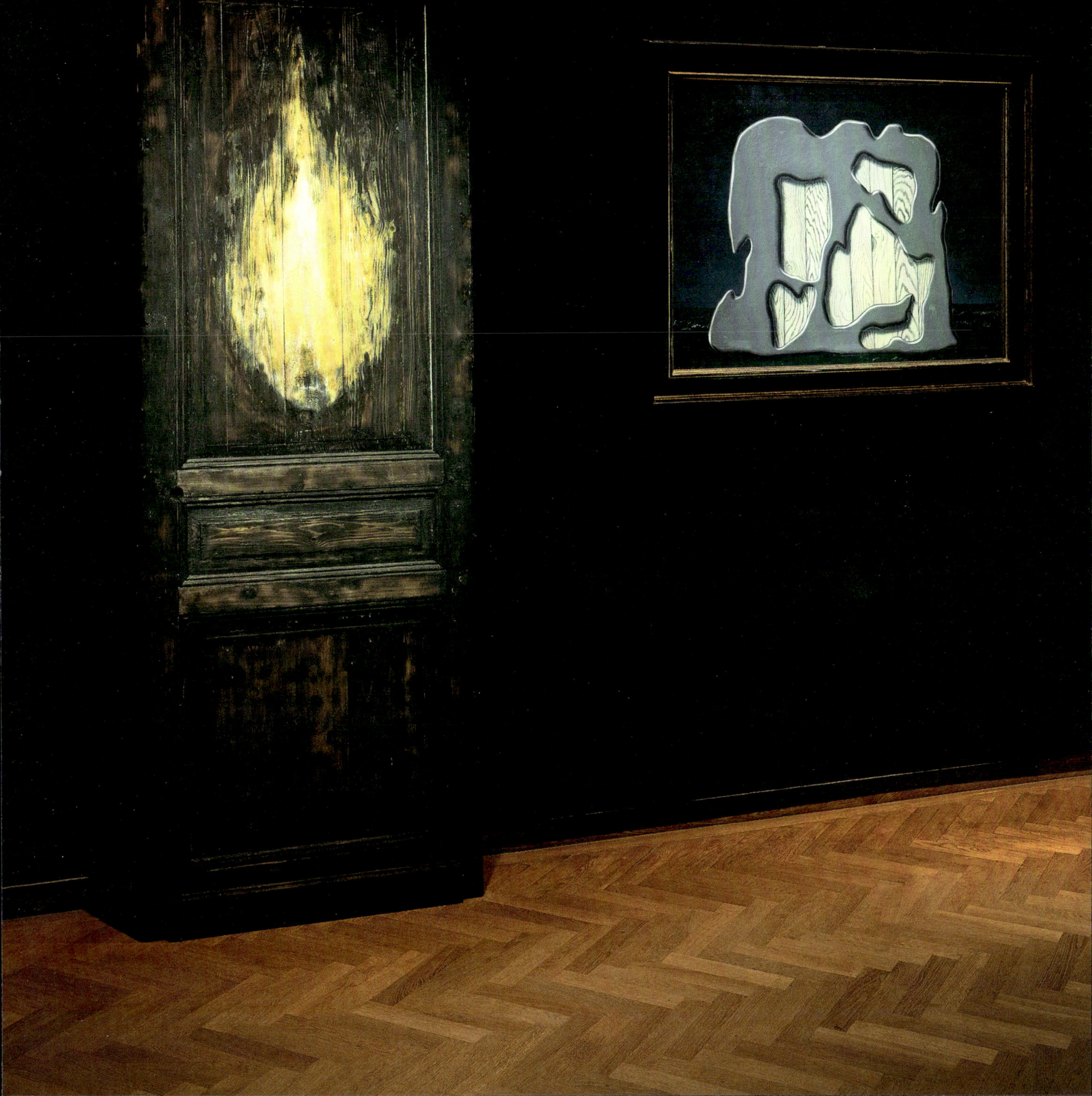

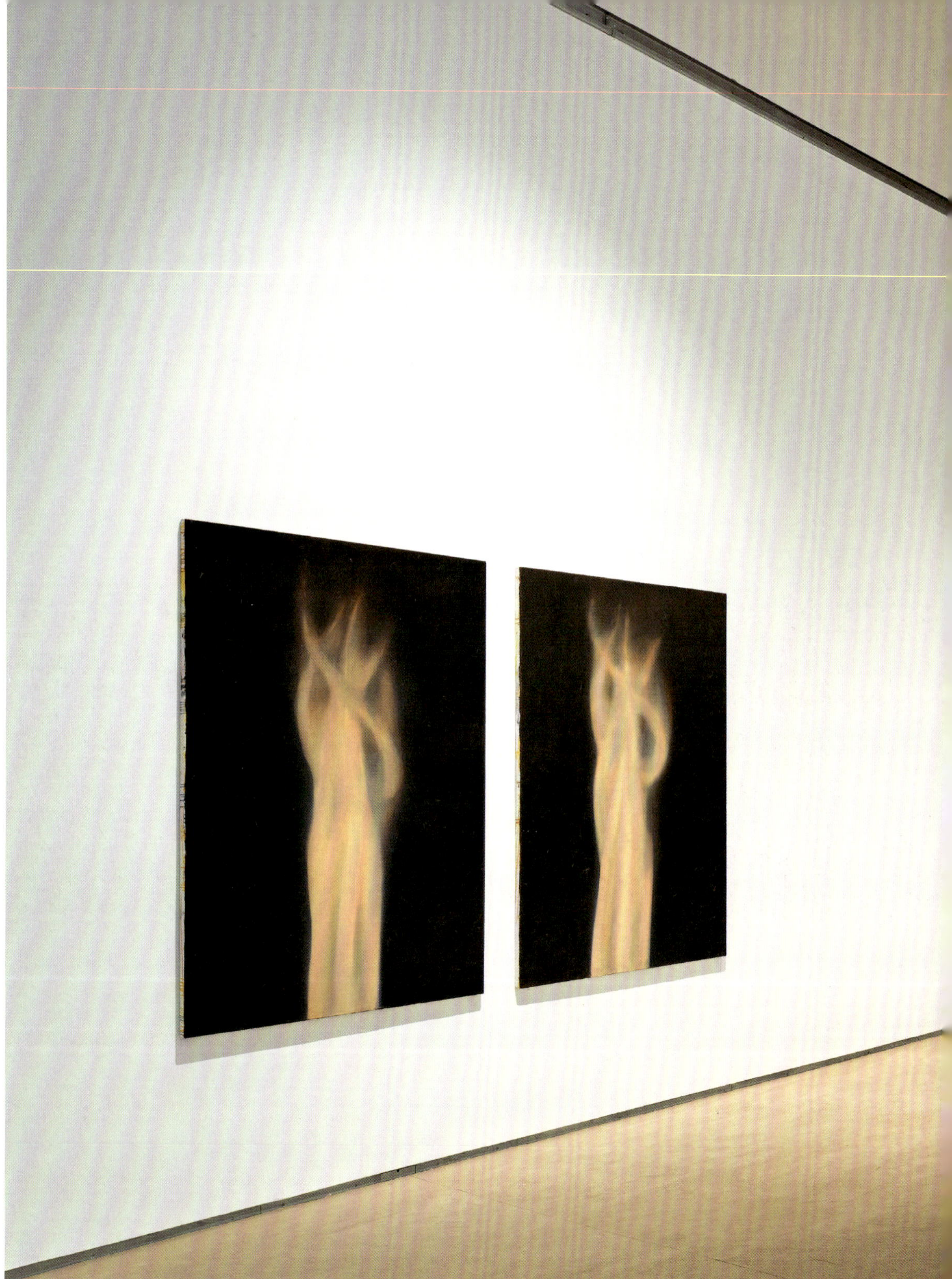

 Exhibition view in the RMFAB, October 2021 (cat. 35 to 38)

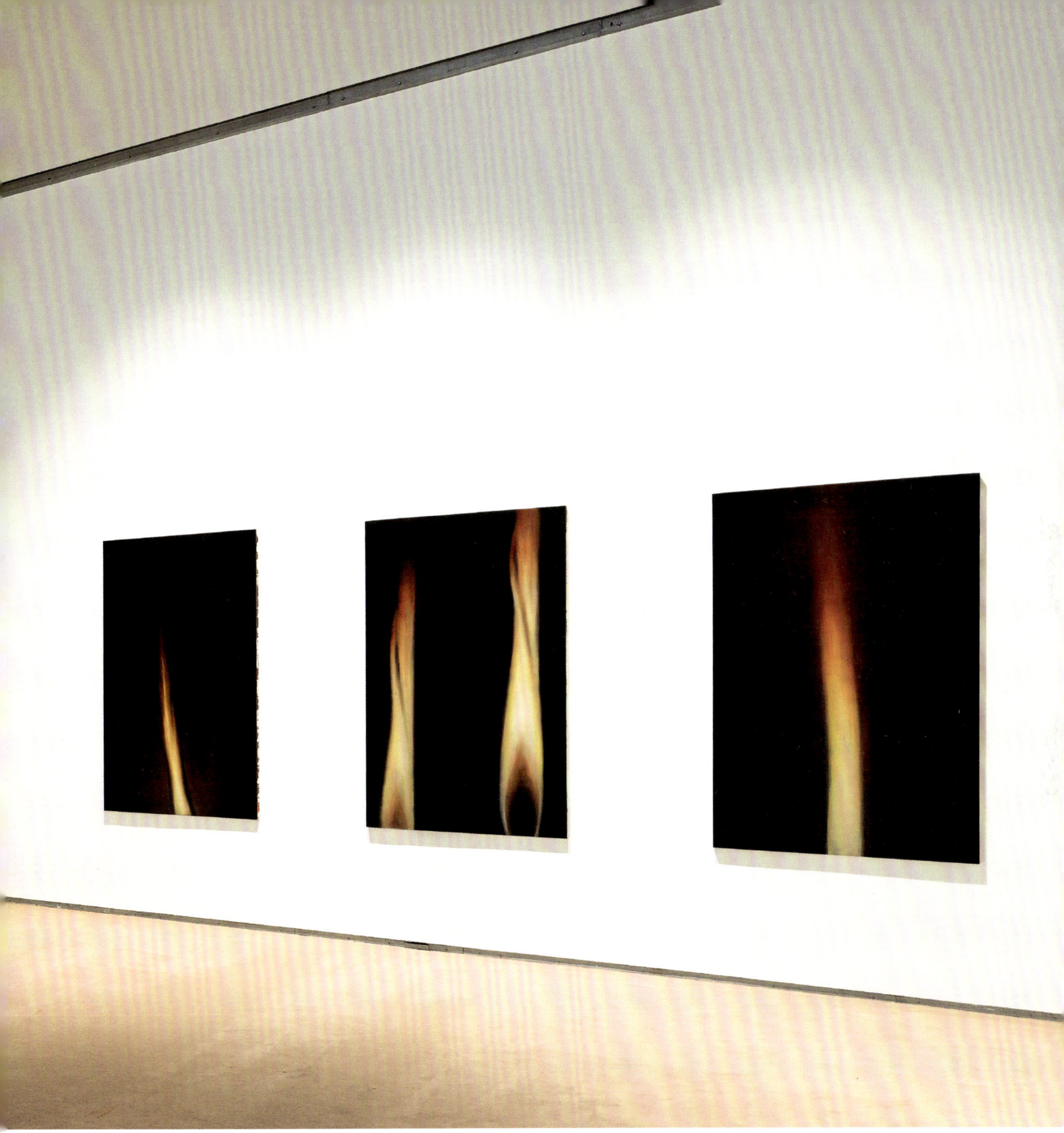

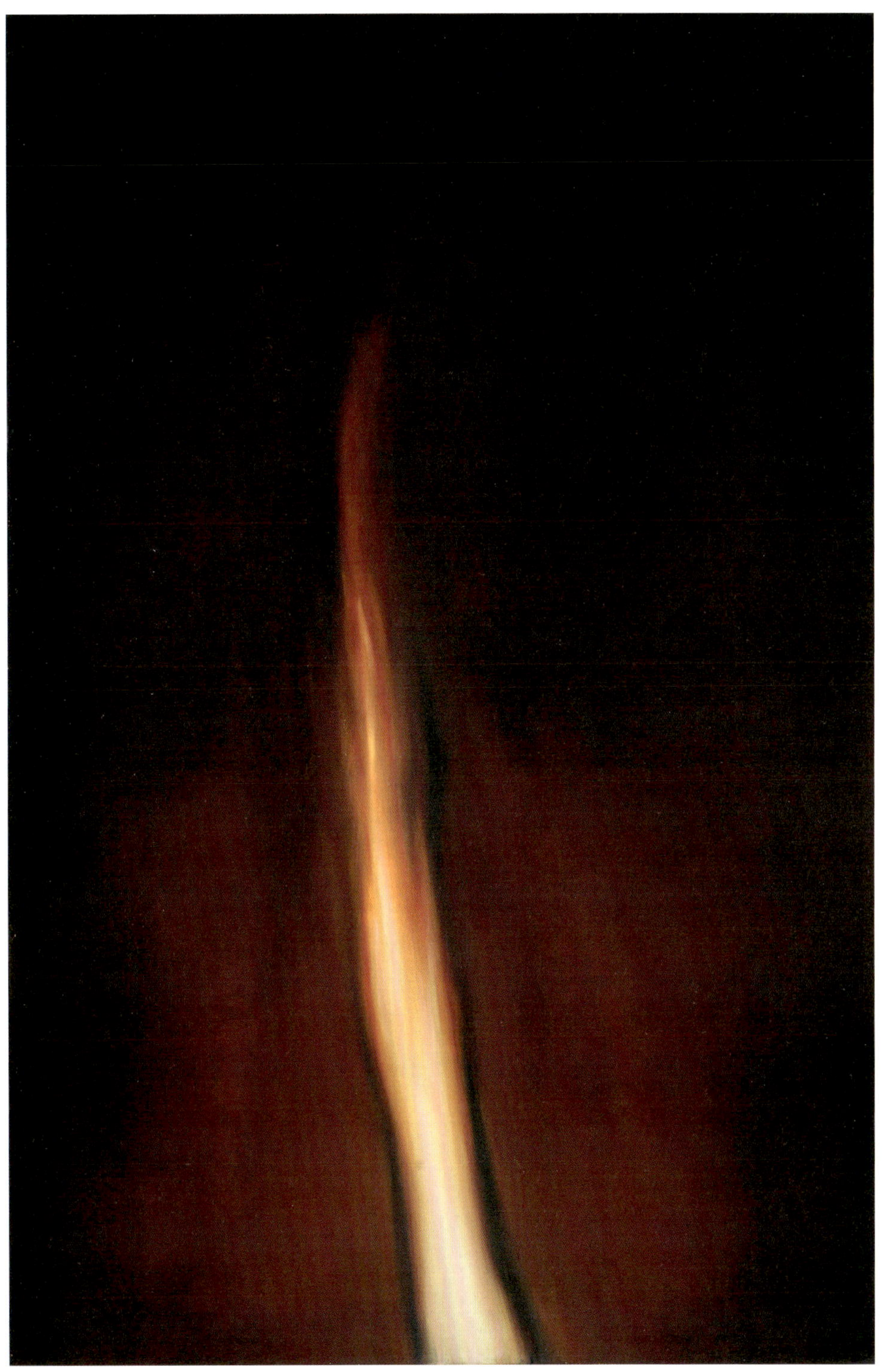

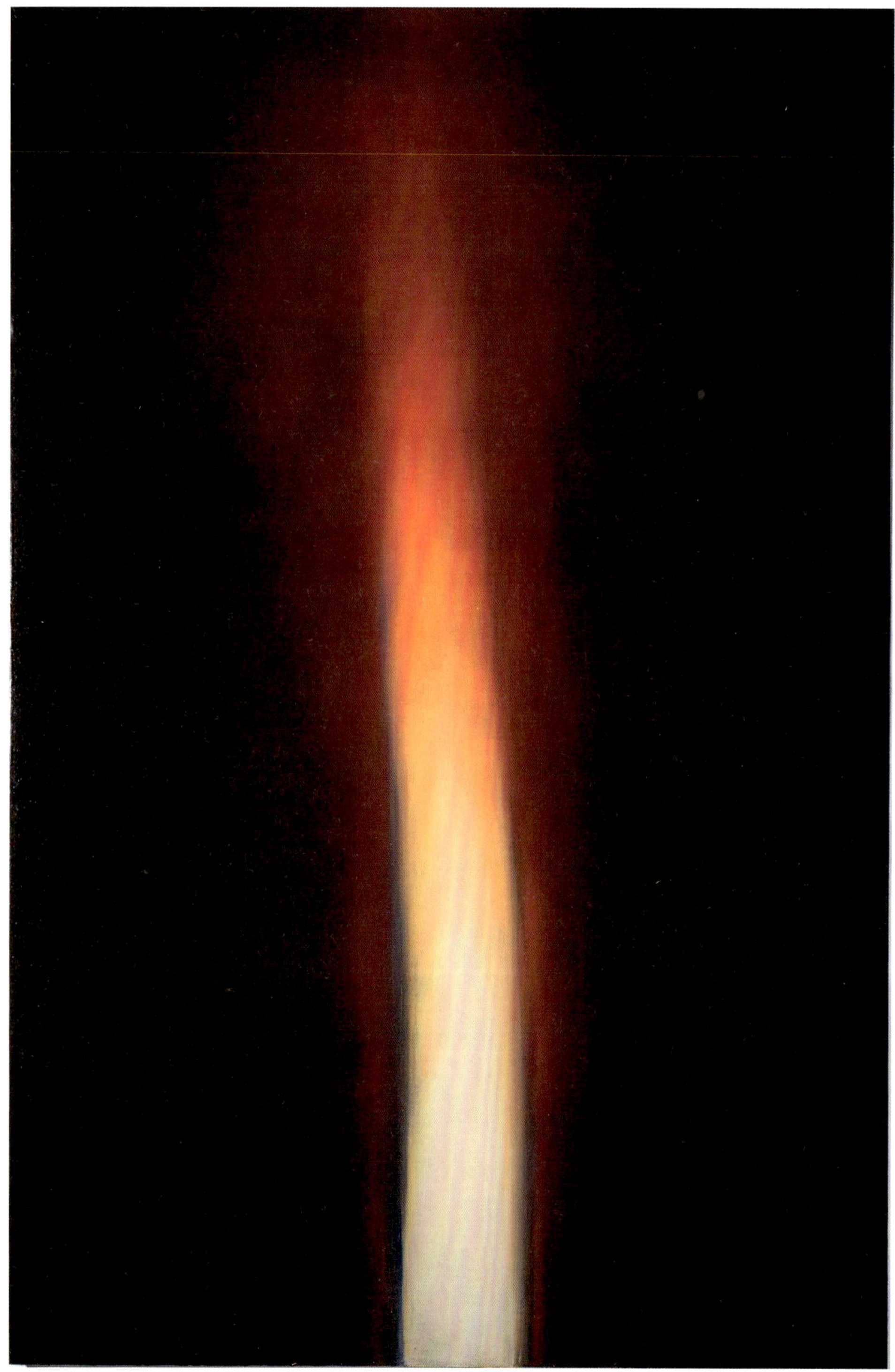

 <u>The Education of the Virgin, Frick Collection, New York</u> (2012)

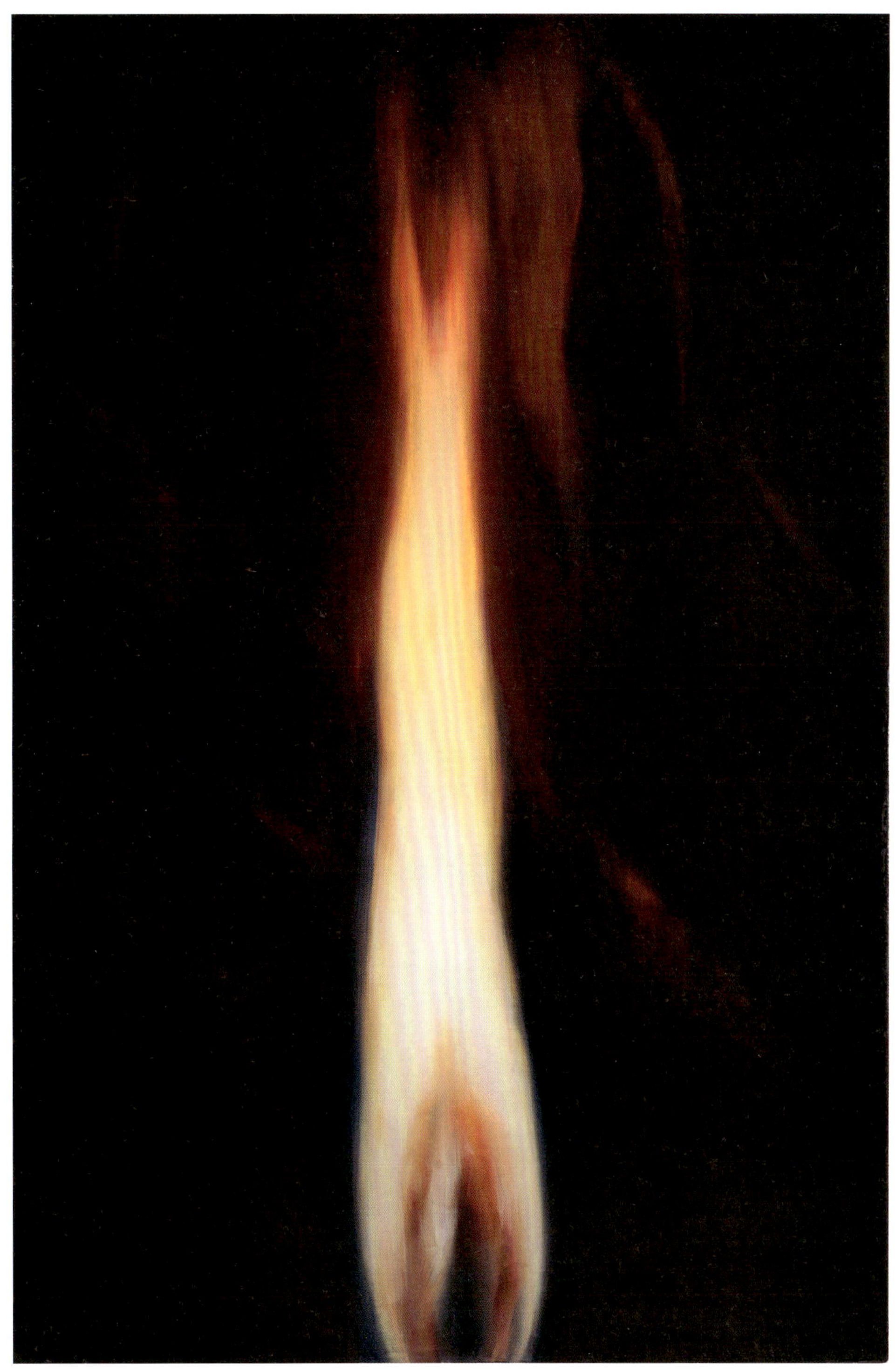

Payment of Taxes, Art Gallery, Lviv, Ukraine (2011)

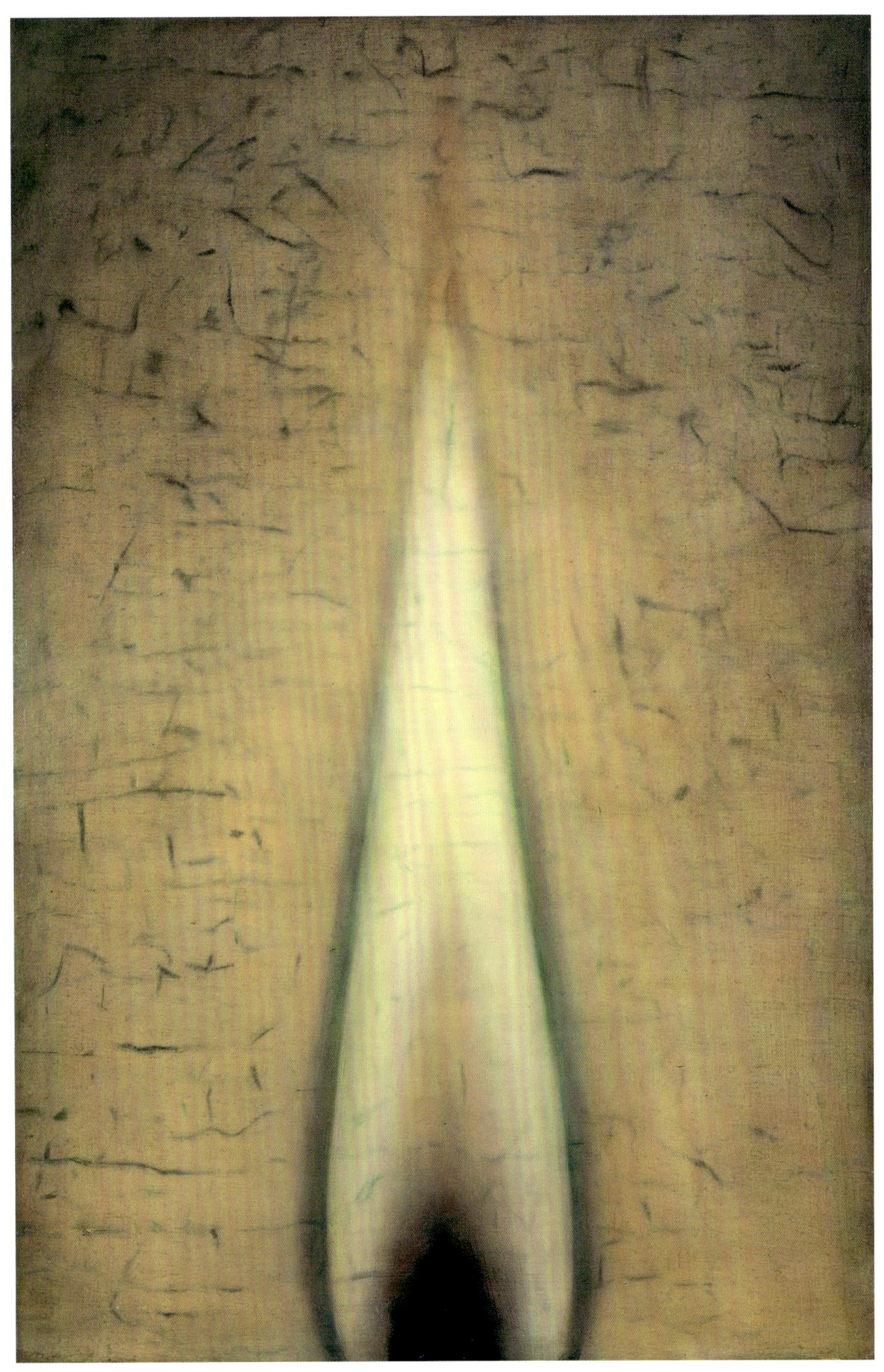

Job Mocked by his Wife, Musée Départemental des Vosges, Epinal (2011)

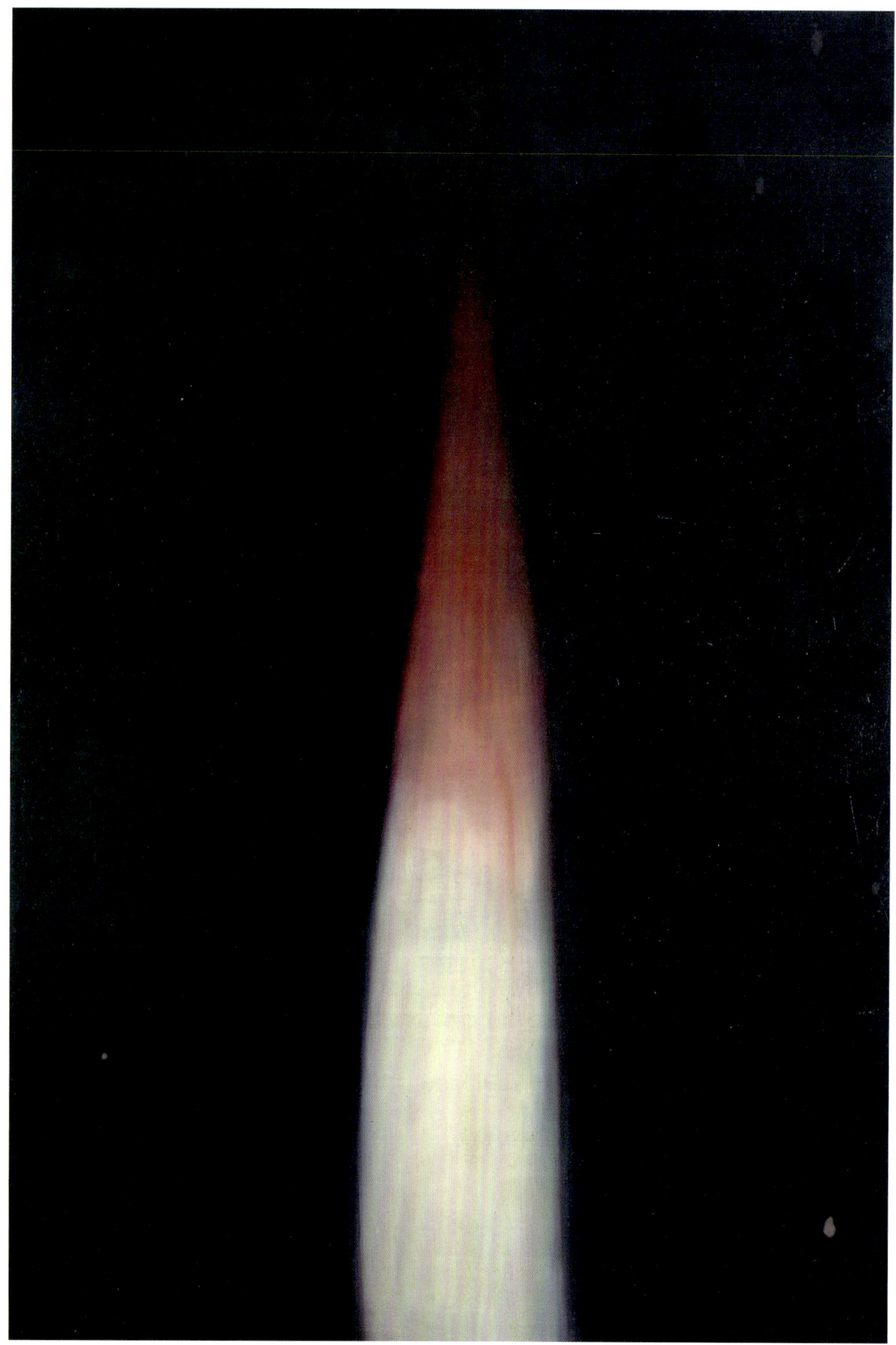

 Magdalene with the Smoking Flame, Musée du Louvre, Paris (2009)

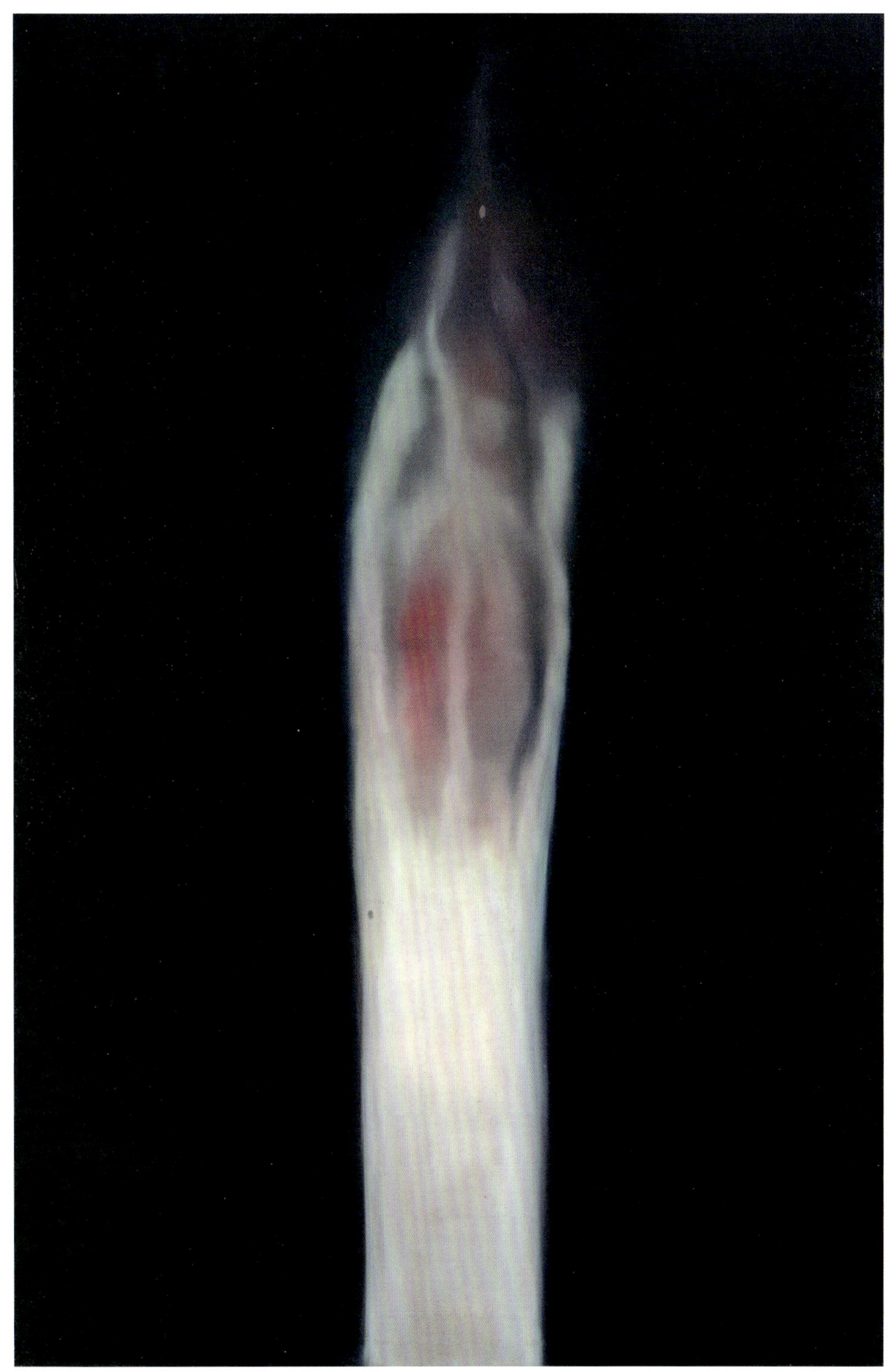

<u>Christ in the Carpenter's Shop, Musée du Louvre, Paris</u> (2009)

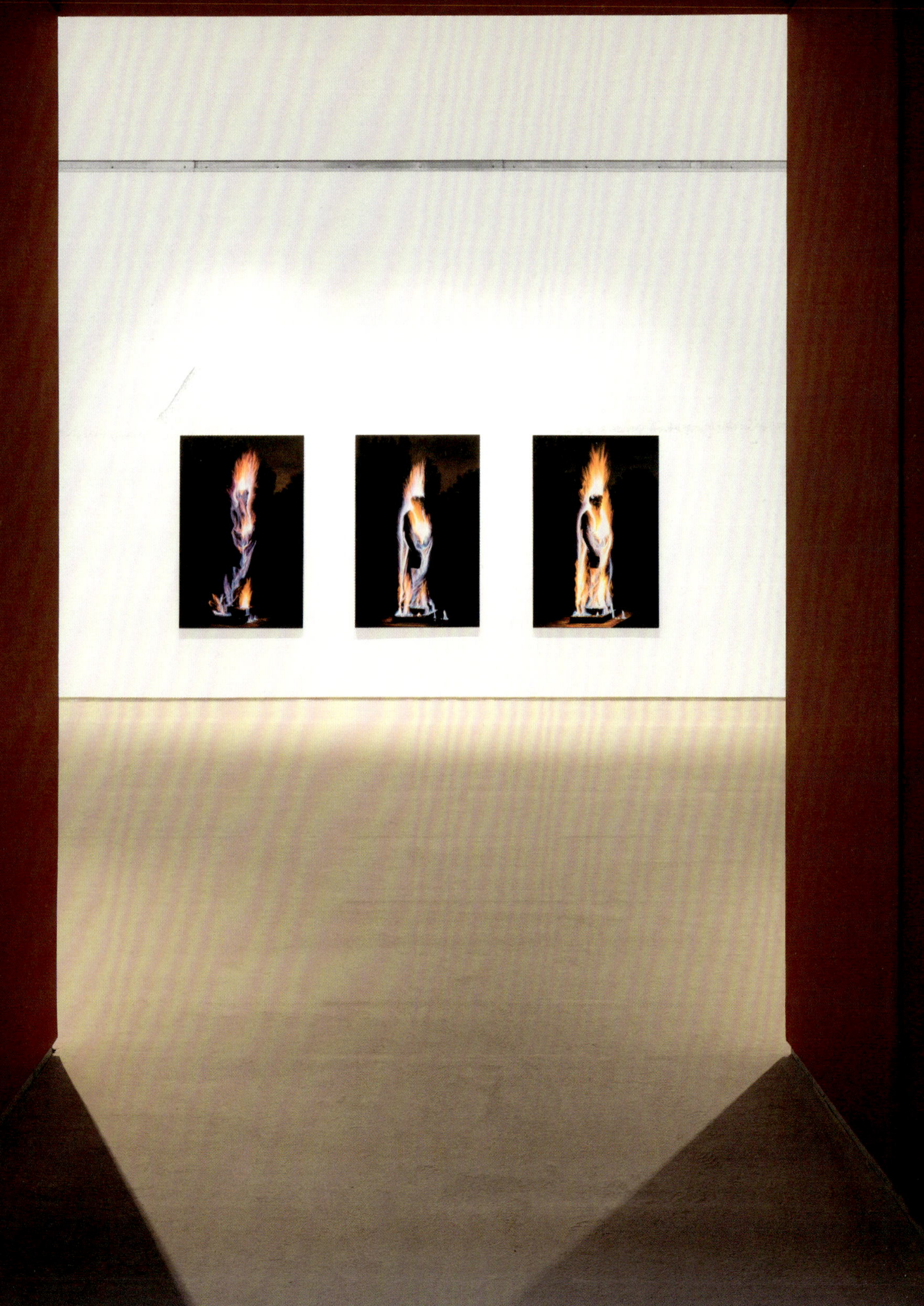

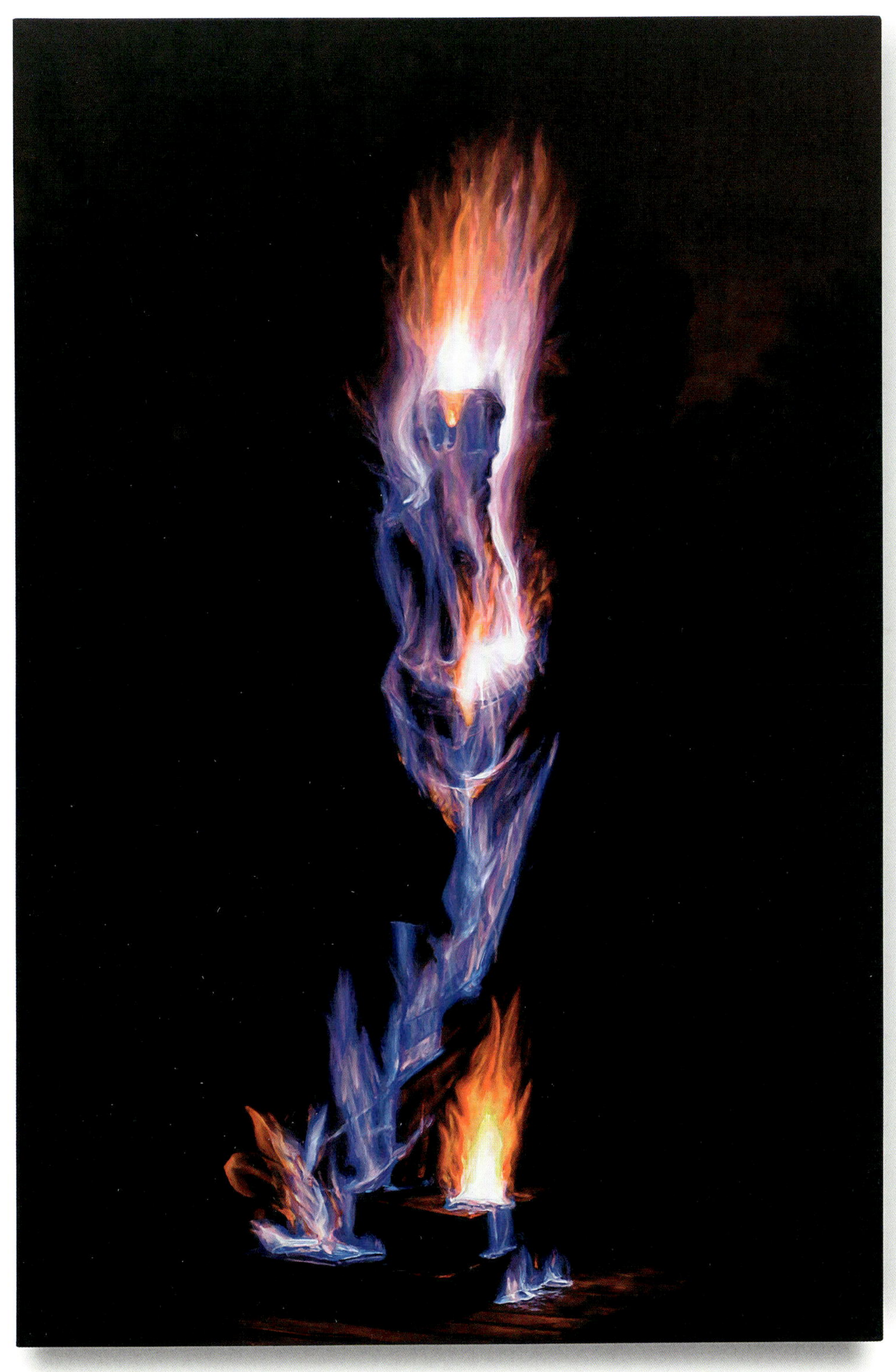

← Exhibition view in the RMFAB, October 2021 (cat. 42 to 44)

↑ <u>Untitled #3</u>, from the "Twilight's Gaze" series (2021)

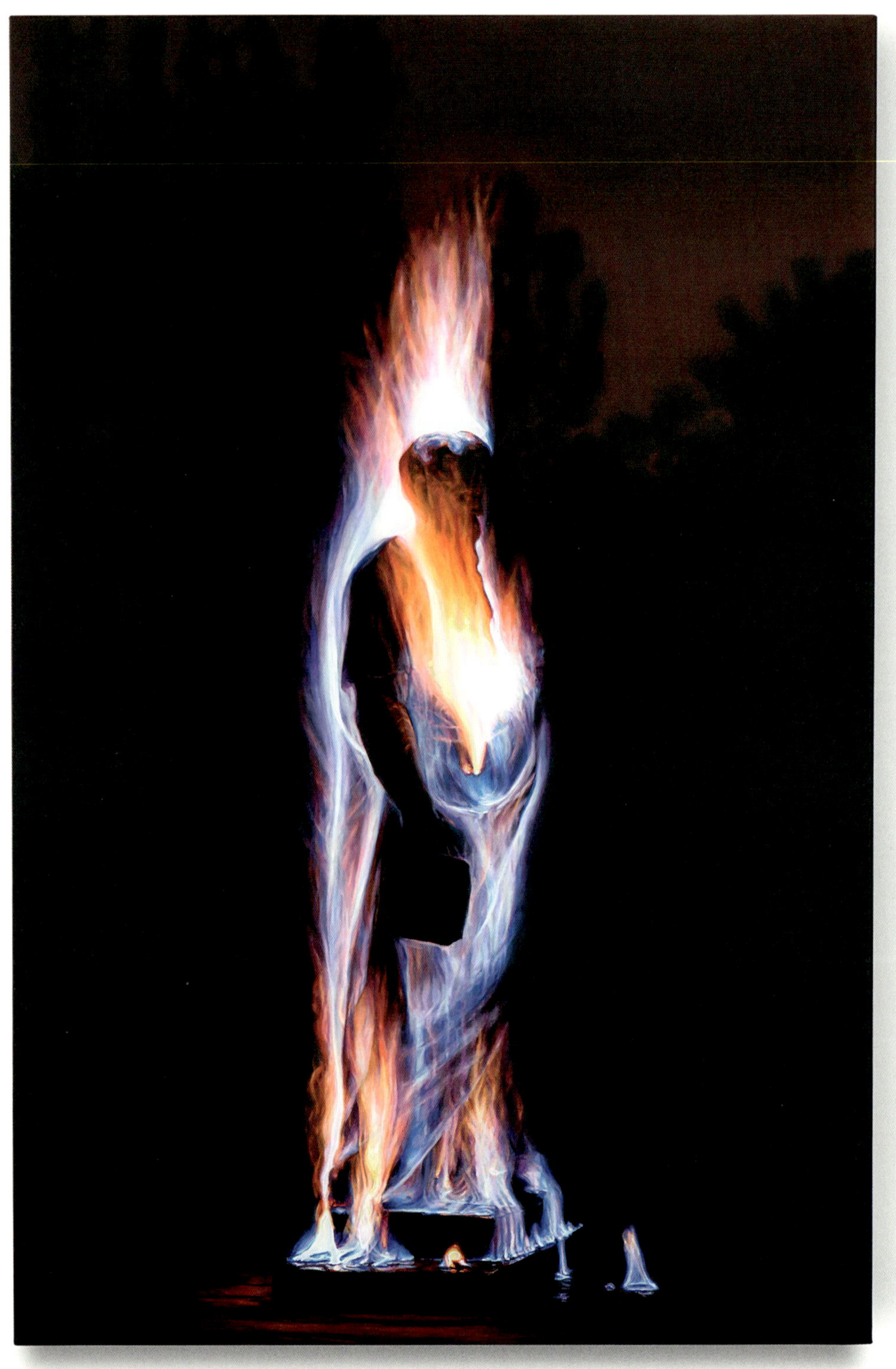

  Untitled #2, from the "Twilight's Gaze" series (2021)

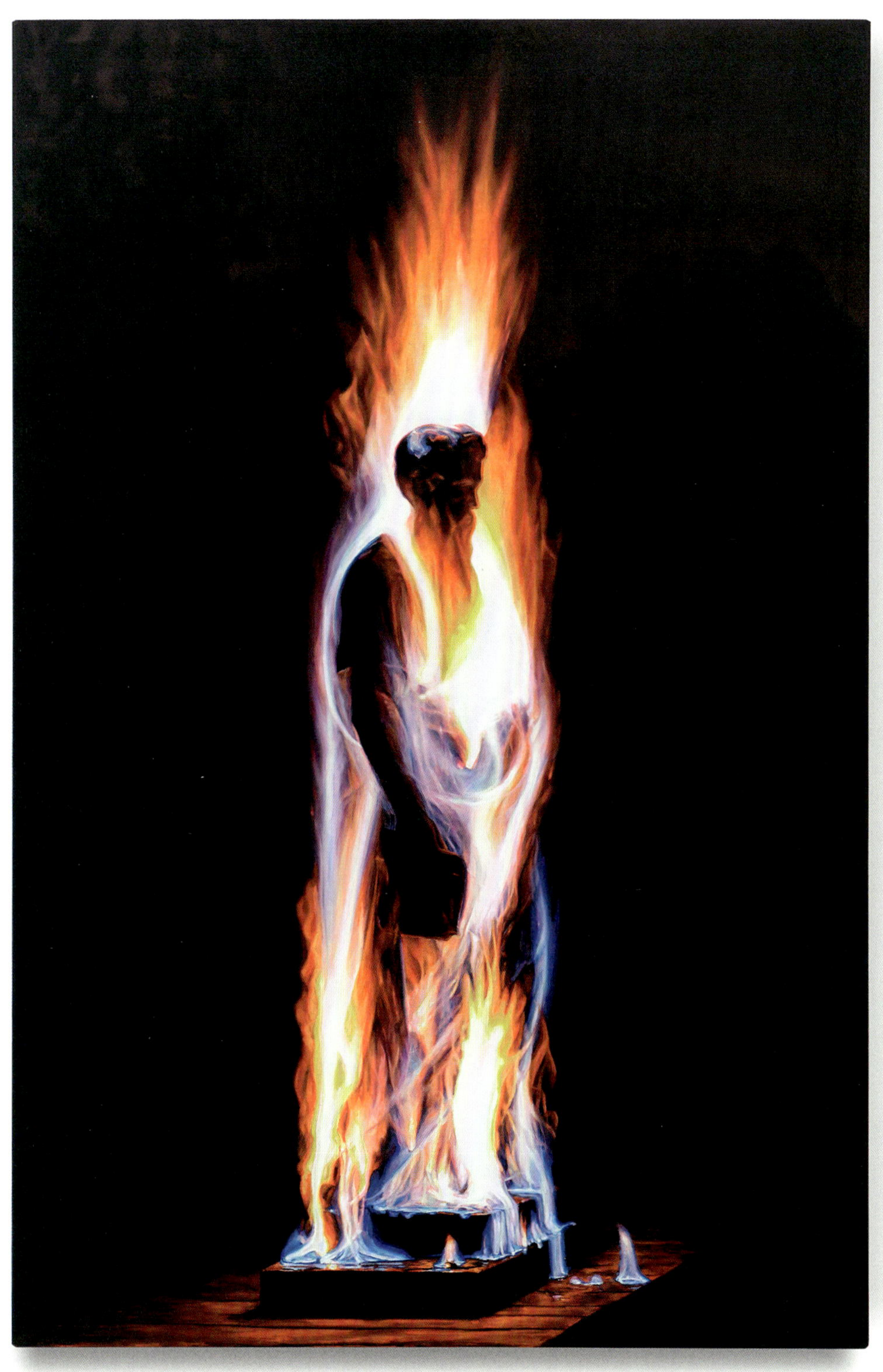

Untitled #1, from the "Twilight's Gaze" series (2021)

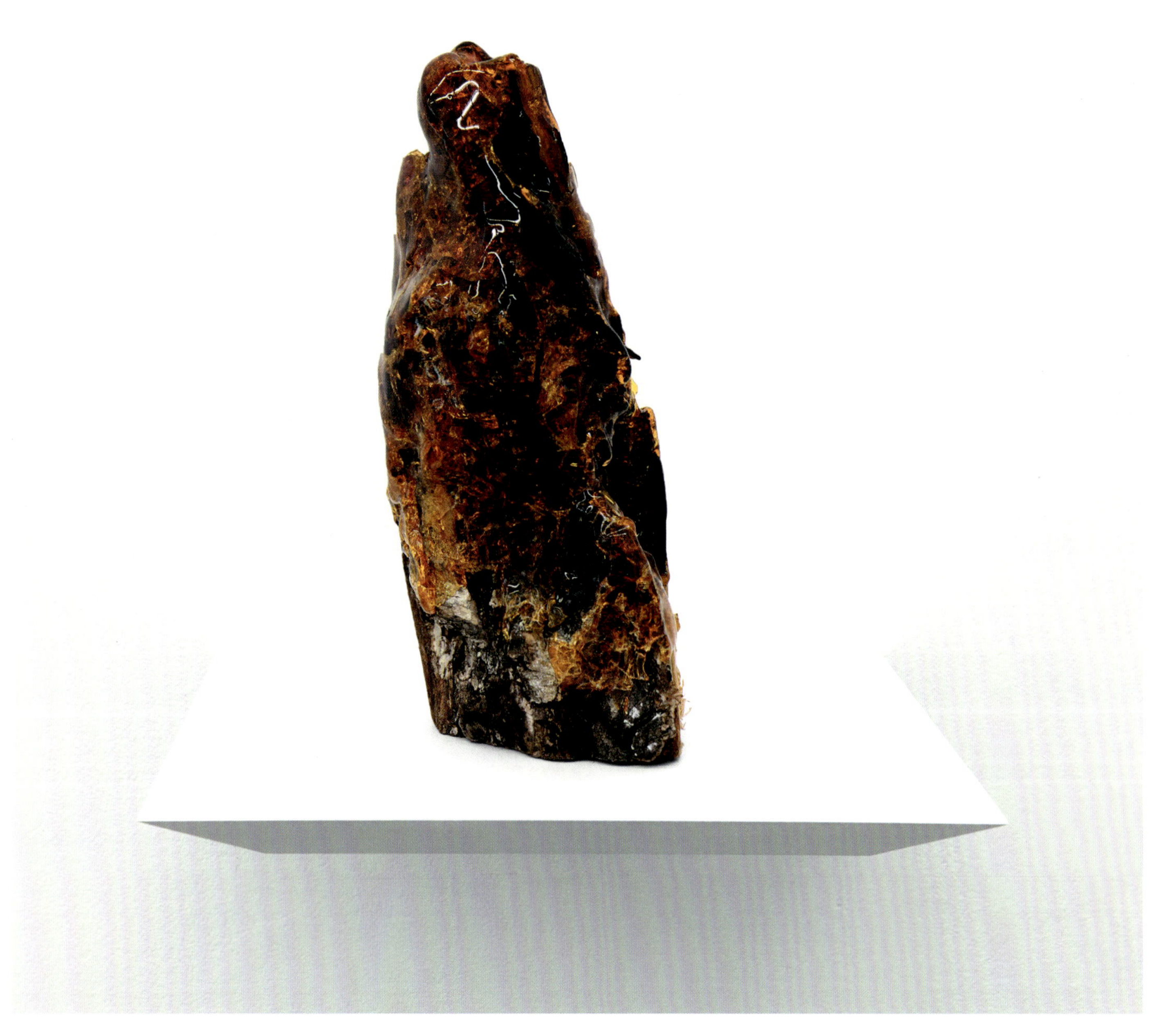

  <u>Untitled</u>, from the "Black is Virgin" series (2016)

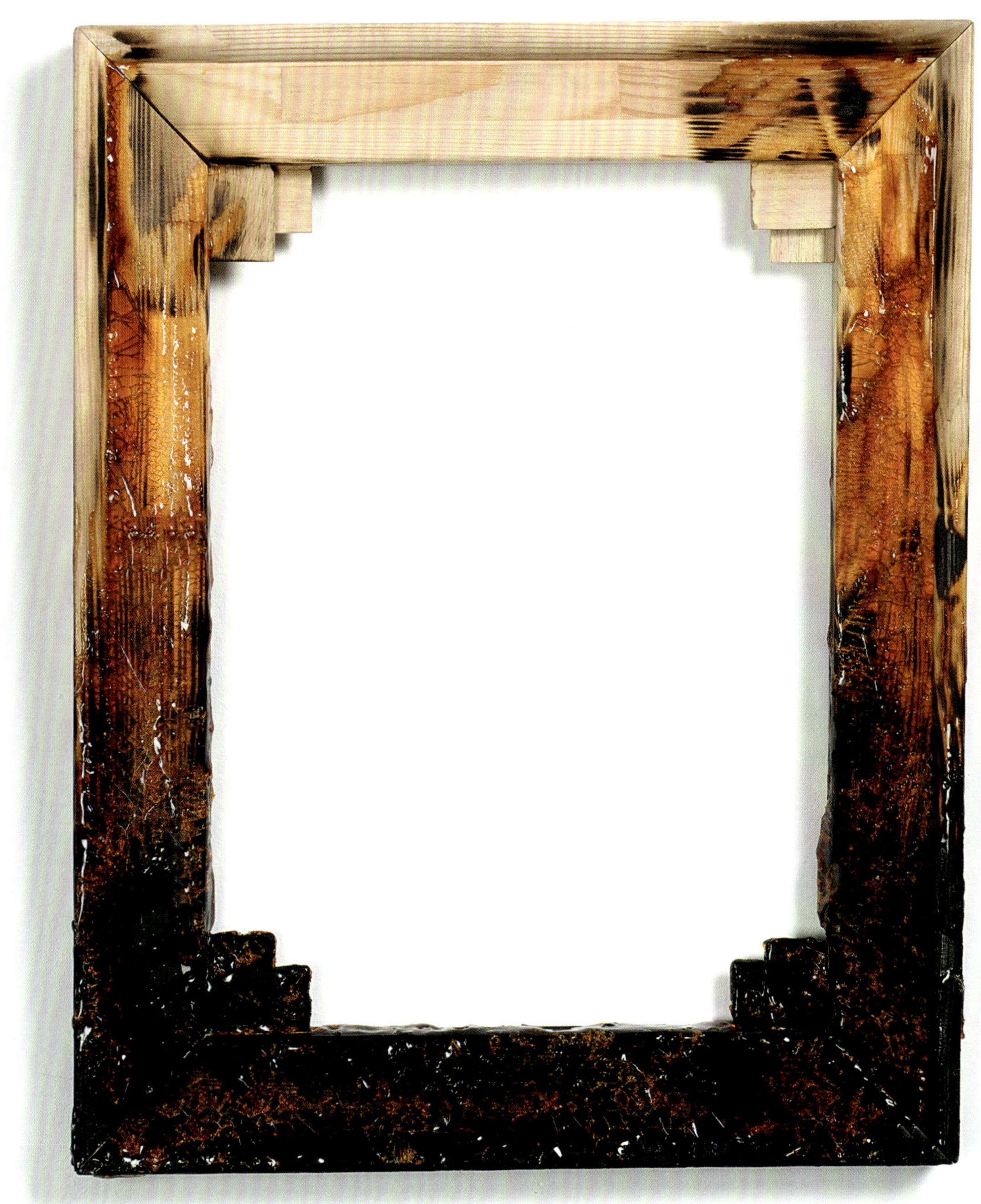

Untitled, from the "Still Fire" series (2016)

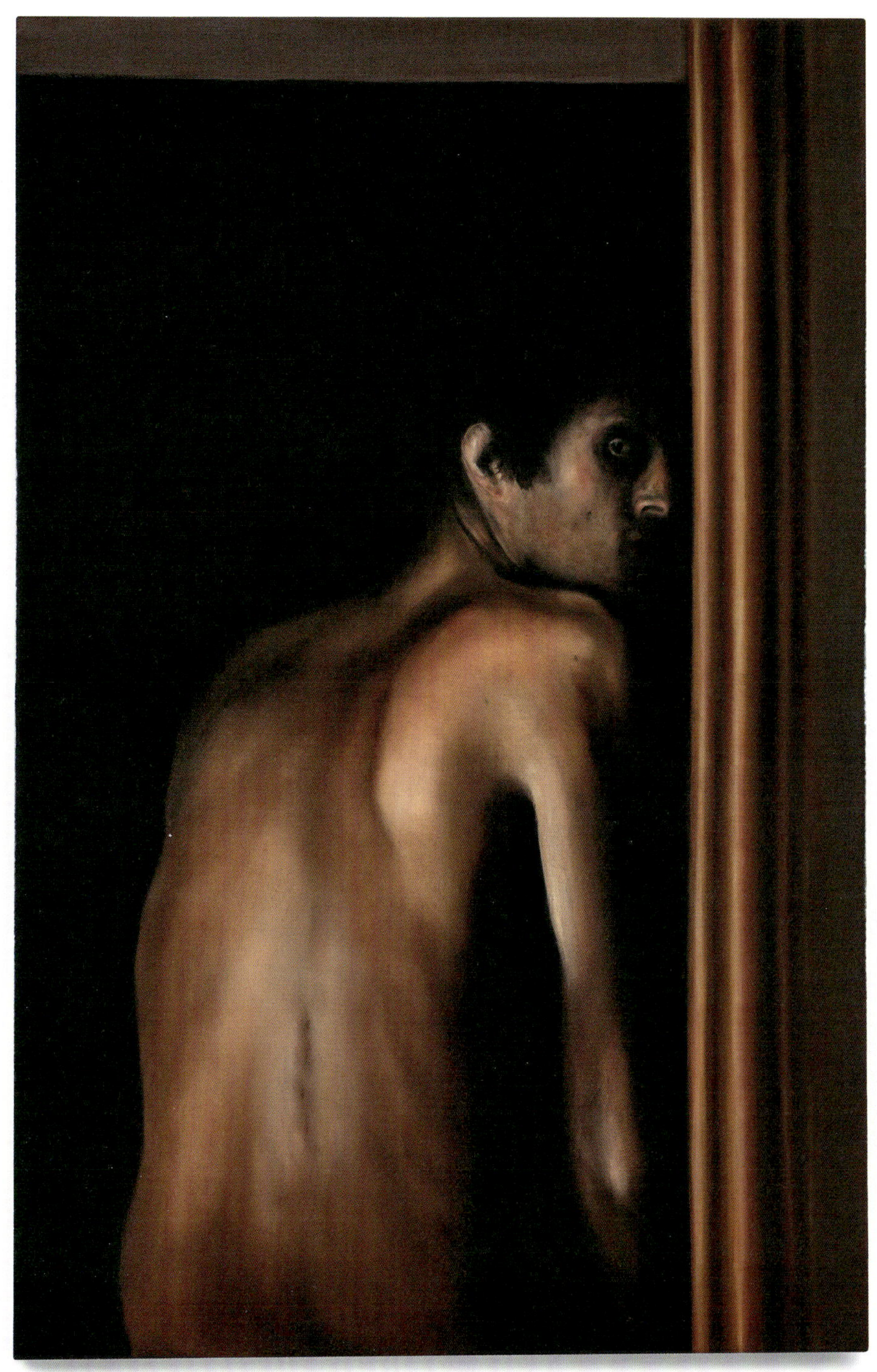

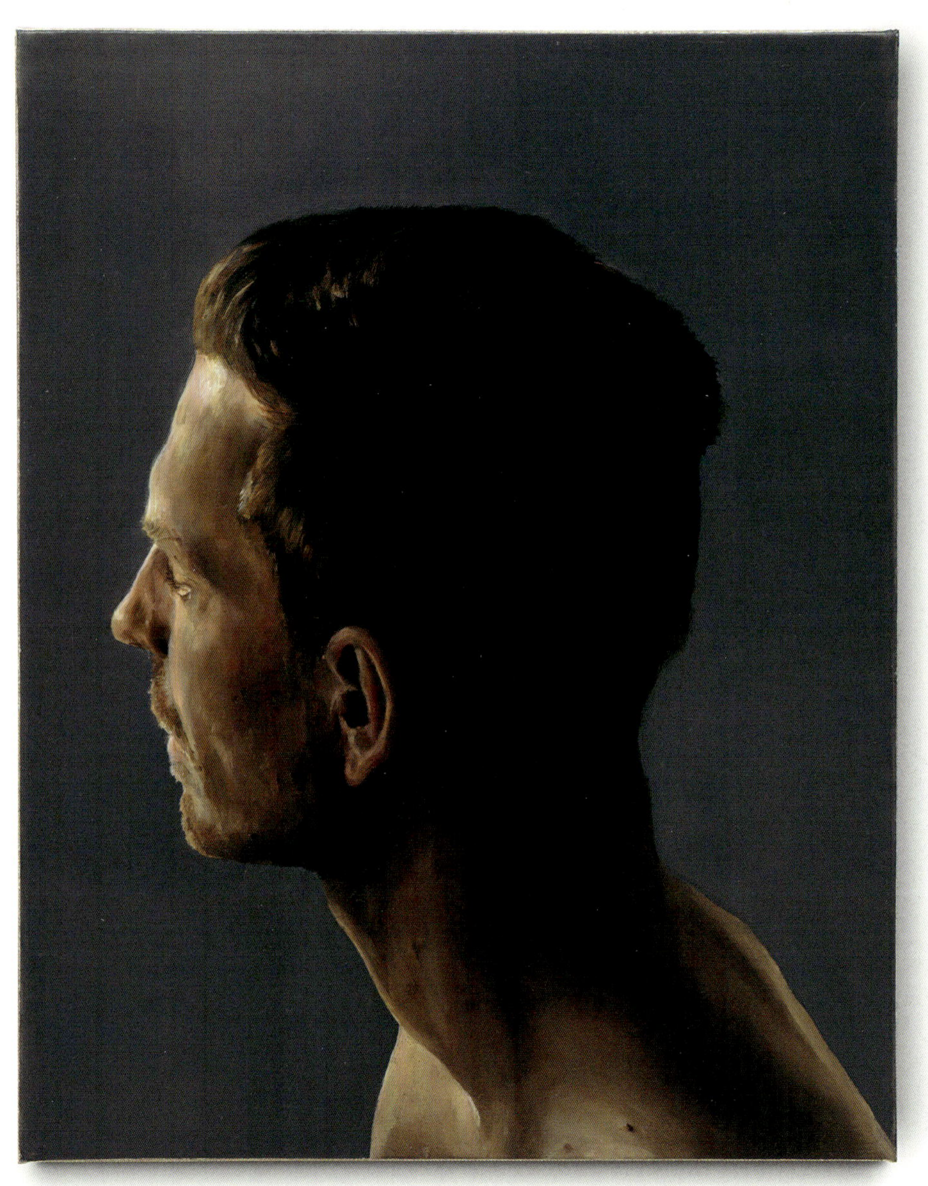

    Listen (2013)

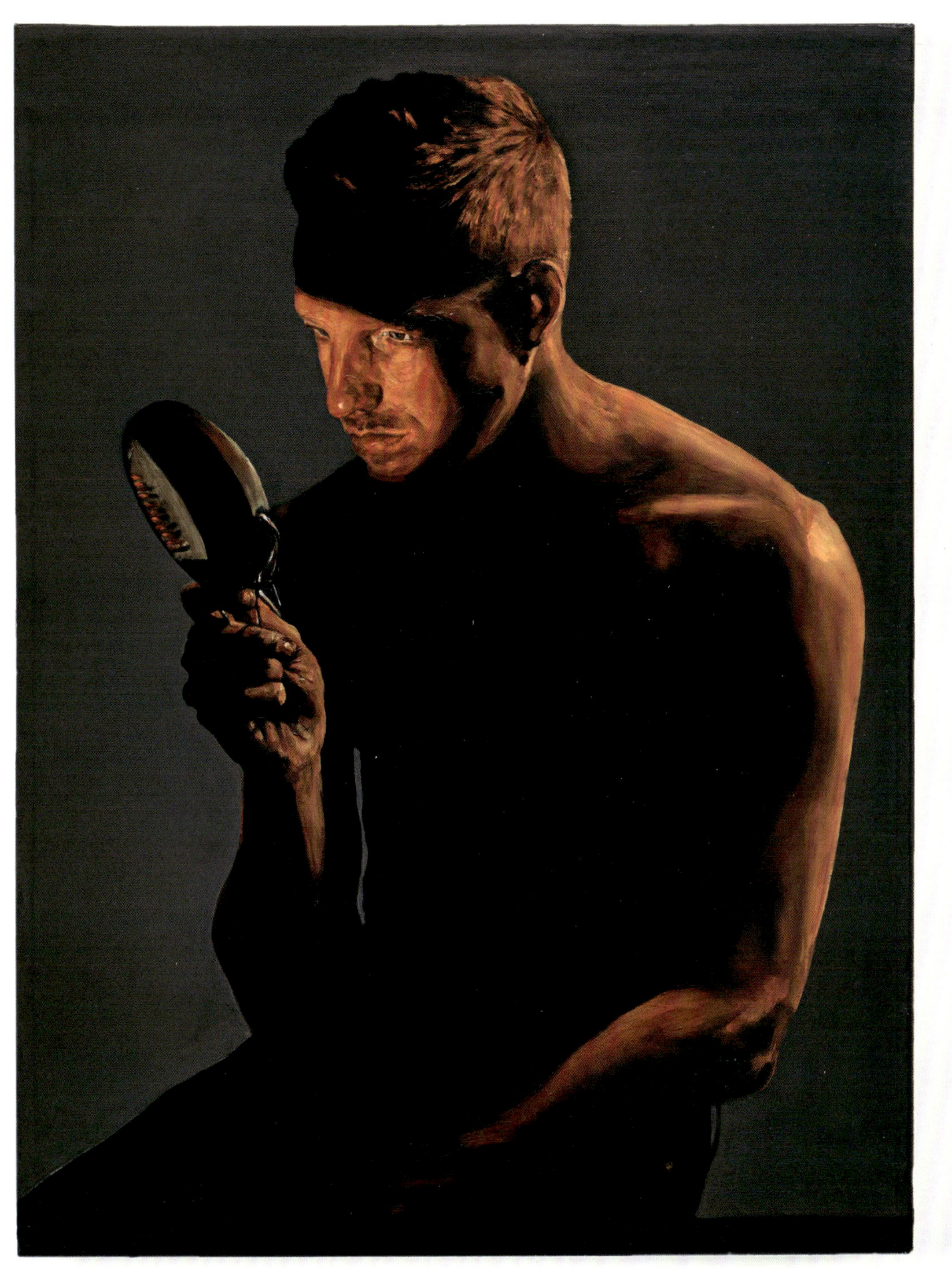

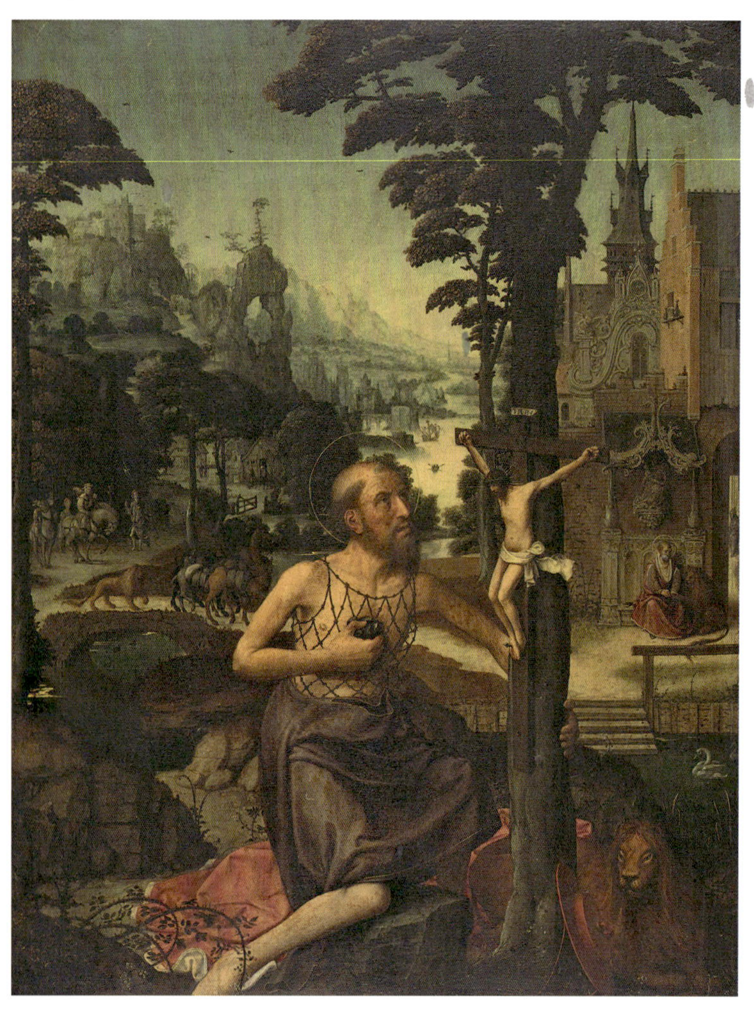

    Jan Provoost St. Jerome Penitent (n.d.)

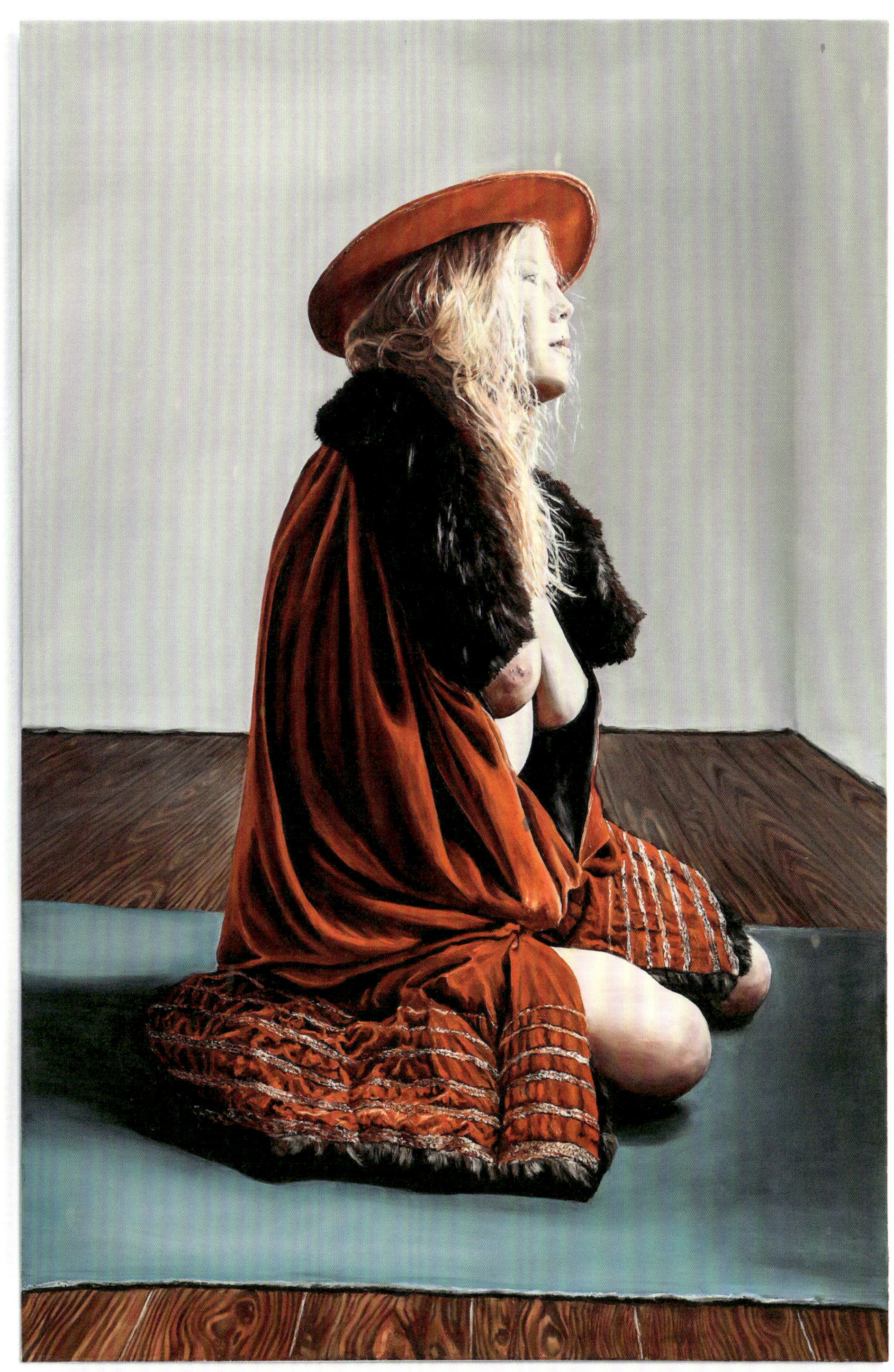

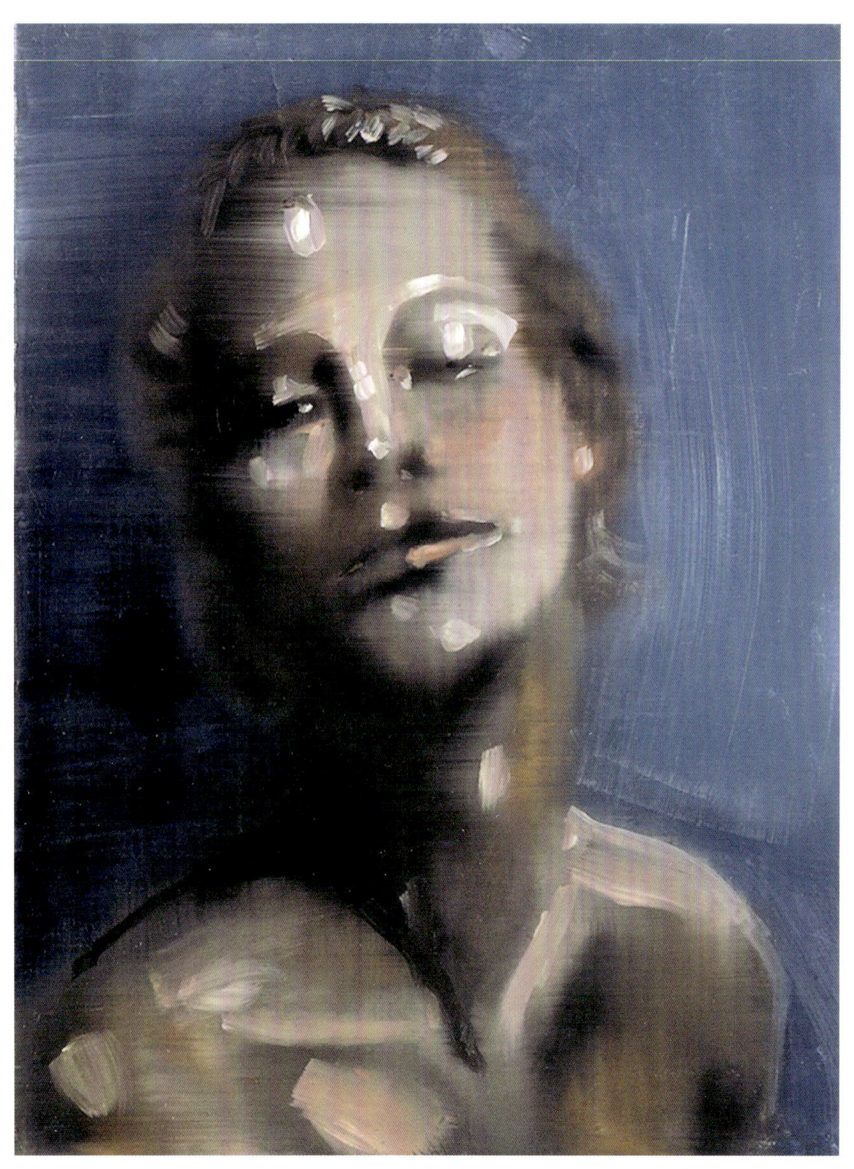

   Narcisso (2009)

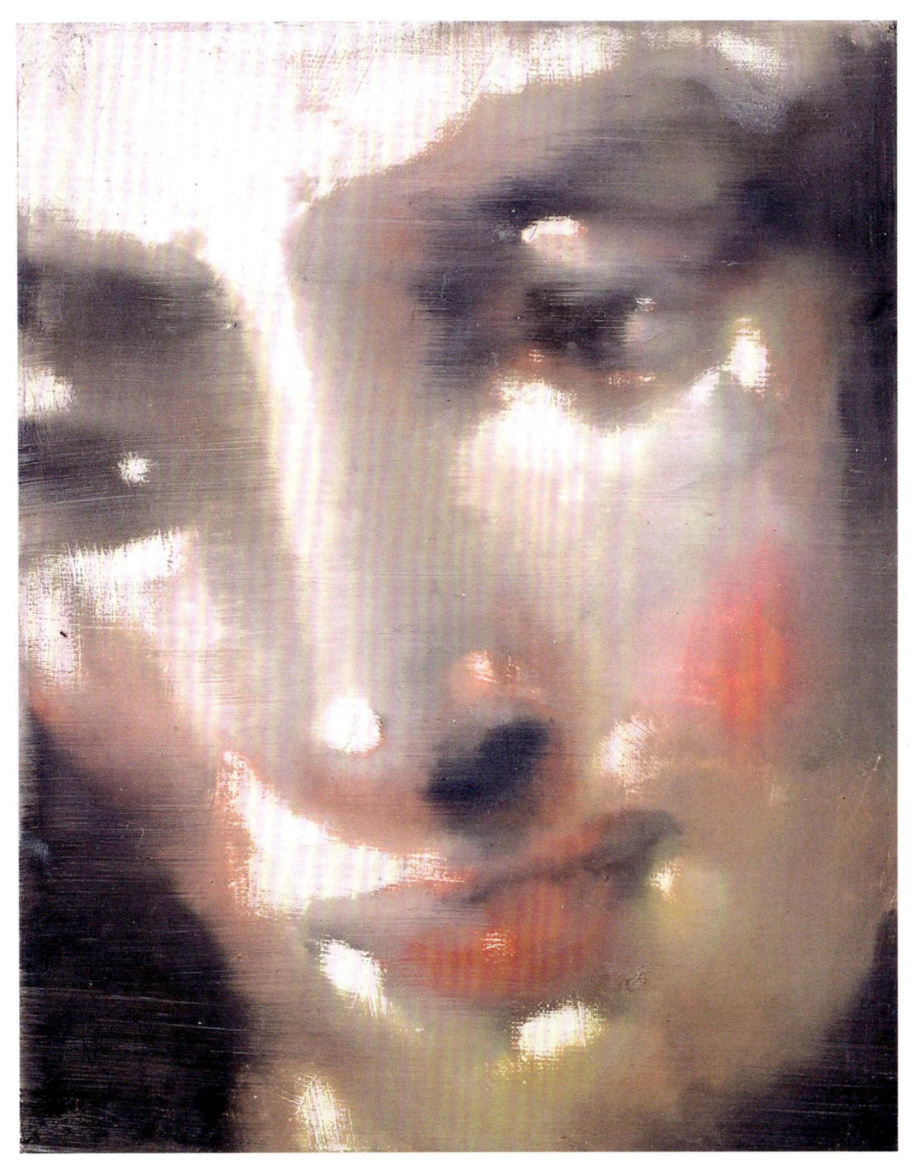

Untitled (2006)

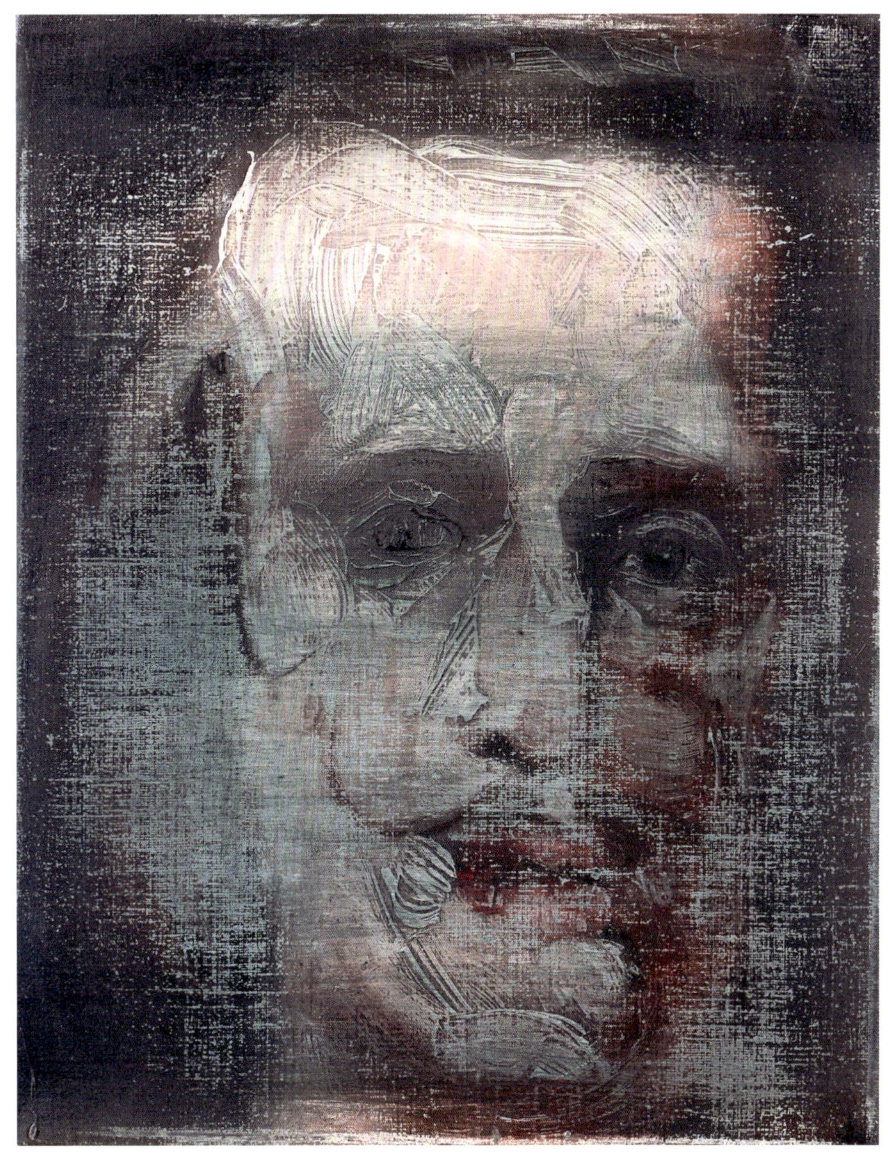

Untitled (Philippe) (2009)

THE OTHER SAMENESS

Laurent Dubreuil

[1]

The other, the other sameness or the very other,
what a difficult idea to explain and to demonstrate.
It is, however, one of the objectives of art, and it's
exactly this difficulty which determines the value
(and I'm not talking about the market price) of
a work. I'm also not talking about the sense of
something "other," the generic designation that
usually refers to a rather vague "non-me." Nor,
above all, am I talking about the *same other*, which
has become known and recognized as part of
twenty-first-century identity. Like other significant
components of our shared experience, the "world
of art" is currently suffering from a delusion, namely
the *reduction of everything to identity*—offensive,
dominant, wounded, oppressed, ancient, new, etc.
Indeed, there exists, within artistic institutions,
an identical version of the "same," the *idem* of the
mainstream tradition, which will always be labeled
academicism, and which sees in artworks a means of
reproducing and preserving power, money and status.
This is something that deserves to be questioned
and, in this context, I could almost understand the
temptation to believe, as a reaction to this déjà vu,
that an alterity of sex, genre or race could alter the
usual whiteness of the museum. But, conversely, is
it enough to speak out under oppression or to claim

one's "dignity," in order to create? Then, it seems,
ways of apparently acting against the established
order actually work in favor of the acceptance of
domination, and are only able to change the meaning:
we transfer some lifeless power over there that was
previously over here, we swap the more and the less.
Thus, from within the system, one claims to redefine
art as *social work*, like an activity regulated by *identities* and *representation* (or, using the latest codified
terms, a combination of the *representativity* of social
categories with the *imitation* of the *mimesis*). So,
maybe things function, but nothing really changes
any longer. The umpteenth reiteration of the *ready-
made* can be seen as the trappings borrowed from a
self-propagating alterity, predetermined, standard-
ized, and finally ready to be sold in the marketplace.

The other, the very other, is not an object,
a reference, a recipe, an index, a fixed result. It is
not a minor declension of the verb "to be." Conse-
quently, it is not white, nor black, nor universalist,
nor cisgender, nor something sexual, nor republican,
nor male, nor bad, nor animal, although it can be all
these things simultaneously. It is happening, here
and now. It is the artistic moment when a metamorphosis suddenly emerges, and which always
questions everything, including the order of order.[1]

[2]

Fabrice Samyn surrenders himself to art, which
means above all that he doesn't restrict himself to
one technique, nor to one format or medium, and
that he is nonconformist and unrestrained, whether
he is using painting or installation, using dust or glass,
assembling or molding, using gold or agave leaves; he
transcends the traditional structures of transaction
and commerce; he even transcends what appears
to be his own set agenda, fluctuating between the
addition of precious materials (like the gilding of a
worm-eaten tree) and the removal of substance
(as with the writing of the word "silence" in *Speech
Act Calligraphy*, where the letters gradually fade

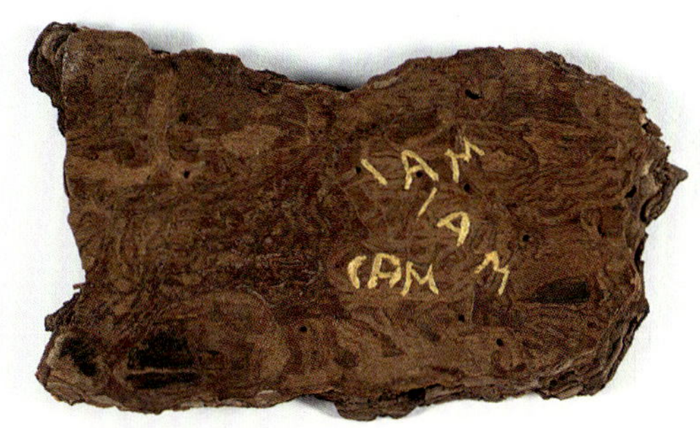

FIG. 1 *Under the Skin* (2020), wood and gold leaf, 16 × 10 cm

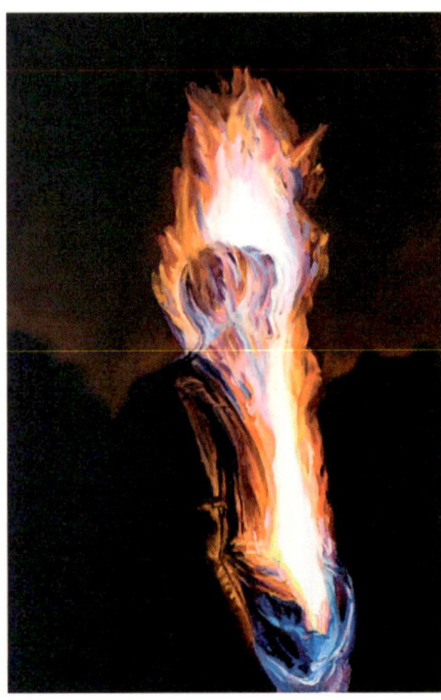

FIG. 2 *Untitled #16*, from the *Twilight's Gaze* series (2021), oil on canvas, 120 × 80 cm

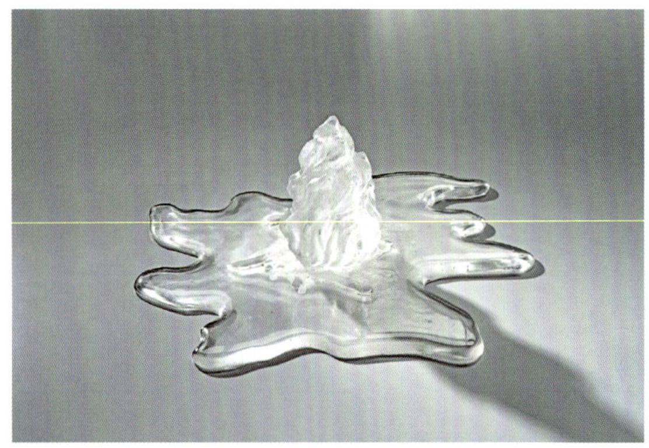

FIG. 3 *Untitled #4*, from the *Feu la vie* series (2010), moulded from funerary flame and cast in crystal, 13 × 40 × 40 cm, private collection

away to nothing; p. 120). With these pieces, Samyn produces *thinking fragments*. In his work, it is no use looking for "single thoughts," neither in the sense of a simple aphorism (as with Blaise Pascal's *pensées*), nor in the sense of a philosophical system. It is more that the thought suddenly appears for Samyn the thinker, ready to fragment, something like what Antonin Artaud calls these "ardes qui ardent duc"[2] like the embers of the soul. Yet these fragments, very often, are fundamental or primal. They lead us to an affirmation of the "other" even through an expressive gesture. I will only track this art through its various dispositions, to experience it, in order to help us in turn to understand how we are "other," if we even ever are.

[3]

Who wouldn't be blinded by it? In Samyn's work fire is certainly often present. In the exhibition *To See with Ellipse* in Brussels, the "small Rubens room" is lit up by images of fire and flames. Samyn continuously shows repeated images of blazing fires and ashes. The series of paintings *Twilight's Gaze* [fig 2 and pp. 69–71] uses multiple angles to outline the different stages of a burning statue of Moses. An ancient pictorial tradition has horns growing from the prophet's head, who is seized with fury on discovering his unbelieving people in adoration of the golden calf. In 2010, Samyn worked on a piece called *Burning Bush*: the artist poured resin over a large juniper shrub and then turned it upside down, producing an image of a permanent amber-colored fire, without the burning flames [p. 16]. In the paintings of *Twilight's Gaze*, and in an unusual theological switch, it is Moses (and not a bush nor a deity) that is consumed by this eternal fire. He finds himself, perhaps like all living beings, caught up in the moment of his own conflagration. On top of that, noting that *Twilight's Gaze* depicts Moses in the form of a statue, we see the pictorial detail revealed of a repeated base.[3] In this way, it is confirmed as art which assumes its theurgical aim and in which fire is one of the most powerful forces.

The idea that emerges is simultaneously both resolutely romantic and classical. The classicism of passion, which translates as *flame* in the refined language of Jean Racine's tragedies. In the same way, *fire* is also a strange, conjugated adjective used in French to signify a deceased person. In the series *Feu la vie* [fig. 3], the flames melt and freeze in a crystalized body. The rhetoric of Racine about the ignition of passion originates in the speech, passed on by Petrarch, and picked up by many other poets, on the impossible coexistence of fire and ice. In *Phèdre*, Hippolyte reproaches his mistress: "When I am on fire, why do you look on me so coldly?"[4] A few decades earlier, Mathurin Régnier, in his first poem, encapsulates the antithesis in the first person and writes:

> And although the blood gathered
> Around my heart was icy,
> My words only spoke of fire.[5]

Going back a little in time, we think above all of Michelangelo, the poet, who begins his most beautiful love sonnet with the lines:

> *Vorrei voler, Signor, quel ch'io non voglio:*
> *tra 'l foco e 'l cor di ghiaccia un vel s'asconde*
> *che 'l foco ammorza, onde non corrisponde*
> *la penna all'opre, e fa bugiardo 'l foglio.*

> I wish I longed for something, Lord, that I do not desire: between the fire and the heart of ice a hidden veil extinguishes the flame, breaks the connection between my pen and my work, and the page becomes false.[6]

I have no doubt, the crystal-clear voice of *Feu la vie* is Buonarotti's incandescent heart of ice—and Samyn's too—as well as ours, made real through sculpture. In the extraordinary experience stirred up by Michelangelo's writing, the passionate flame that simultaneously fiery and icy, is what releases the poetry, what makes "the page become false."

Incidentally, regarding falsity, the syntax of the original Italian in the poem is ambiguous. It is just as correct to read "the heart of ice" (*il cor di ghiaccia*) as "a veil of ice" (*di ghiaccia un vel*, a grammatical inversion). This disconnection between the work and the pen, from self to self, which opens the poem, is the falsity. Nothing Samyn shows us of fire is real. Even the series *Still Fire* [fig. 4] reproduces large flames with a technique of treating wood grain with different finishes; but these panels don't burn and turn into ash. Nothing is real if everything is unstable; but all this really exists in the moment, as something "other."

I mentioned the romanticism of fire: it's the romanticism of an inner energy that burns and expires. If Samyn's work sometimes inspires in us a contemplative calm, for example with the magical iridescence of the glass domes in *The Color of Time* [p. 102], his main source of energy remains the strong creative power of fire in all its forms. In this way, Samyn joins the group of visitors to the volcano

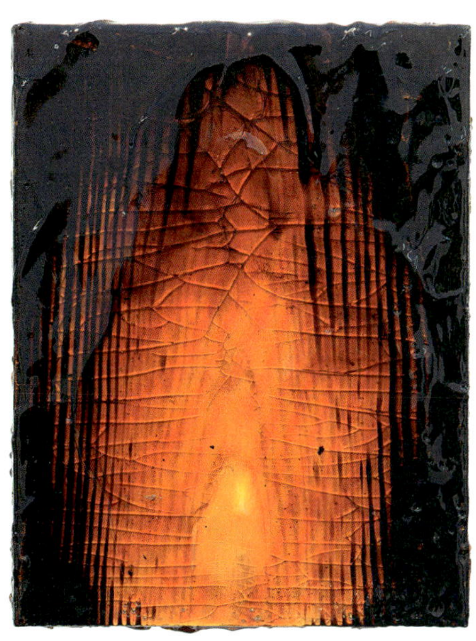

FIG. 4 *Untitled*, from the *Still Fire* series (2011), wood and pine resin, 32.5 × 25.5 × 2.5 cm

that I talked about in *Génération romantique* (*The Romantic Generation*), in the chapter titled "Playing with Fire." The great romantics knew that fire was as necessary as it was dangerous. Samyn doesn't try to hide from the effects of intense fire; he exhibits burnt frames for missing pictures [fig. 5]. Also, with *Kundalini* [fig. 6], he carefully places, on a plush red velvet cushion, a calcinated head from a decapitated wooden statue, brushed with gold dust. The phoenix is an emblem for this artist. But his resurrection is about something else; it's not to do with a suspension of life or a rebirth: it's about survival with, and through, the artwork.

[4]

Fire for Samyn is much like the *elements* were for the ancient philosophers who were contemplating the fundamental nature of the universe. In Greek, such thinkers were called physicians, because they were discussing *physis*, or more precisely, the *nature* of *nature*. Through a later semantic shift we would today call them *meta*-physicians. Among them can be found advocates for water, for earth, or for air, as well as admirers of fire, the force of life and energy.

Let's jettison chronology: I would like to reposition Fabrice Samyn among the pre-Socratics. His thinking fragments are like the remnants leftover from old forgotten authors, scraps which, taken together, nevertheless outline parts of a vast dreamlike knowledge of reality. I read and translate a quotation that comes to us from Heraclitus: "This very world, the same for all of us, none of the gods and none of the humans created it, but it has always been and it is, and it will be, an everlasting fire, which ignites and weakens as things goes on."[7] I take from this that there is only one world, this one, the *same* one. The same one: it belongs to everyone. Identity is not for each individual to define from what they understand from "everyone"; it is limited to this world in which we live, which is one. This world, the same for everyone, which has not been created, is eternal and undergoes change. It's an "everlasting" fire that changes (grows and dwindles) and is therefore never "the same" in the sense of being in a fixed state, something balanced, something stable. "The same for all of us" does not mean the same identity for all, nor even less the same sense of identity, but it is *this*, which allows the possibility of change.

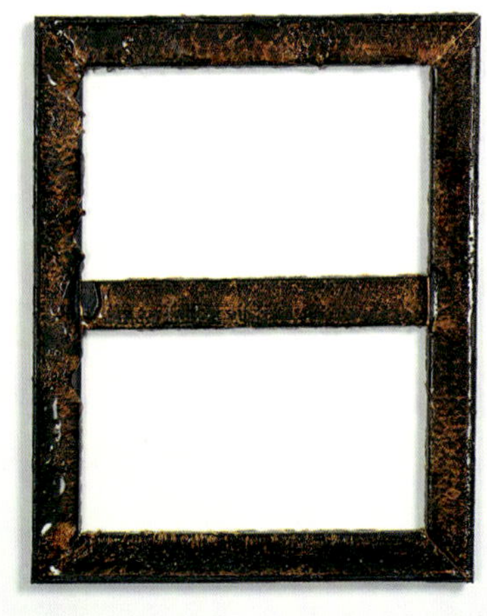

FIG. 5 *Untitled*, from the *Still Fire* series (2016), wood and pine resin, 49.7 × 40.5 × 1.8 cm

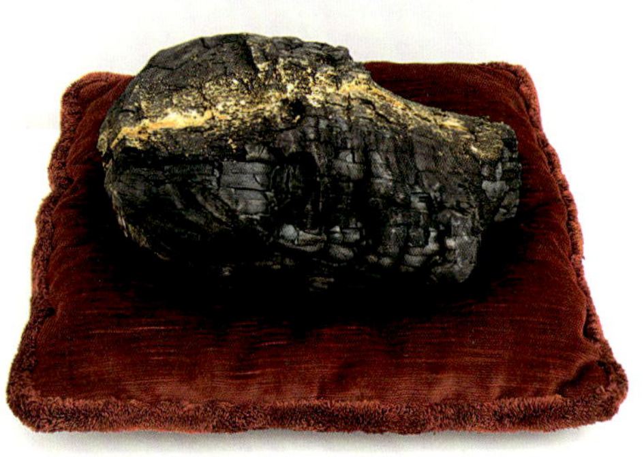

FIG. 6 *Kundalini* (2012), wood, gold and velvet, 17 × 38.5 × 38.5 cm, private collection

Many translators make the mistake of translating the final verbs in the quotation as "to light" and "to extinguish," which misrepresents the Heraclitan insistence on "everlasting," repeated through the shifting time scales of the imperfect, the present, and the future tenses. We know that without suddenly dying out, the sacred fire can sometimes subside or flare up even more. These changes in intensity touch us, they exist. But Heraclitus's promise, and Samyn's maybe, is of an eternal fire that survives individual incidents, or death. The burnt wood still glows: *From Fire to Fire* [p. 54].

[5]

Among Samyn's depictions of flames, consider those taken from the old masters. Look at his pictures of the enlargements of light sources illuminating the chiaroscuro scenes in Georges de La Tour's paintings. *The Dream of Joseph*, *Job Mocked by his Wife*, *Saint Joseph the Carpenter*, *Magdalene with the Smoking Flame*, *Magdalene with Two Flames*, *The Payment of Taxes*, *The Education of the Virgin*, *Saint Sebastian Tended by Saint Irene* [fig. 7], are some of the De La Tour paintings which are *cropped*, *enlarged*, and *inverted* by Samyn. *Cropped* in the sense that the artist only retains a detail from the older painting, the wick of a burning candle, the halo of light created by a lantern, the light from a torch, while the rest of the picture is discarded. Literally *enlarged*, because the new canvases measure 1.8 by 1.2 meters (a painted surface larger than those of the originals of *Saint Sebastian* or of *Magdalene with the Smoking Flame*), and also because, thanks to the enlargement, the genius of De La Tour appears to be magnified, even taking on an abstract power in the full close-ups. *Inverted* because with De La Tour the candle or the flame, following on from the example of Caravaggio, becomes "this obscure clarity," allowing the dark shadows to transform the scene. The pictorial sample turns the usual sense of representational logic on its head and makes the

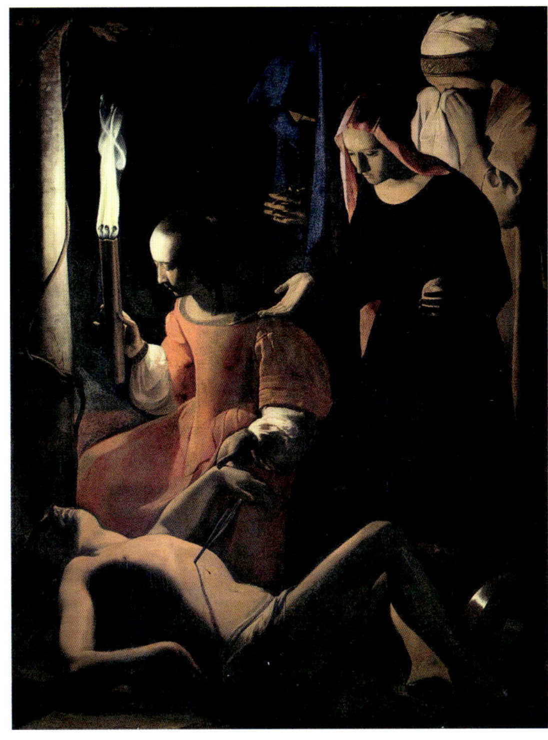

FIG. 7 Georges de La Tour, *Saint Sebastian Tended by Irene* (ca. 1649), oil on canvas, 167 × 131 cm, Paris, Musée du Louvre

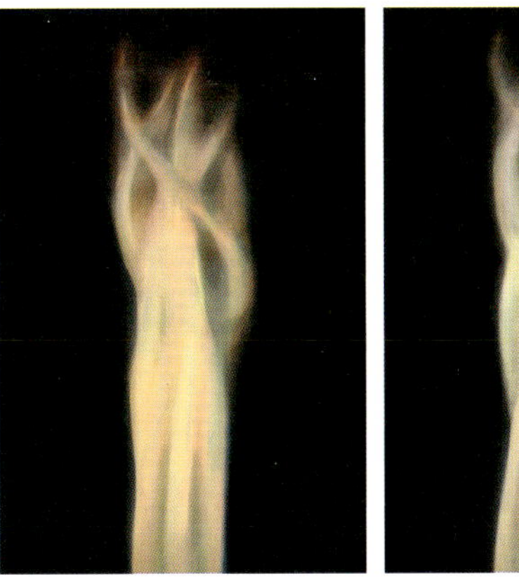
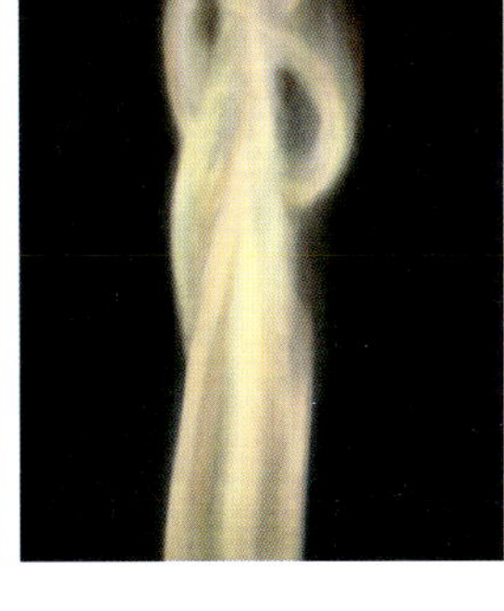

FIG. 8 *Saint Sebastian Tended by Irene, Musée du Louvre, Paris / Saint Sebastian Tended by Irene, Staatliche Museen, Gemäldegalerie, Berlin* (2007), diptych, oil on canvas, 180 × 120 cm (each), private collection

means of the painting—the glimmering light in the dark that illuminates the figures—the *end* of the painting. Samyn reflects on the act of painting by showing that without the artificial light which provides the light source for the painting, or the painted natural light, nothing can be seen. Never is Fabrice Samyn so clear about this as in his reactivation of the long-lost past. I should rather say that he imagines the *re-presentation* of the past. Indeed, if yesterday is the past, it is recreated for us, here, transformed. As well as the recreation of De La Tour's flickering light, empowering the luminous touch of the painting, Samyn, in the diptych *Between Vanishing Points* [fig. 9], is also searching for Raphael's and Perugino's vanishing points, once again cropping, enlarging, and inverting old masters through the depiction of these infinite, hazy landscapes, where the depth of the surface image has no beginning and no end.

At first glance, Samyn's interaction with one of the Adam and Eve paintings by Lucas Cranach is along similar lines. *Lucas Cranach's Studio* [p. 47] is focused on the stag behind the sixteenth-century Eve, and its large eye in which the distorted reflection of a window can be seen. The Flemish Renaissance artists were masters of painting reflections in eyes and of anamorphic art in general. In their portraits, the convex mirrors in a Van Eyck or a Memling painting become like painted eyes, where images of the windows in the artist's studio are reflected. Cranach produced many variations on the theme of the fall of Adam and Eve, and sometimes even depicted other mythical figures in a similar pose and setting (like the Apollo and Diana from 1526 which is in the Royal Collection in London). A stag often appeared with Adam and Eve. In the eyes of the animal the hint of an outside reflection can be found, but not always the

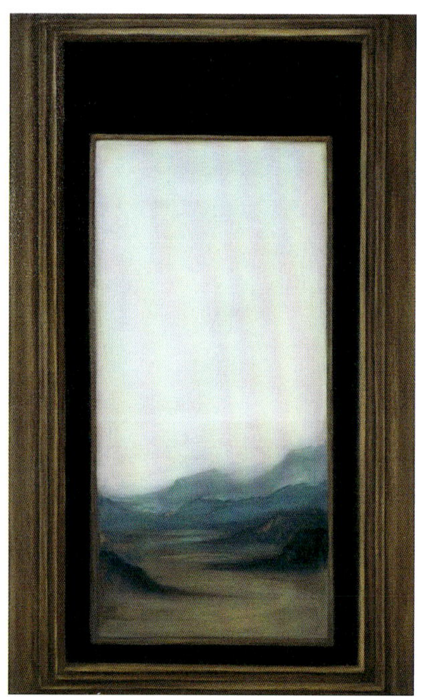
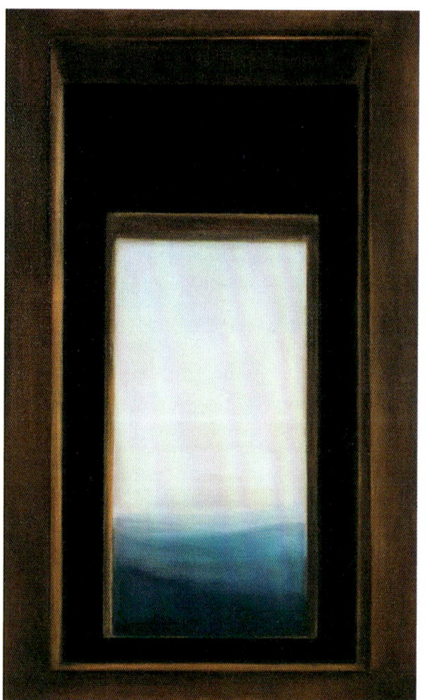

FIG. 9 *Between Vanishing Points* (2012), diptych, oil on canvas, 150 × 94 cm (each), private collection

same one. Looking at Cranach's painting from 1528, now in Detroit in the United States, and that of 1537, which is in Vienna, Austria, a white mark in the stag's eye shows the reflection of the sun. In the Apollo and Diana from the Royal Collection, and in the versions of Adam and Eve found in Münster, Antwerp, and in Brussels, attentive observers can spot, not just a blemish, but the curved image of a window. By exploiting this barely visible image, Fabrice Samyn once again uses and underlines the effect of cropping and enlarging. Is it once again, however, an inversion of the original artistic composition? I don't think so, as the original is on a different scale. With Cranach, in fact, the subtle inclusion of the window in the stag's eye is only a superficial indication of the light source. We're dealing more with the creation of an impossibility, especially in contrast with the white mark that I can see in certain of his other paintings, which are only representing the sun. Neither Adam, nor Eve, nor the animals in the garden of Eden would know about interiors, even less about the process of posing in an artist's studio with a window. So, what is the particular significance of this detail? It's to show us the *art* and *artifice* of painting, which simultaneously offers us a vision of this world and a simulation of it, which both reveals reality and, conclusively, its "otherness." Through the reproduction of the reflection in the stag's eye, Samyn, is interested, as the title indicates, in the artist's *studio*. After all, this incongruous detail (a window in the garden of Eden?) could be an error made by a junior pupil in the master's studio, an addition made by a foolish and clumsy apprentice who adds the finishing touches to complete the pictures; or, on the contrary, it could be an intentional jest (in other words, *a studio prank*); or, my preferred option, a premeditated gesture, a sign that reminds us of the artificial nature of the work.[8] Between Magritte and Cranach, Samyn thus participates in an age-old communal reflection on the *treachery of images*—revealing the alteration of reality through painting.

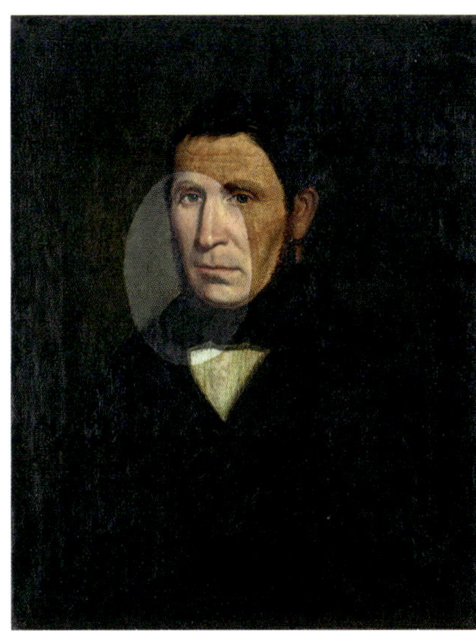

FIG. 10 *Blinder* (2009), locally devarnished antique painting, 63 × 50 cm, private collection

The presence of the past can also be seen in the old oil paintings, acquired and reworked by Samyn, with the old varnish partly removed in such a way that other elements appear on the canvas. In *Blinder* [fig. 10], the removal of the varnish reveals, through the resulting contrast, the dark appearance of the man. *The Pupil's Mask* [p. 10] makes a domino mask appear on the face of a woman. This mask, instead of concealing the face, casts its outline onto the darkened canvas. It's no coincidence that this removal technique is part of the range of art restoration procedures that, usually, removes varnish before retouching occurs. Samyn, effectively, is *restoring* a potent artistic practice on what is often a modest painting. It is also no coincidence that the only term possible for this technique in French is *dé-vernissage*, literally de-varnishing, as if Samyn's art was questioning, to the point of immediately canceling, the social rituals of the professional art world: as an answer to the public exhibition opening (*vernissage* in French is literally "the varnishing") we are presented with its opposite, an idiosyncratic "exhibition de-varnishing."

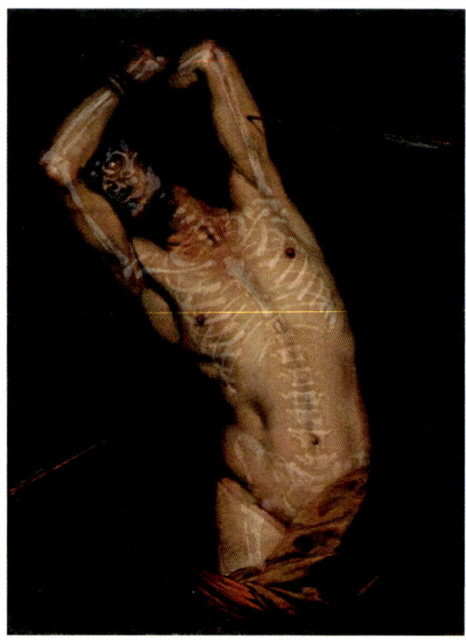

FIG. 11 *Beyond Eros and Thanatos* (1625–2012),
locally devarnished antique painting,
118 × 89 cm, private collection

I observe this even more in *Beyond Eros and Thanatos* [fig. 11], where the twisted body of a Saint Sebastian is not only pierced by arrows, but is also penetrated by invisible X-rays, revealing, thanks to the removal of varnish, the bone structure of the skeleton within the body. This painting plays with conventional limits (the "theme" of Saint Sebastian, the masochistic eroticism of a tortured human body, the components of a *vanitas* or of the dance of death, preservation by varnish) and, above all, with the use of a professional device—the use of resin as a protective layer—and it shows evidence of radiation other than that from the ghostly X-ray light, like a substantiation of the invisible, through pictural vision.

[6]

This is how Samyn's work functions and this is the way it is shown in the exhibition at the Royal Museums in Brussels. Is the confrontation between the actual work and the trace presence of art from the past (I haven't said *outdated art*) a game of smoke and mirrors? Yes, probably, in the way that these baroque elements multiply, through reflection, these images within the image. Also yes, on condition that we *re-view* what a mirror really is, which the artist constantly asks us to do. Historically, mirror technology has developed gradually. Before reflecting glass, a polished metal surface was sufficient. Samyn repolishes old bronze mirrors from China that becomes *Partial Eclipse* or phases of an eclipse in *In The Glimpse of an I*. This "*glimpse of an I*," this fleeting "I" moment, is described in this way because the mirror always projects back the unstable image of the unobtainable "me." Pursuing this theme, Samyn even asks *Is Looking in the Mirror Always Looking Back?* [p. 75]. This painting shows the movement of a man looking askance in a mirror. It's a response to the elements on show in those "reborn" Italian self-portraits that, like Giovanni Savoldo's in the Louvre, with its multiple reflecting surfaces, are produced by combining highly skilled representational technique and the use of mirrors, which were new at the time. In *The Mask of Your Image* [p. 77], Samyn's mirror is like a lamp projecting light onto the face of a nude man. *Suppose You Don't Exist* [fig. 13] shows the same model, or maybe a different one, viewed from behind, not from the front, with nothing

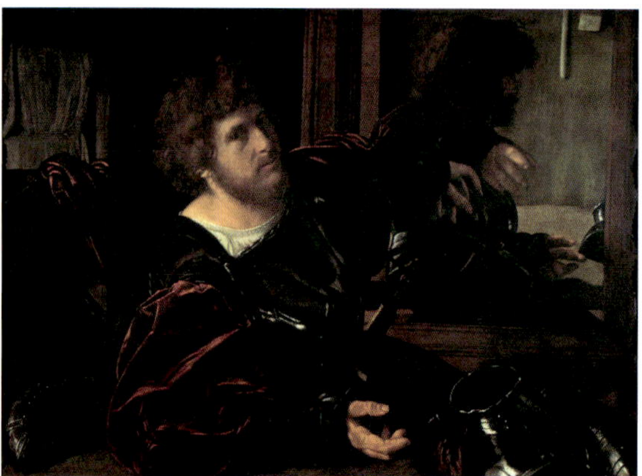

FIG. 12 Giovanni Gerolamo Savoldo, *Selfportrait* (ca. 1529),
oil on canvas, 91 × 123 cm, Paris, Musée du Louvre

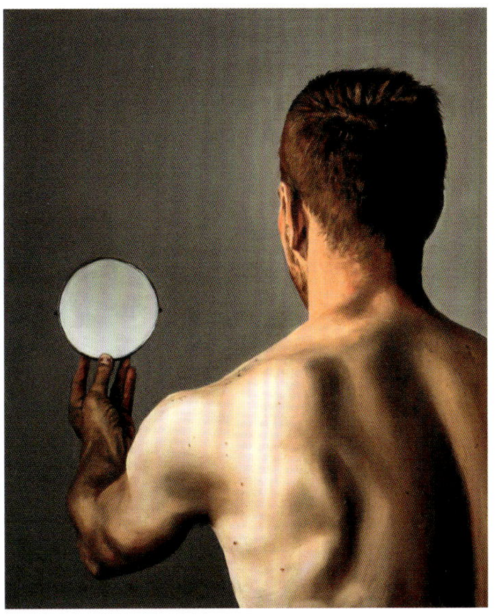

 Suppose You Don't Exist (2013),
oil on canvas, 65 × 54 cm, private collection

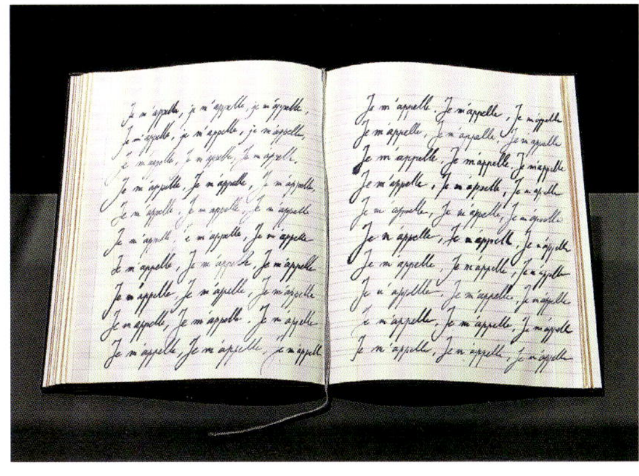

 Je m'appelle (2014), mixed media
(metal, wood, ink on paper), 75 × 110 × 80 cm

reflected in the mirror held in his hand. I'm not going to dwell on the allogenic nature of these mirrors. At this point, we couldn't think for a moment that, with Samyn, we would be considering something fixed or identical, like Stendhal's proverbial, realistic, and fantastical "mirror that we carry with us for the length of a journey." There is no use repeating all that. I would however add two variations.

The first one is the school notebook placed on a desk where one or several different hands have written the repeated lines "My name is" [fig. 14]. These three words are missing a name, like the mirror in *Suppose You Don't Exist*, which doesn't reflect anything. But what if, however, the phrase in the school notebook was not incomplete? We are not reading a specific Christian name, but are hearing a voice without a name, belonging to nobody, saying "my name is." The accepted version is that "my name is . . .," and even more, that I am it. It's the basic grammatical way of identifying someone. In fact, at best, calling myself Laurent or Fabrice, I name

myself, and my name is what I can spell. This has nothing to do with describing your own personal or group identity, where art reflects its setting and its time, or where the clarity of the work reveals certain things about how it was produced.

The second variation is taken from *Narcissus?* [p. 9]. In this work, Samyn takes a detail from the Caravaggio painting of a young man gazing at his reflection in the water. Samyn only takes one of the hands, and its reflection, and rotates the image vertically. A virtual and imperfect sermon no doubt, expressed by these two hands coming together in prayer, beyond the bounds of the visual differences of their composition. But also, Fabrice is questioning this narcissism, this "homoeroticism" that we see so clearly in such paintings and in those of Caravaggio in particular. After all, Narcissus is not in love with himself, but with his reflection; that is to say, of someone "other" than himself, someone evanescent. Is he therefore even Narcissus, in full size as well in close-up?

We have really offended people by telling them that they are either hetero- or homosexual. Above all, we have made them believe in simplistic categorizations, as well as saying *love=friendship=attraction= eroticism=desire=sexuality=gender identity*, like some psychopathological or analytical ancient Bible text. By reducing everything down, we have quickly ended up with—and this is our current situation— a one-dimensional existence, as flat as the latest smartphone. This vocabulary then has helped support the incorrect nonsense such as *a woman loving a man loves the other* or *homos love the same*. Samyn shows us a simple experiment: put a man and a woman next to each other, with short hair, call them *Eve & Adam* [p. 43], clothe them in old vests with holes positioned over their nipples, and see what the result is. The message is ambiguous. These two are the same, even though they differ. Is it just that the small difference only comes from the respective

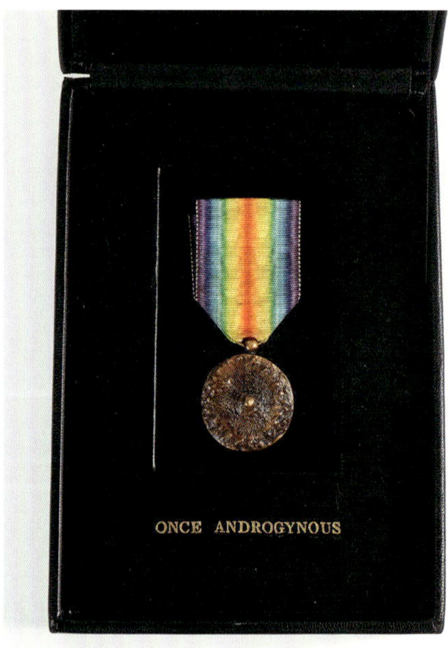

<u>FIG. 15</u> *Once Androgynous* (2014), the artist's nipple cast from World War I medals, 7 × 12 × 18 cm

size of their nipples, or the presence or absence of stubble, or does it come from her more direct, colder gaze, or from the bags under his eyes and his slight pout? If I get carried away and feel attracted to both painted images, I am told I am *bisexual* (although some would disagree, because you have to choose). Here, we touch on the third error in the *homo-hetero* discussion. In Greek, *homoios* means the *same*; and the *other* means *heteros*. Except that it is even more precise than that. For the most part, the Greek *heteros* means the choice between two. *Heteros* is the second designation of a duality. With our use of *heteros* and *homos*, we are immediately admitting that there is only a binary choice (male or female), and even further, ratifying that in the matter that it's either A or non-A. And what about you? Is this your idea of love? Do you think that your affections, your feelings, are always expressing the underlying structure, following ordinary logic or the genetic code (either *xx*, or *xy*)? Really and truly? Admittedly, it's sometimes about that, but it's not only about that.

In ancient Greek another word for *heteros* is *allos*: *other*. This adjective is an unusual one. Using it, we don't know in advance if we are dealing with amusing adventures from 0 and 1, but *in principle* probably not, and that we can count higher and see more alternatives than from the base of two. Comparing exotic and different finery, a character in *The Phoenicians* by Euripides uses the phrase "this other manner other"[9] where *allos* can in turn change without either having to fall into a simple variation of the theme, nor naturally, on the same thing. The philosophers, Aristotle in particular, speak about *alloiosis*, alteration in the sense of transformation, becoming something else. On the other hand, *heteroiosis* isn't used, because that means the passage between two contrasting entities, which modern thinking defines as *dialectic*. For us it's not enough. Neither "one and the same," present everywhere: not the well-regulated movement between "this" and "that." Neither do we need "other things"; we want something else. And that's what Fabrice wants, who I talk to online on June 19, 2021; he being close to Saint-Paul, above some sacred forest beloved by the arts and the muses; me, on Mount Parnassus. Samyn talks to me about the coincidences of opposites, of Nicholas of Cusa, of alternative formats, of body pains and the feelings of movements, and I outline to him this idea of the *very other* or *other sameness*, which I hold on to during the extreme haste in which I write this piece, until the moment when, once again, I *move back* to Ithaca where I've been living for sixteen years, and during the summer change house and hillside (no longer the southern one, but the one in the east). Fabrice and I hardly know each other, but we recognize each other, particularly through this formula of the "other," or ours, which is only a limitless desire for transformation.

[7+1]

I've written at least once *the art of Samyn*; in French, *l'art de Samyn*. You read "art by him" and you are right. A few years ago, the Michelangelo exhibition at The Metropolitan Museum of Art paid particular attention to Buonarotti's clients, who asked that the work being acquired was actually "by him" (and not completed by his studio, after drawings by or from instructions by the master), by the *hand* of the artist himself, a complete and perfect design:[10] in French, *l'art de sa main*. On the one hand, these demands are understandable: yes, the art by the artist should be by him. On the other hand, Samyn suggests a completely different way of working that, on the contrary, removes, even ridicules, the need for an original. When a work is attributed to Samyn, could we gently skate around the essential truth of whose hand completed the work, not forever, but just for now? Mind you, a distracted ear might still hear different words when hearing Samyn, such as "*sa mien*" in French, literally "her own," through a clash of gender and grammatical structure. These variations don't exclude him, because the artist is really looking for his own

way of working in a style that may not be exclusively "his own." That one of the objectives of this body of work should be the other sameness, does in no way mean that the fragmentation of thought tries —guiltily, the rumor of our time whispers to us— to override radical activism. On the contrary, adopting such a gesture could not be more radical today, as it goes against the doctrine of the globalized world, with its deceitful straight talking, and its foot soldiers of uniformity broadcasting soliloquies nonstop on the airwaves about their prefabricated mini-egos, as and when they are asked to do so by the distribution system of speech and thought. The nature of Fabrice Samyn's work is therefore inevitably political. But thankfully, it seeks fresh horizons and goes beyond that. That is to say, toward its "otherness," its very other sameness.

1. I explain this in much more detail in *La Dictature des identités* (The Dictatorship of Identities) (Paris, 2019).
2. Antonin Artaud, *Œuvres complètes* vol. XXII (Paris, 1986), p. 437.
3. We can recognize the melted statue in the sculpture that Samyn titles *Moshe*, the remains of a process captured on canvas; a magical painting.
4. Jean Racine, *Phèdre*, act V, scene 1.
5. Mathurin Regnier, *Odes*, I.
6. Translated from Michelangelo, poème LXXXVII, *Rime* (Bari, 1960).
7. In the Diels-Krantz numbering, fragment B30: *kosmon tonde, ton auton apantôn, oute tis theôn oute anthrôpôn epoiêsen, all'hèn aei kai estin kai estai pur aeizôon, haptomenon metra kai aposbennumenon metra*. The Greek text and the French translation are different, with a different interpretation of the passage in Jean Bollack and Heinz Wismann, *Héraclite ou la séparation* (Paris, 1972). A reminder that, in the fresco *The School of Athens*, Raphael depicts Heraclitus (the philosopher who is crying) using Michelangelo's features.
8. In old French, *l'astelier* is an alignment of wooden poles or beams attached together.
9. Euripides, *The Phoenicians*, v. 132: *allos allos ode . . . tropos*.
10. We can consult the catalogue edited by Carmen Bambach, *Michelangelo: Divine Draftsman and Designer*, exh. cat. The Metropolitan Museum of Art (New York, 2017).

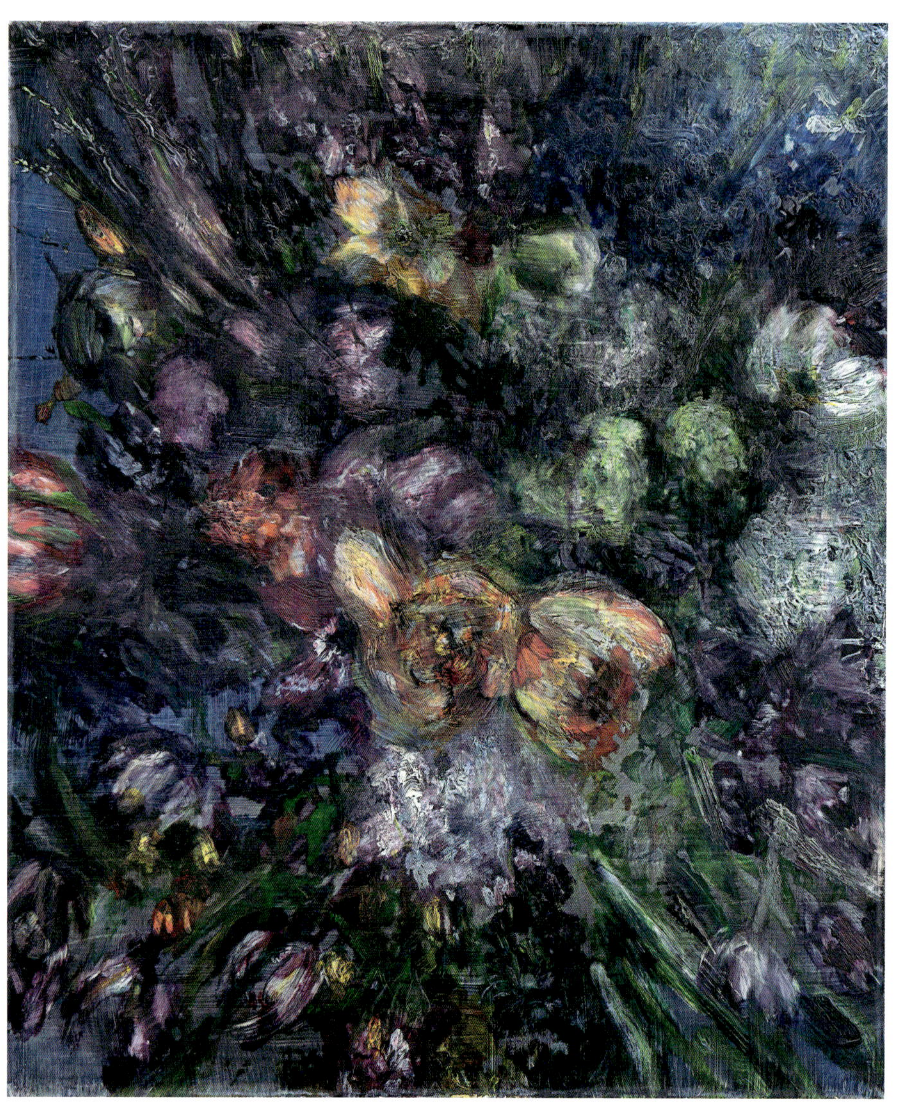

 <u>Still Night</u> (2014)

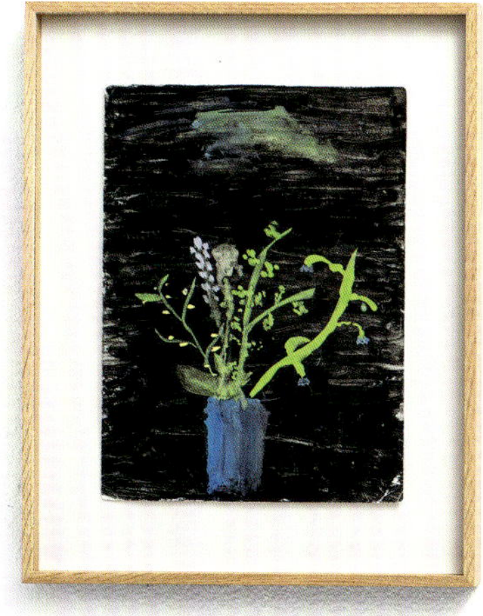

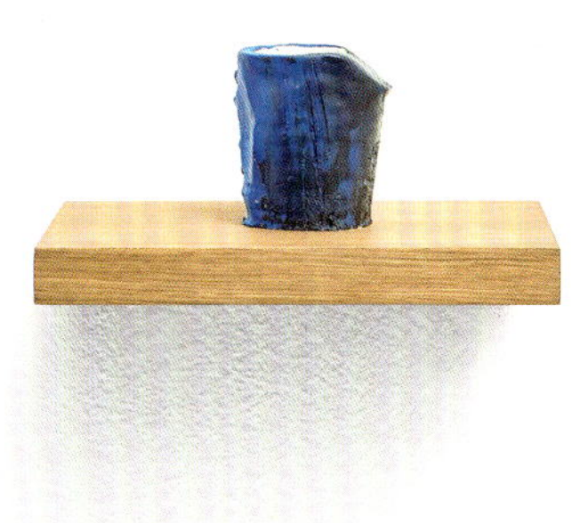

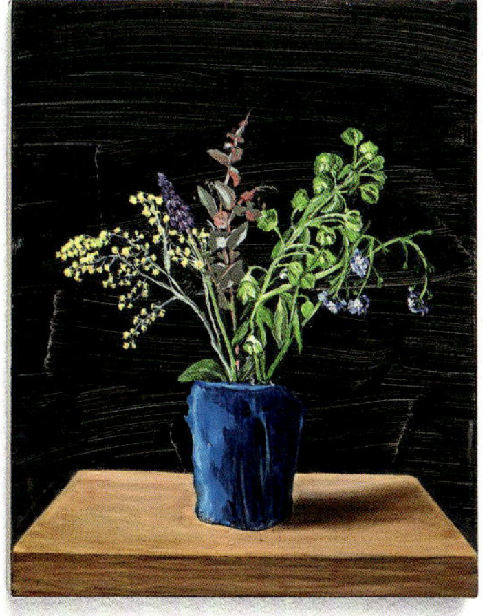

This work, consisting of a watercolor, a ceramic vase on a board, and a painting, revisits the depths of identity. Samyn takes as his starting point one of his own childhood paintings produced between the ages of six and seven, a floral composition. With the desire to regenerate reality, he invited florist Thierry Boutemy to identify the flowers and reconstruct the original bouquet. This was arranged in a most accurate reconstruction of the earthenware vase in the drawing, and then painted again by the artist. The traditional practice of painting still life is a step back in time for Samyn, recreating reality from childish interpretations of the world. The exact replica of an object alludes to the inevitable change that a child's gaze undergoes when developing into that of an adult, but also to what is constant as part of one's unique personality.

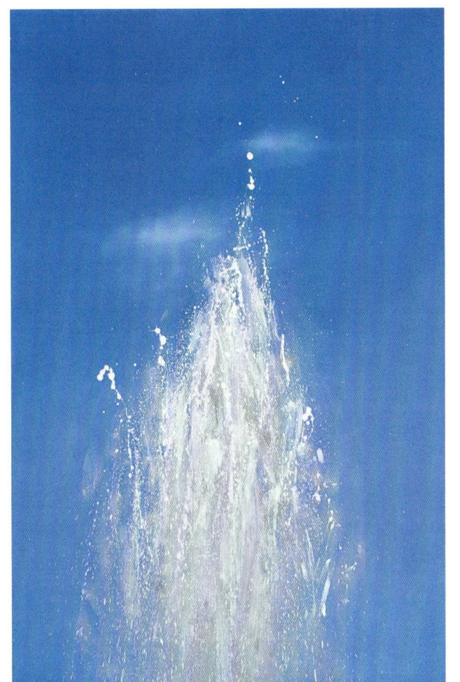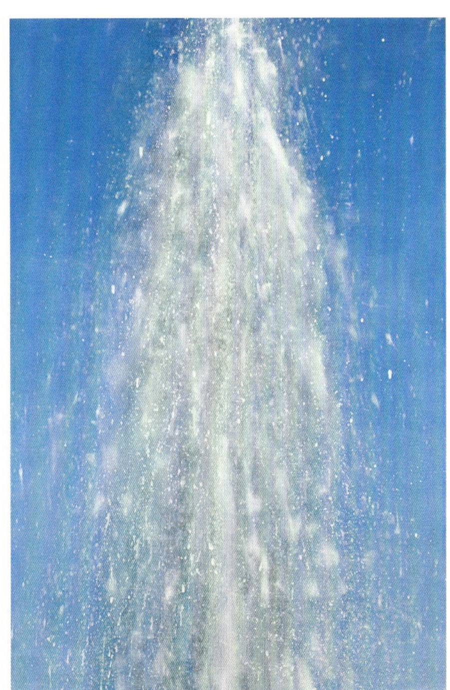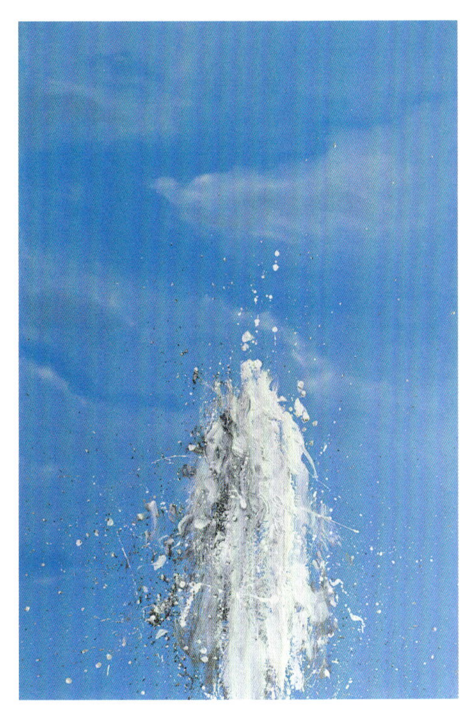

 Untitled (Fountain #5, 9, 2, 1, 3, 4) (2010–2013)

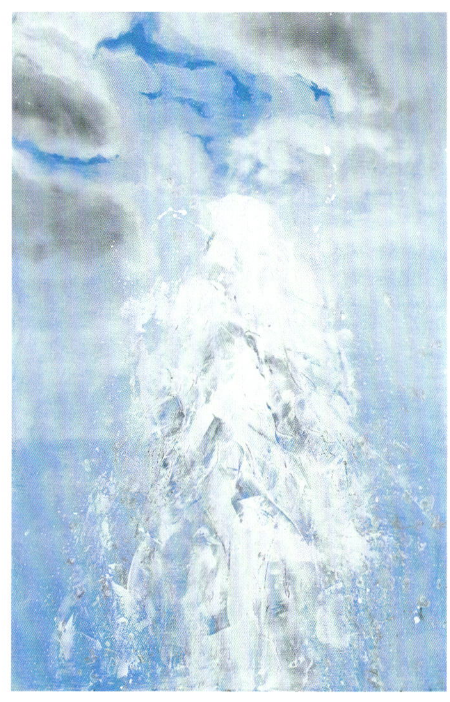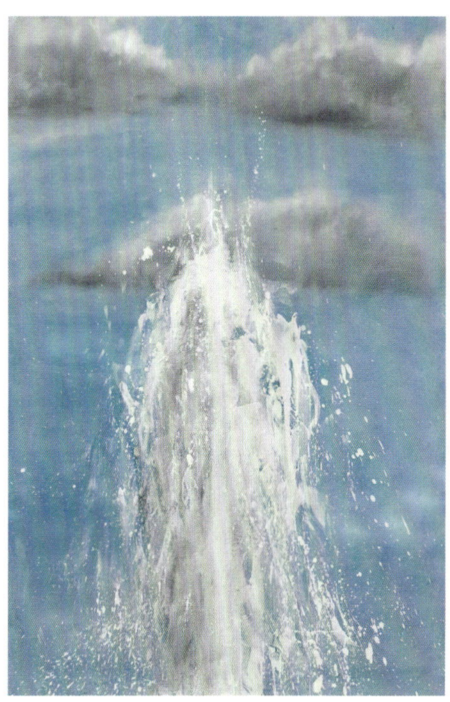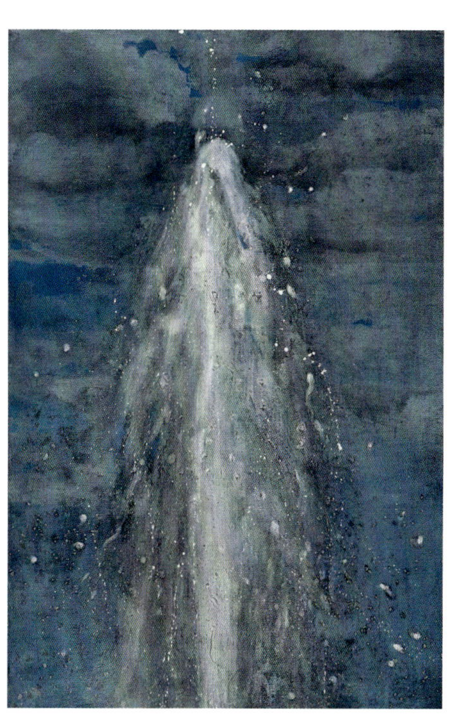

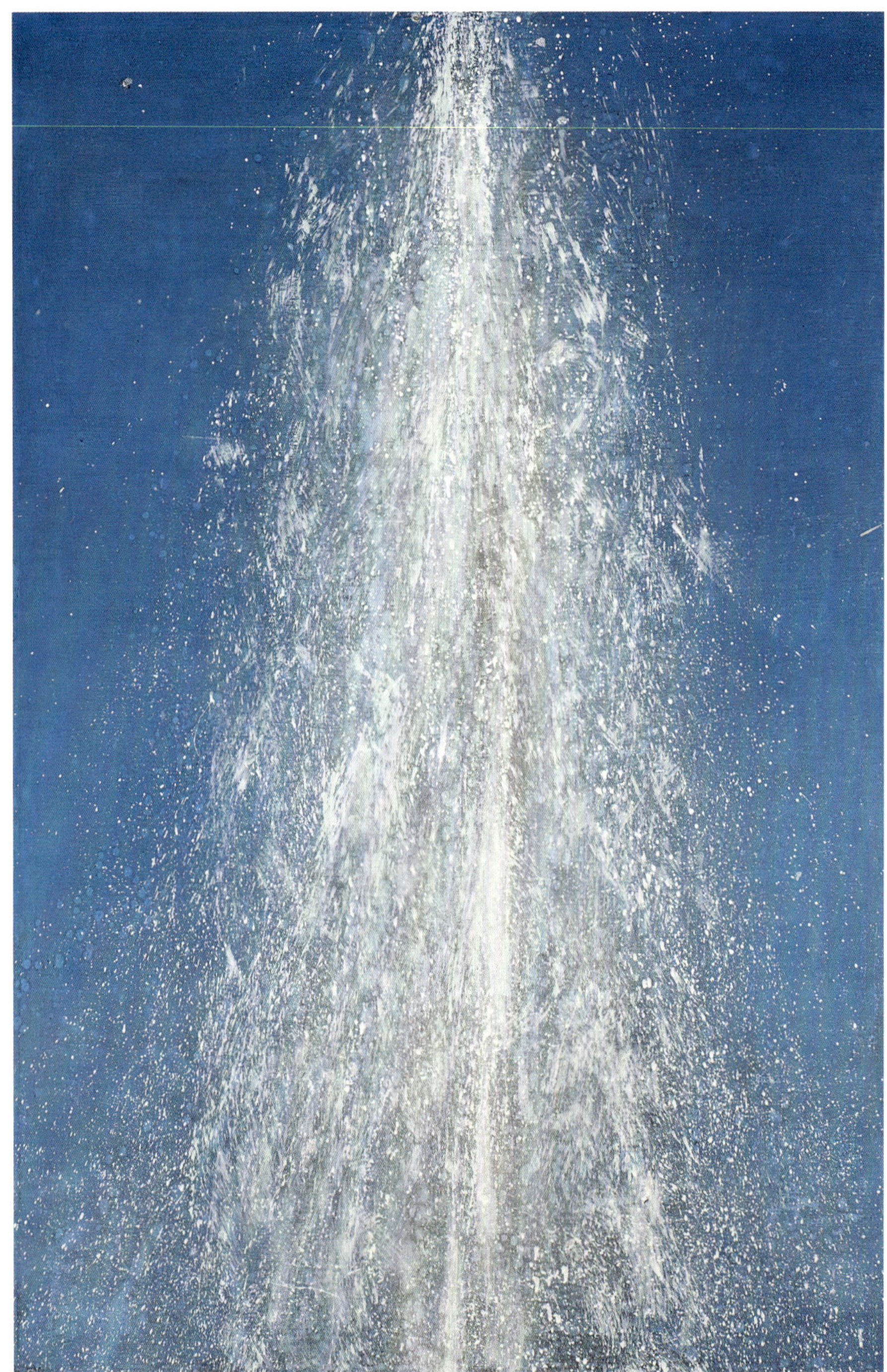

  Untitled (Fountain #10) (2013)

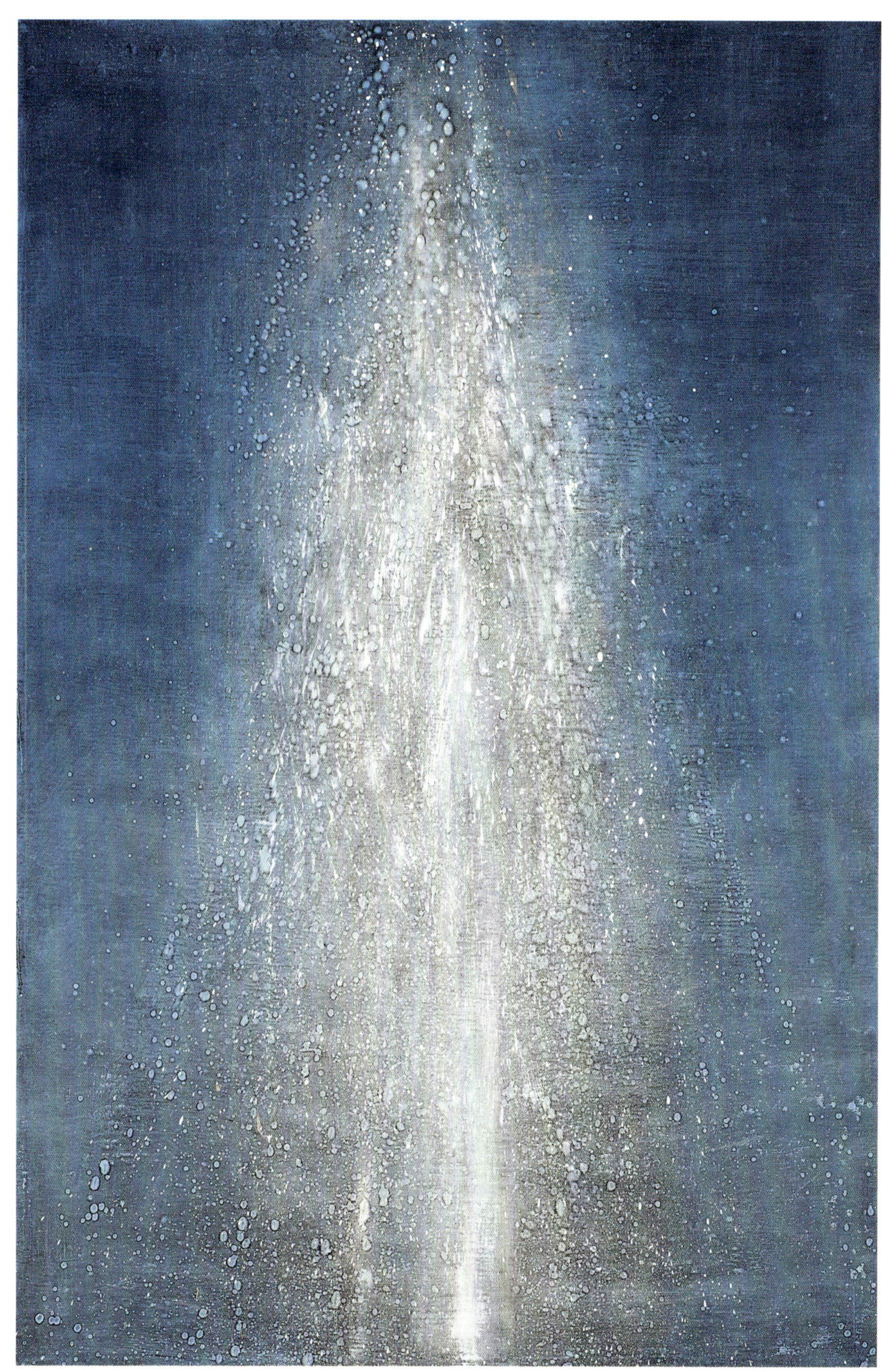

Untitled (Fountain #8) (2013)

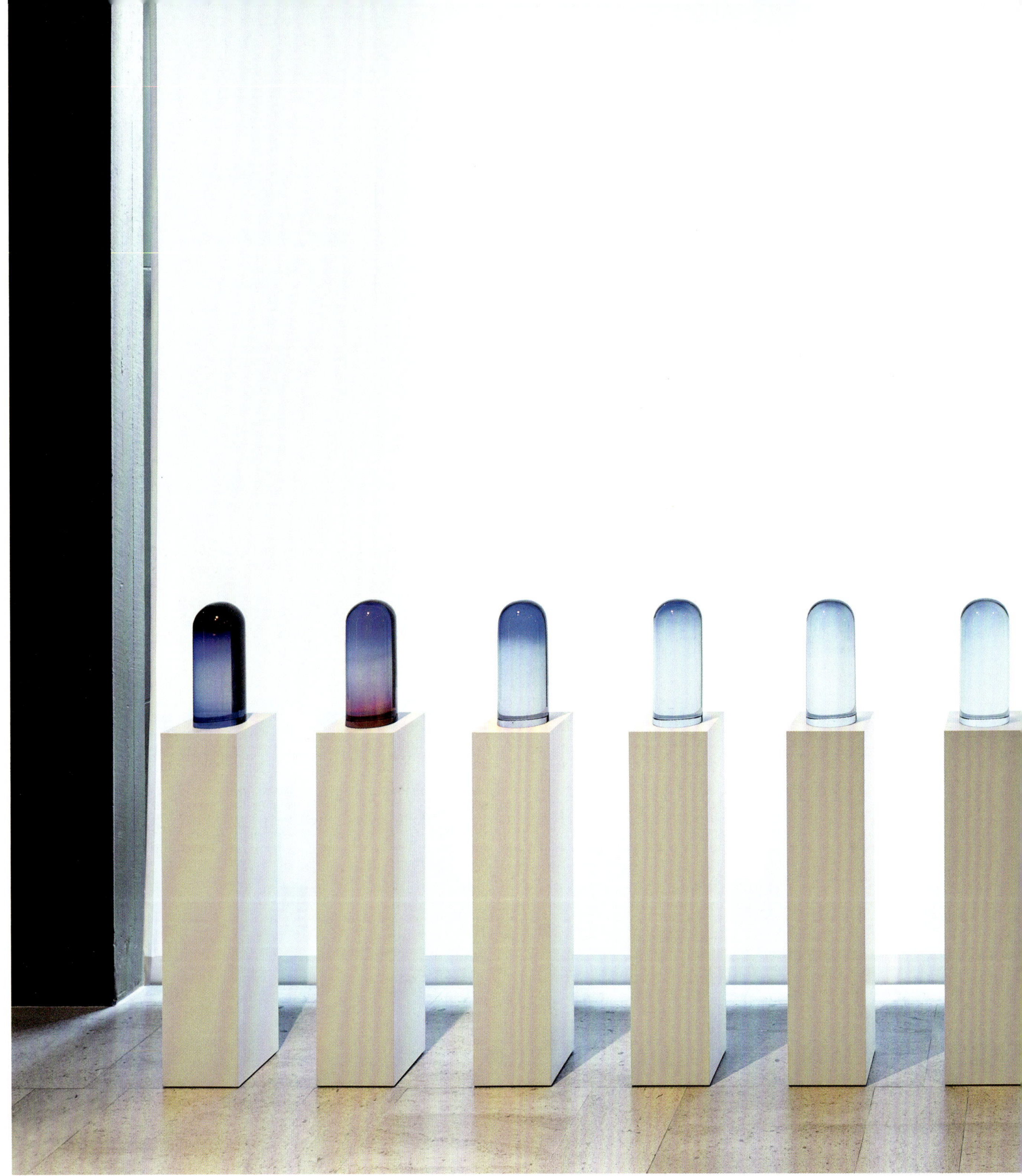

   <u>Untitled</u>, from "The Color of Time" series (2016)

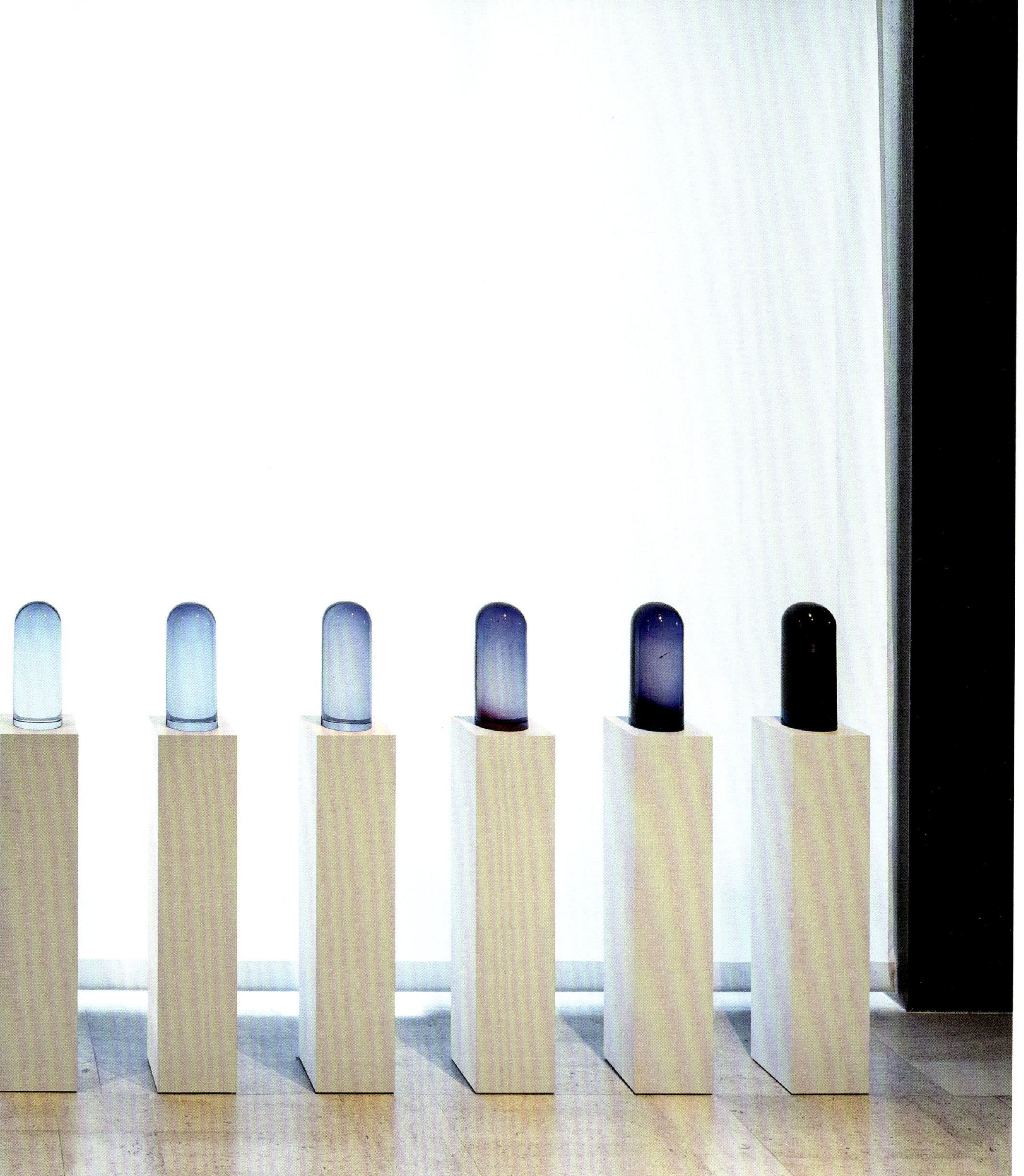

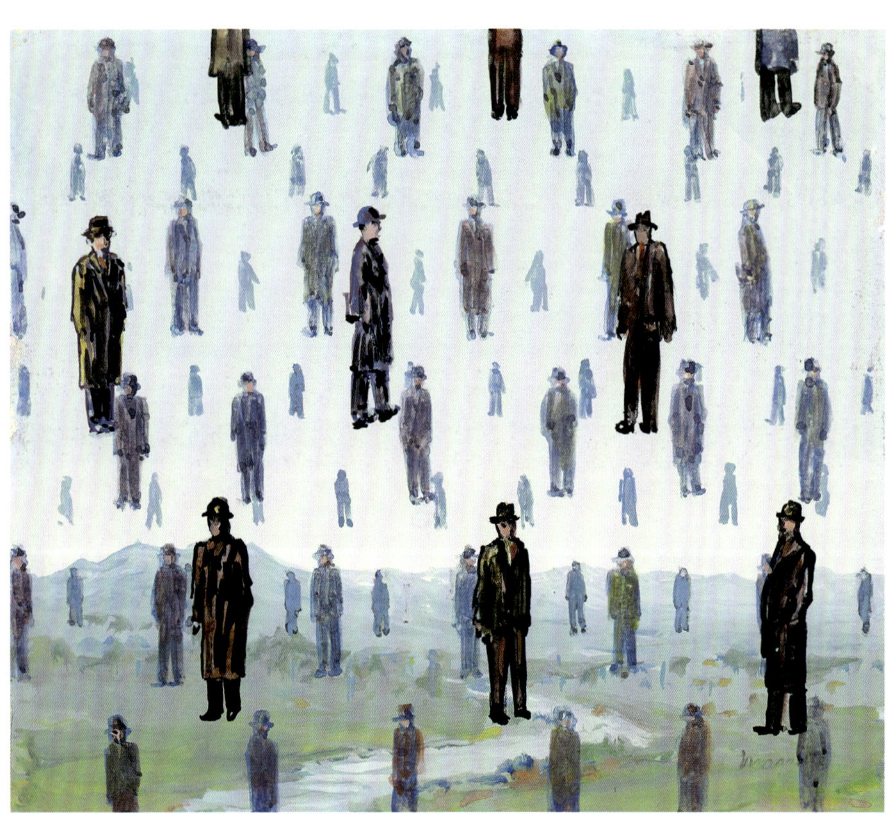

↑ René Magritte <u>Golconde</u> (1953)

→ <u>In Between Between</u> (2013) / <u>Brussels Said Silence</u> (2012)

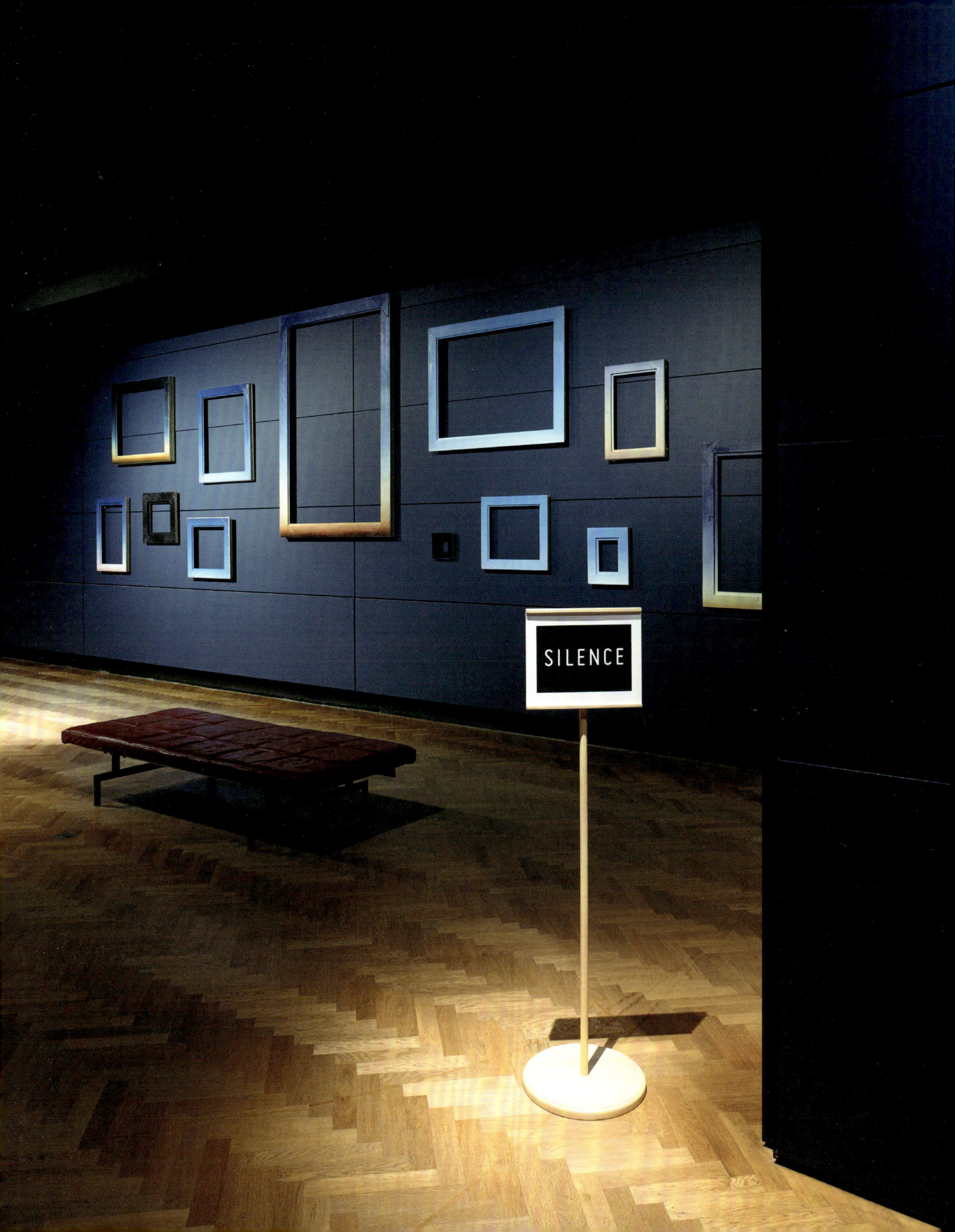
SILENCE

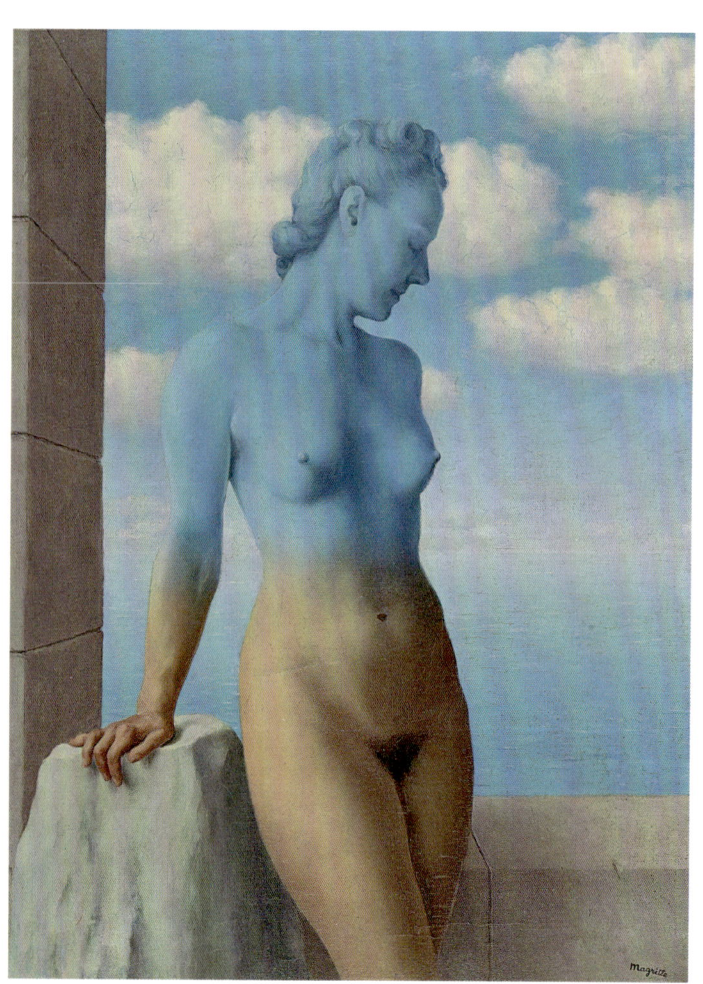

106   René Magritte   <u>Black Magic</u> (1945)

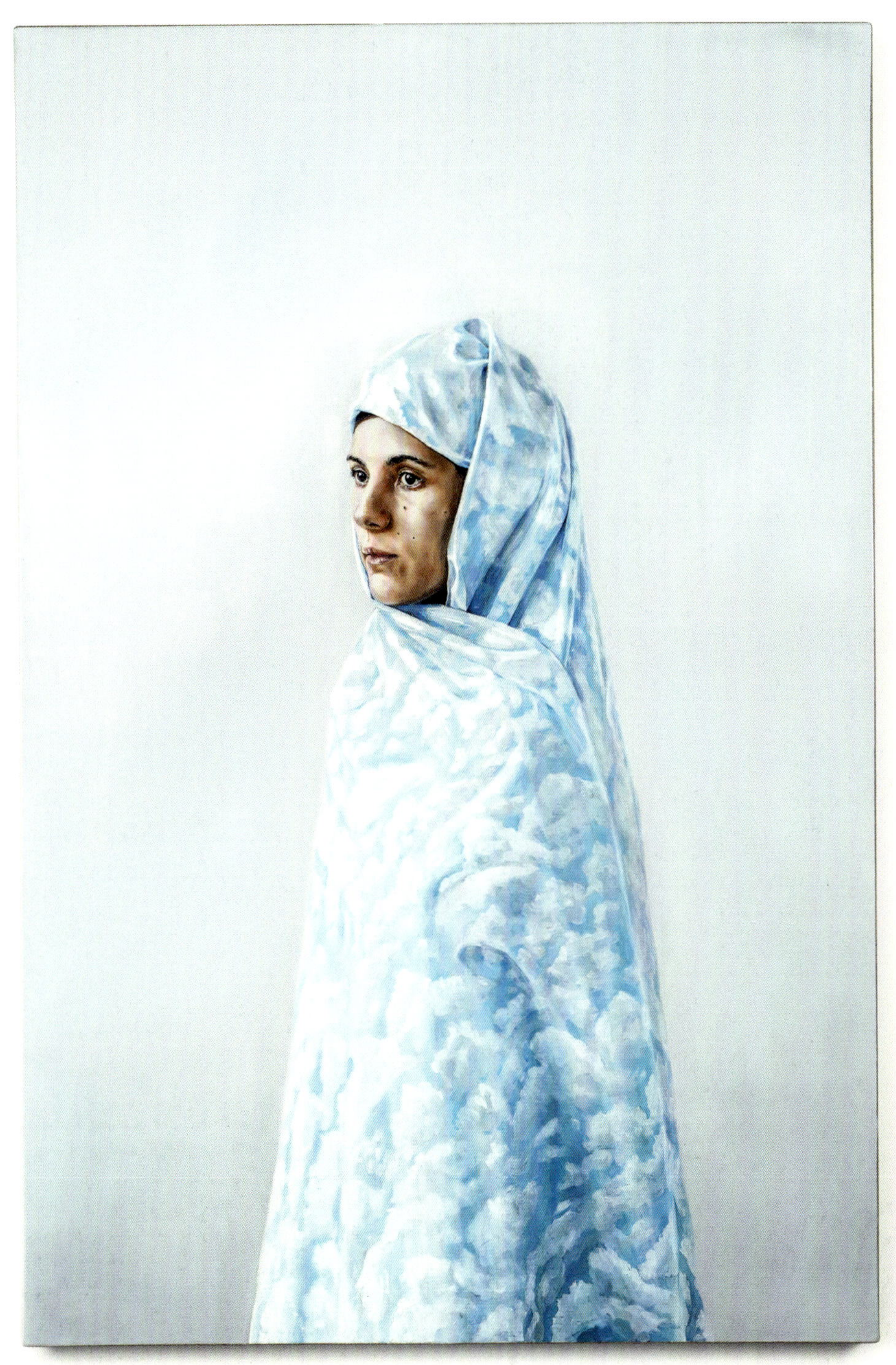

Our Veil (2018)

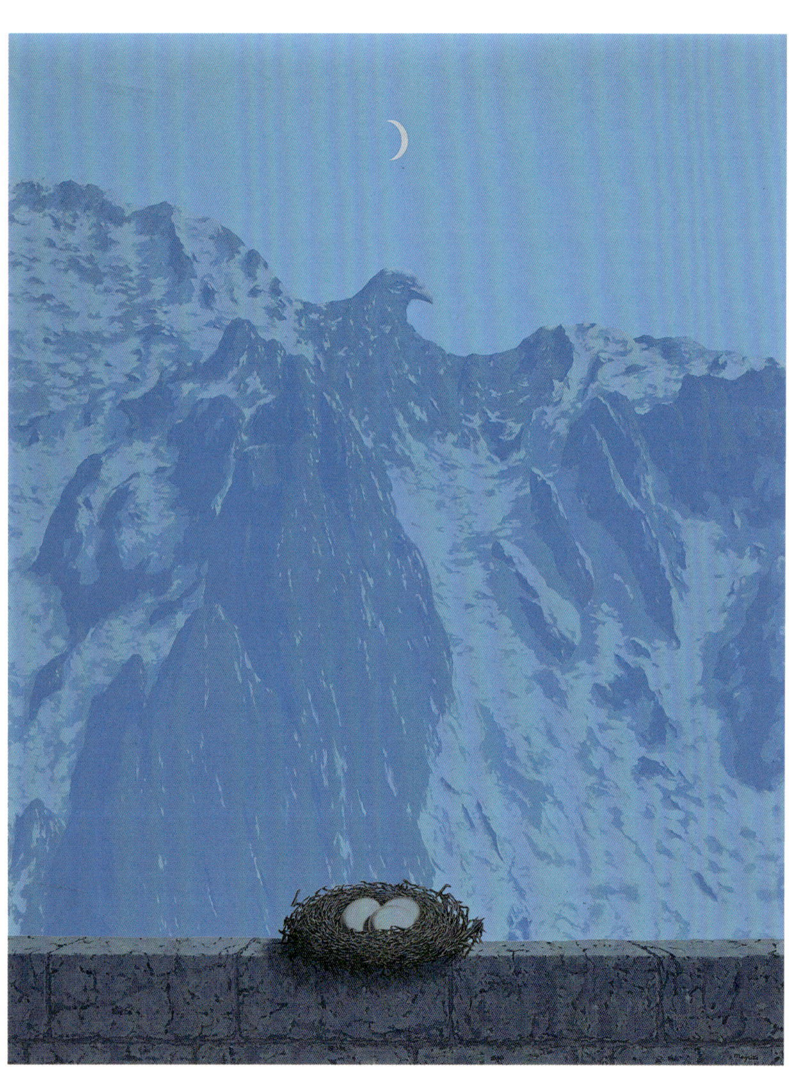

↑ René Magritte <u>The Domain of Arnheim</u> (1962)

→ Marianne Berenhaut & Fabrice Samyn <u>À nous deux</u> (2021)

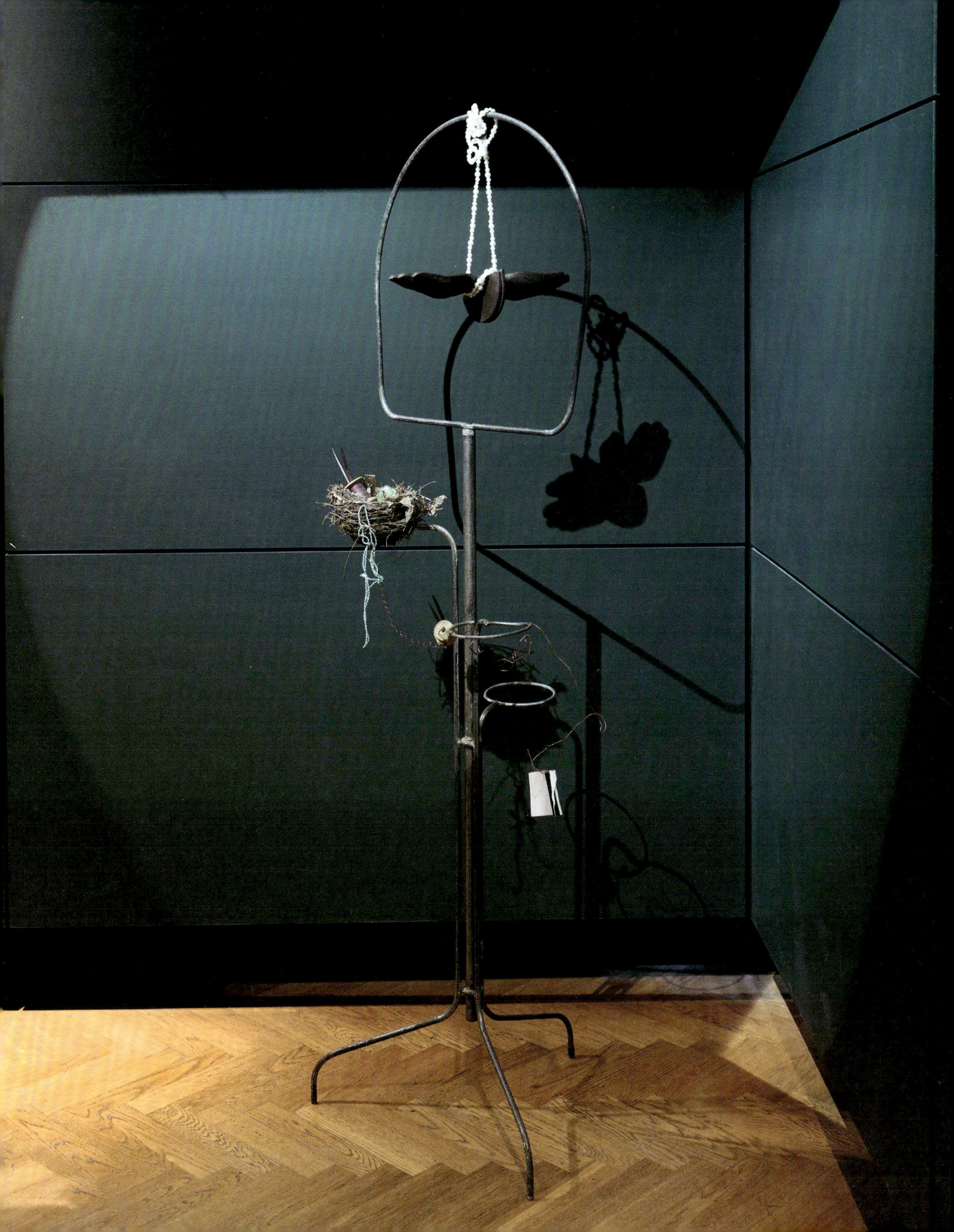

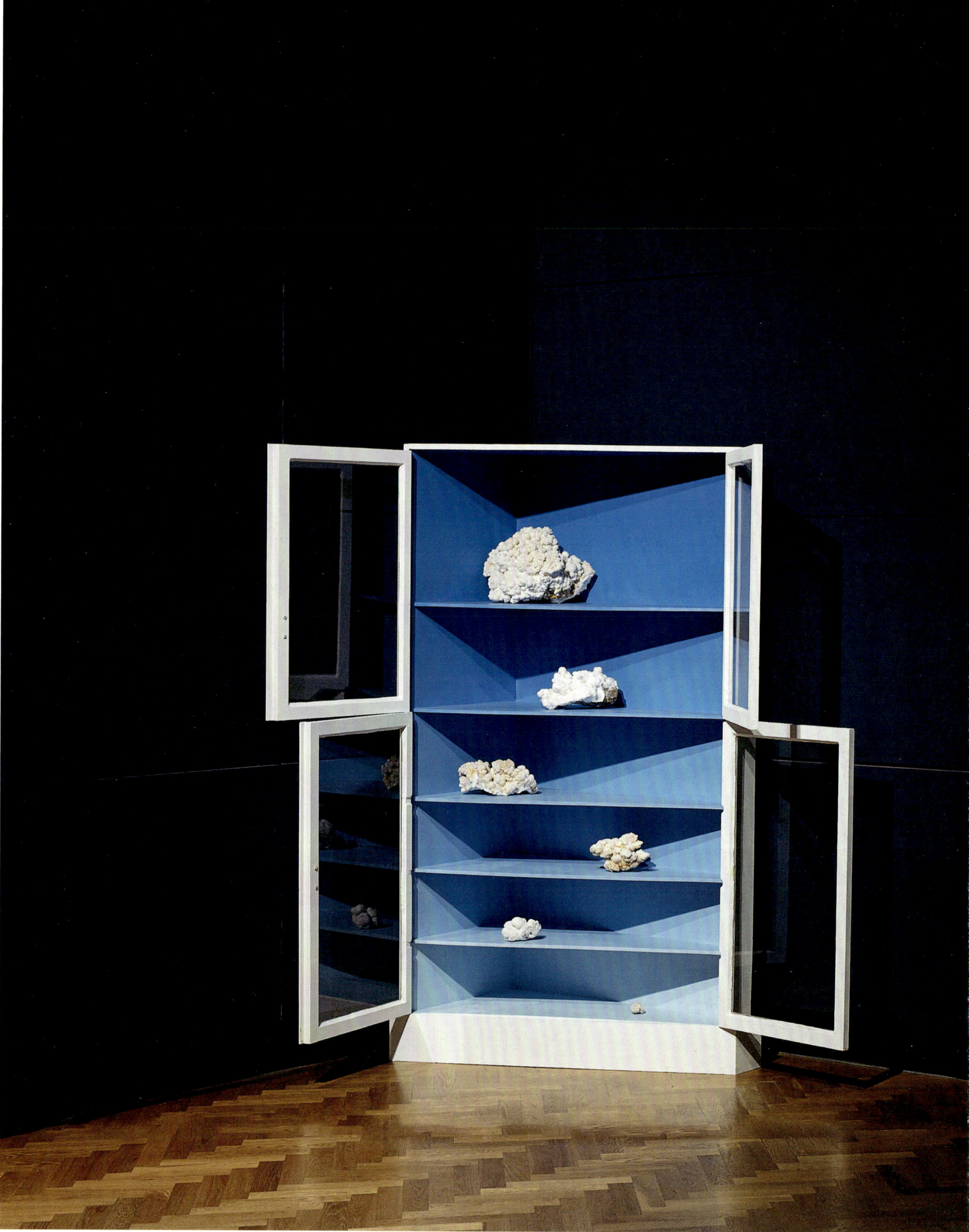

Depth of Sky (2019) / René Magritte The Empire of Lights (1954)

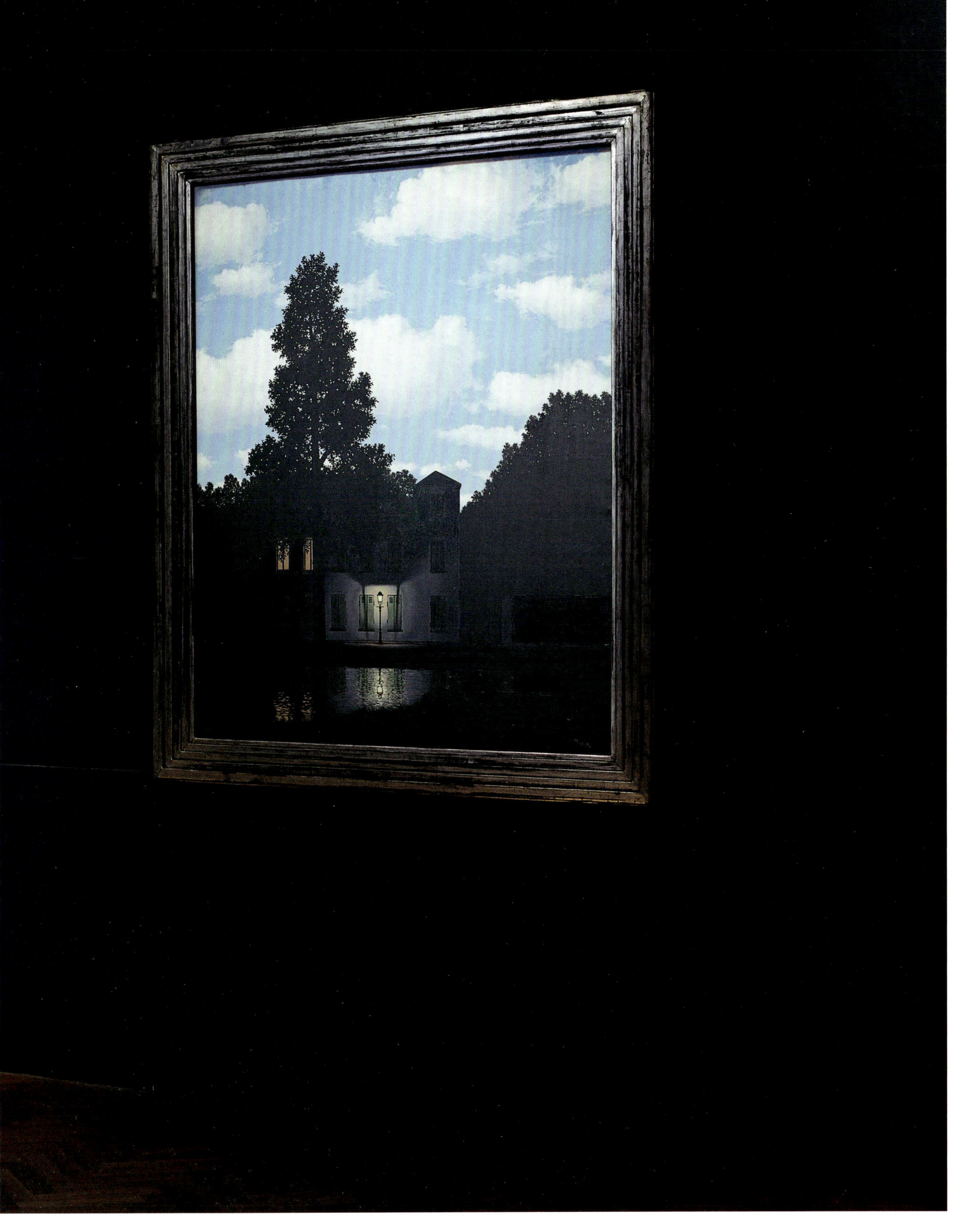

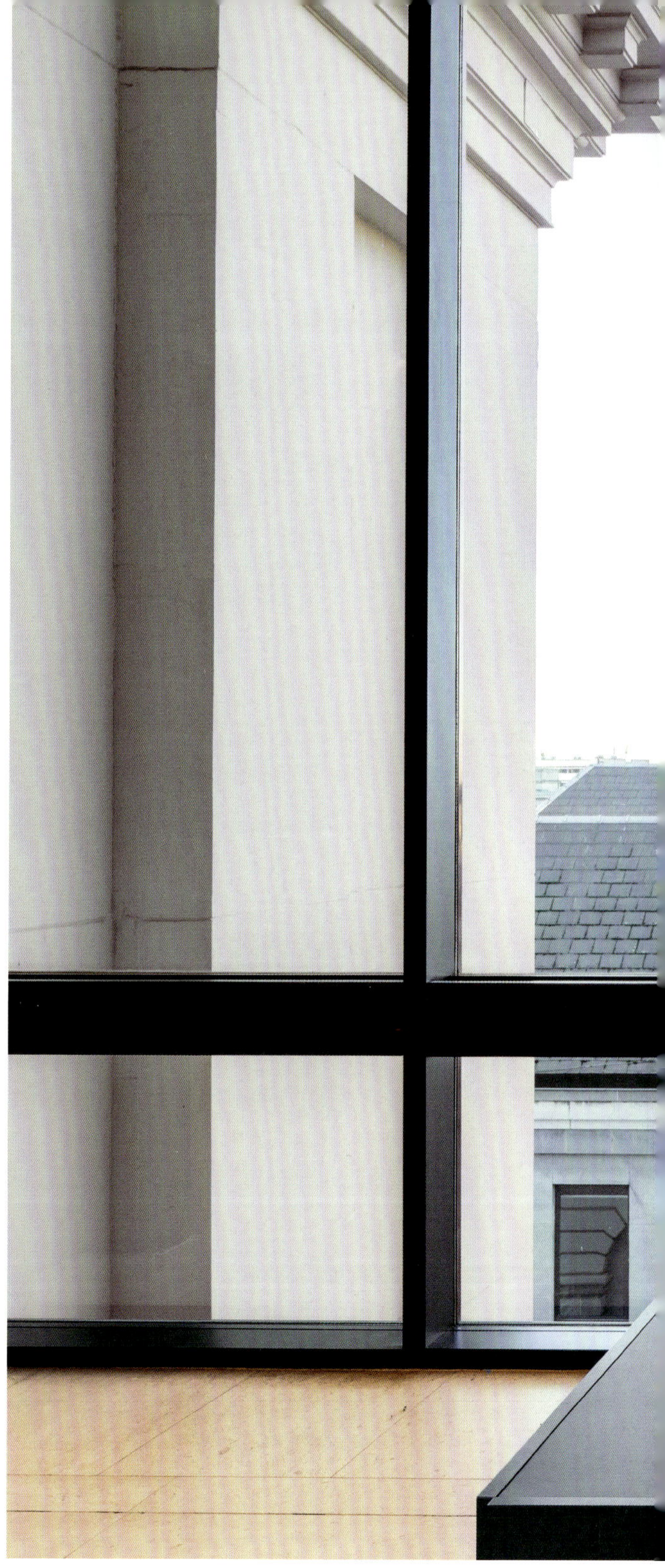

　The Hatching of the Cloud (2021)

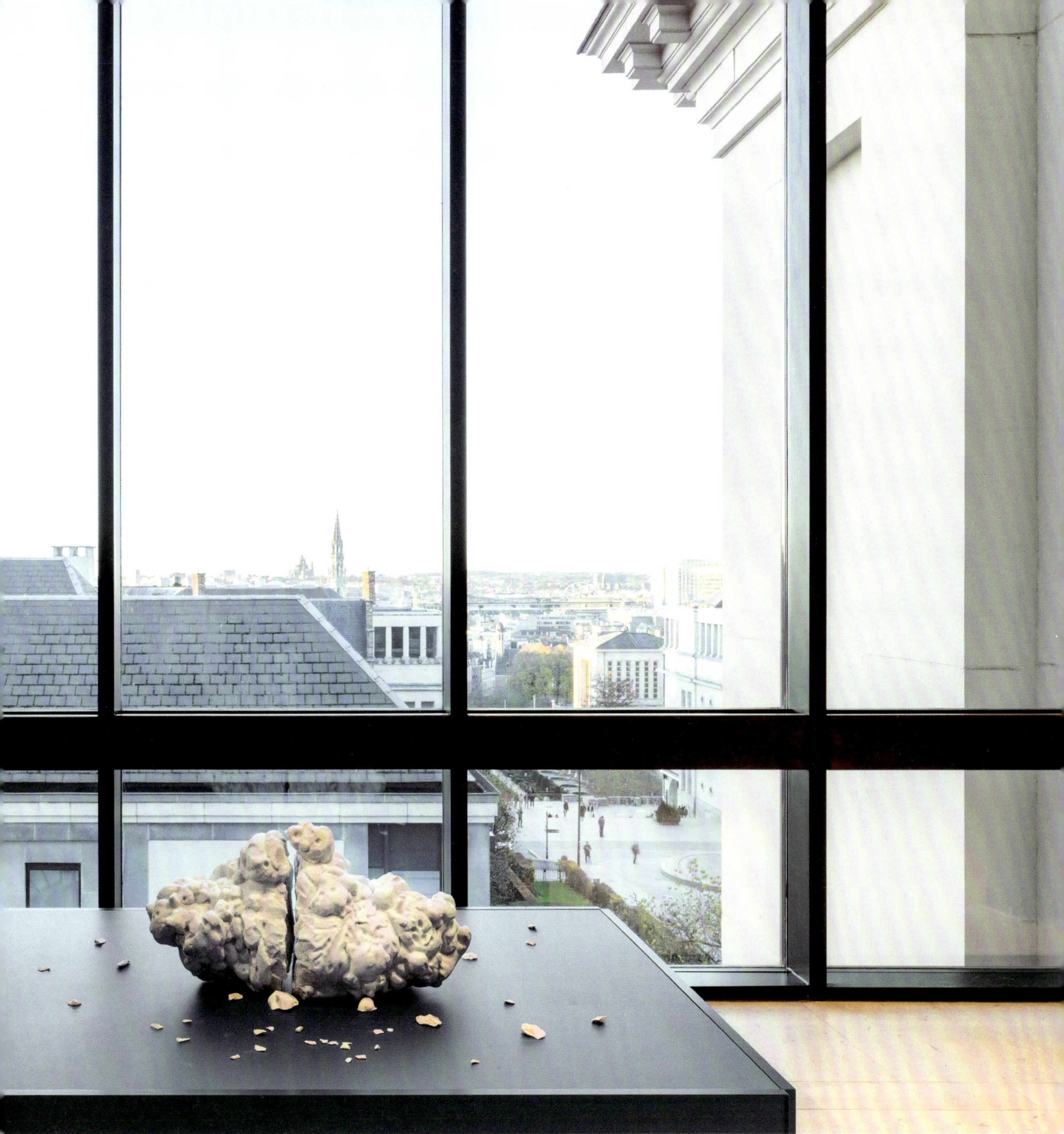

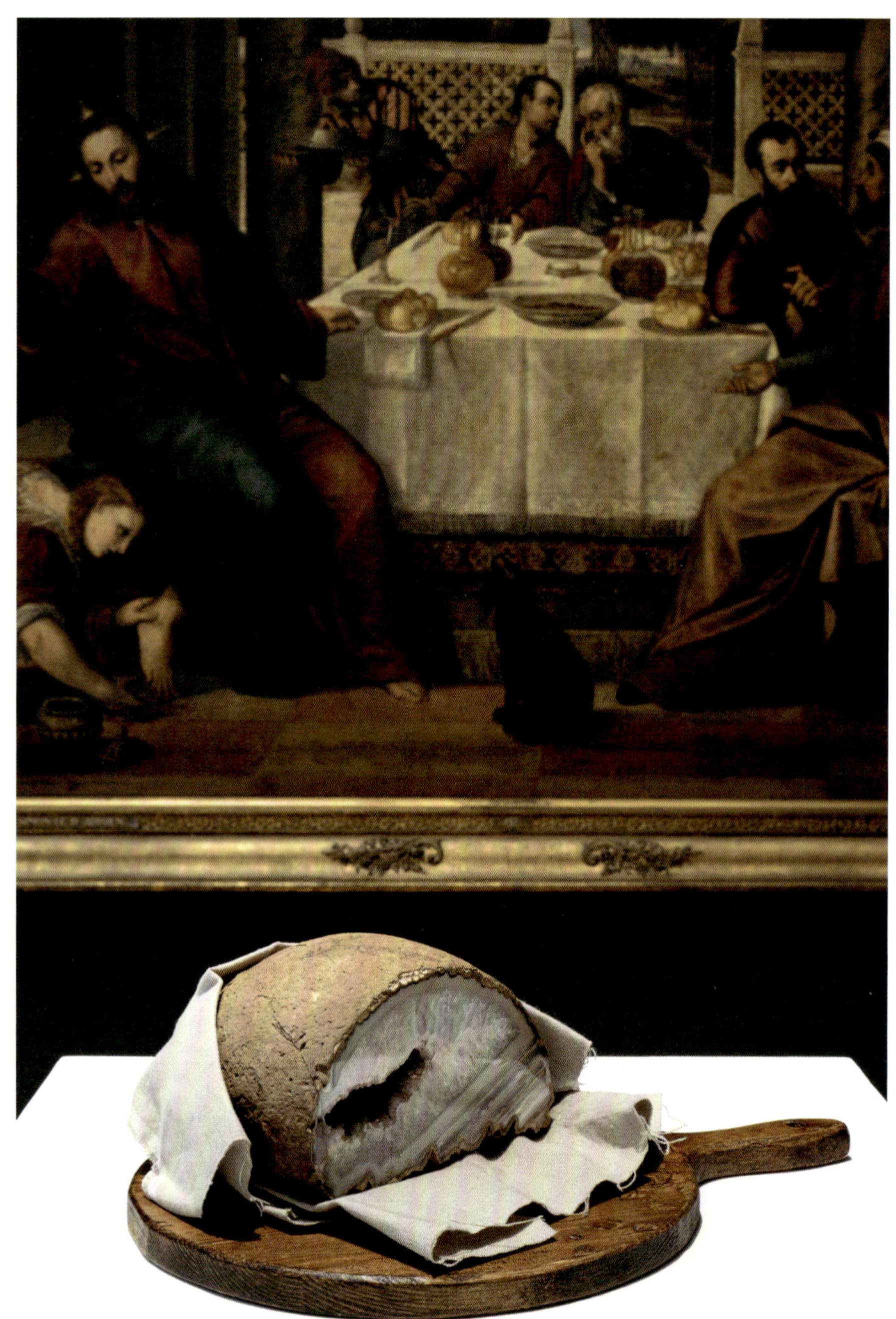

    The Temptation of the Image (2020)

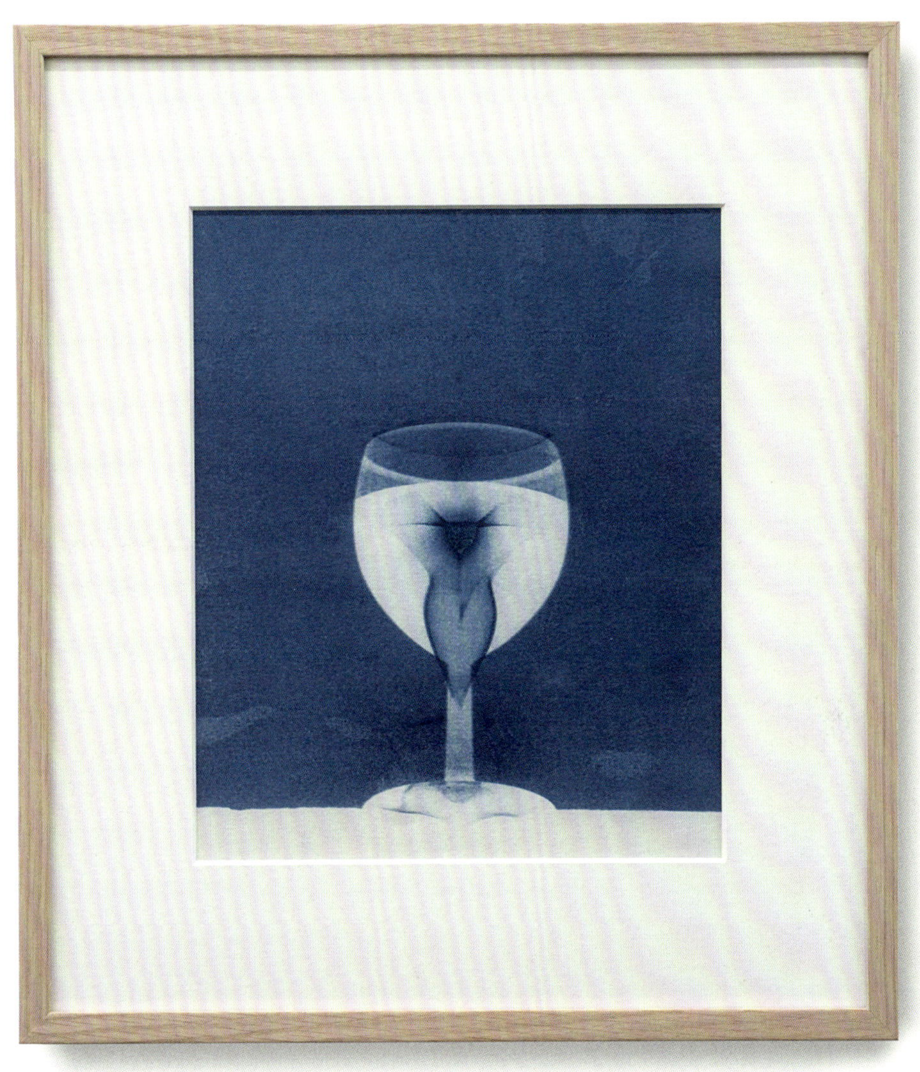

Untitled #6, from the "Burning Chalice" series (2012)   115

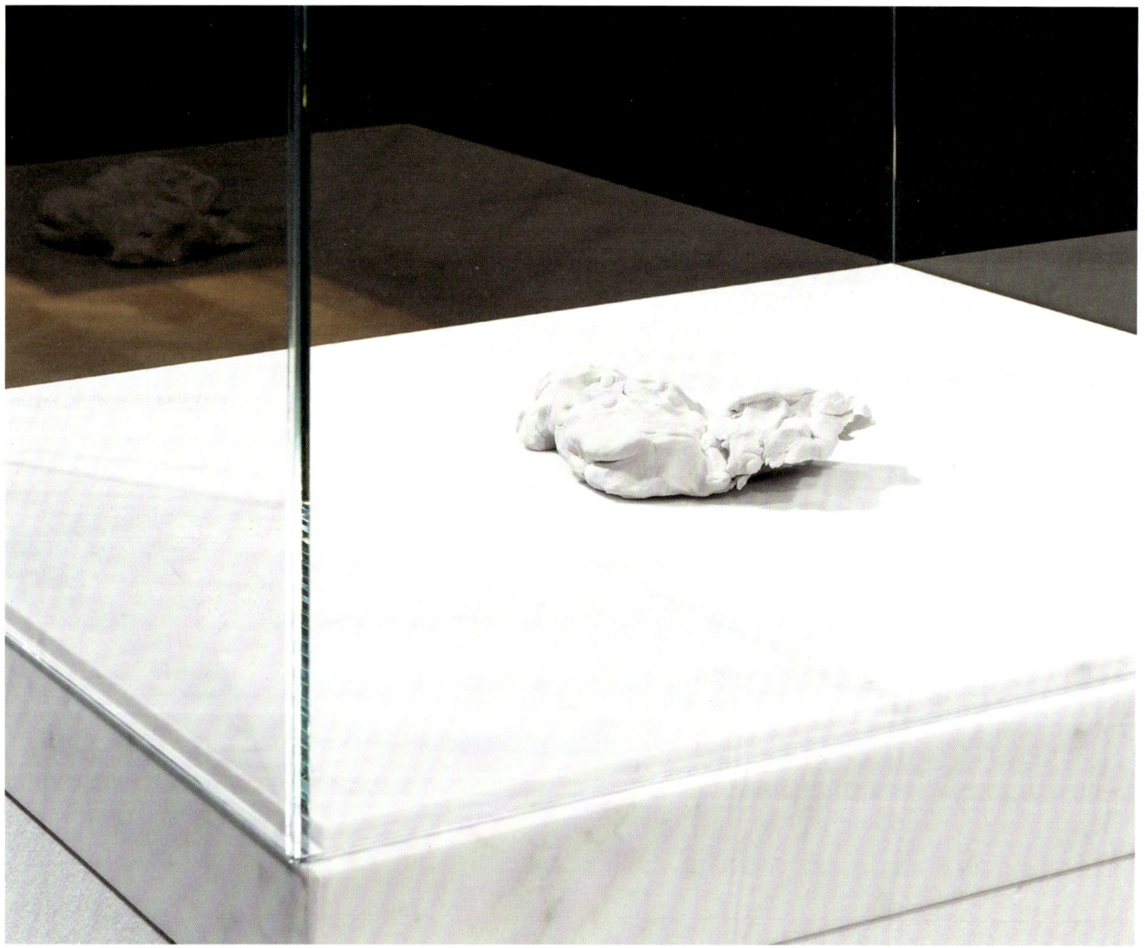

Each work is made up from a letter addressed to someone blind since birth in order to describe a cloud to him or her in the form of a poem. The first one was addressed to Ibrahim after he asked: "No one has ever told me about clouds. Can you describe one to me?" This letter is engraved in Braille on the base and as such only a blind person is able to read it. And based on this letter the person receiving it will sculpt a cloud in fibrous porcelain, which will be placed on the platform base of the exhibit. From time to time a visually impaired person will come and activate the work by removing the glass cover and reading the poem to all the visitors.

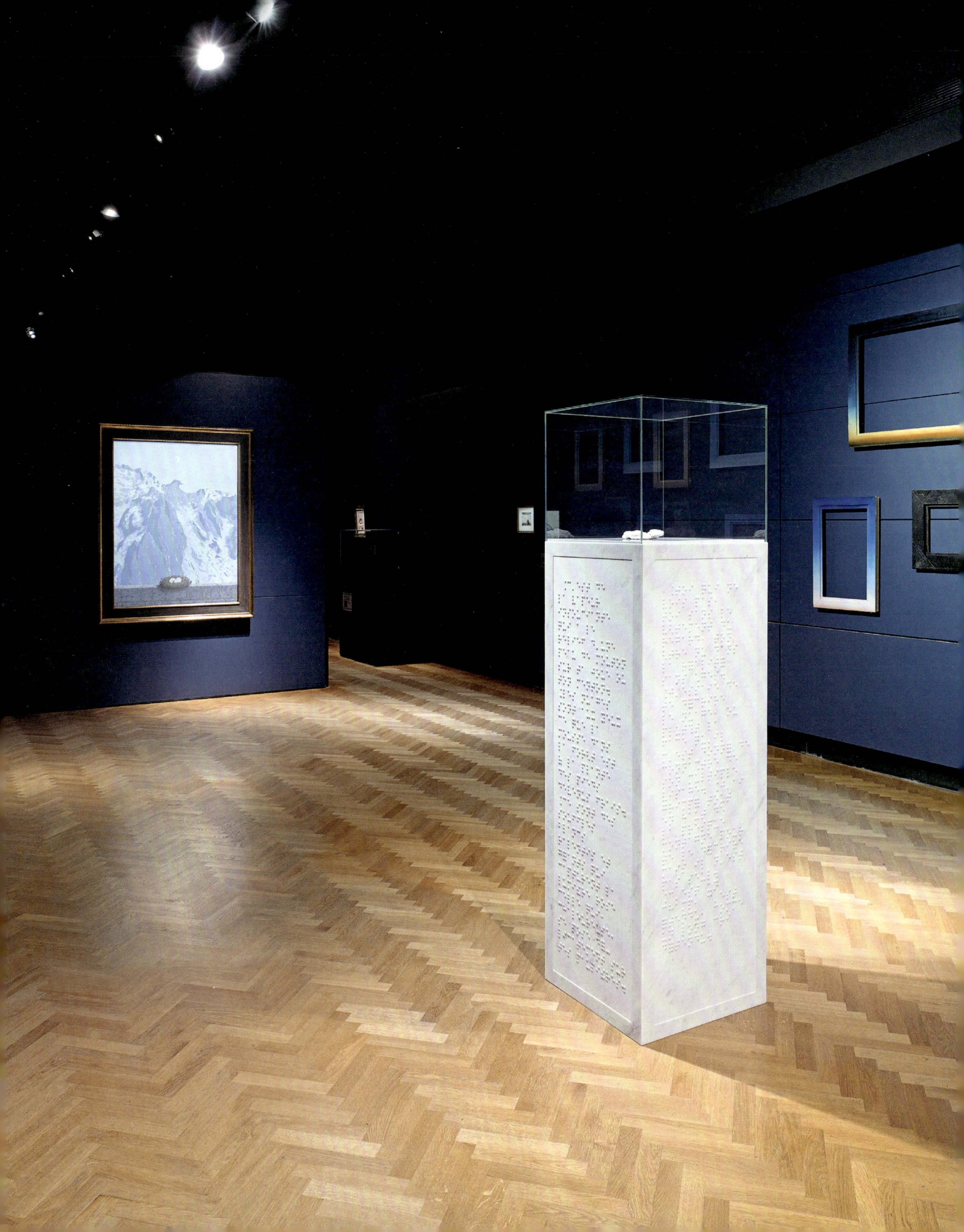

For *Love Letter to an Unknown Person* the artist asked seventeen translators from different countries to translate, one after the other, a love letter. He sent this letter from country to country, following the line of latitude on which Belgium is situated (fifty degrees north). The letter encircled the globe because French was the language it began in and the language it ended up in, and it allows us to appreciate the impossibility of being completely faithful to the subtleties of language. The text becomes loaded with the translators' particular sensibilities, and it is interesting to note that some of them translate it in a lyrical style, showing the inclination of certain cultures to associate love with romanticism.

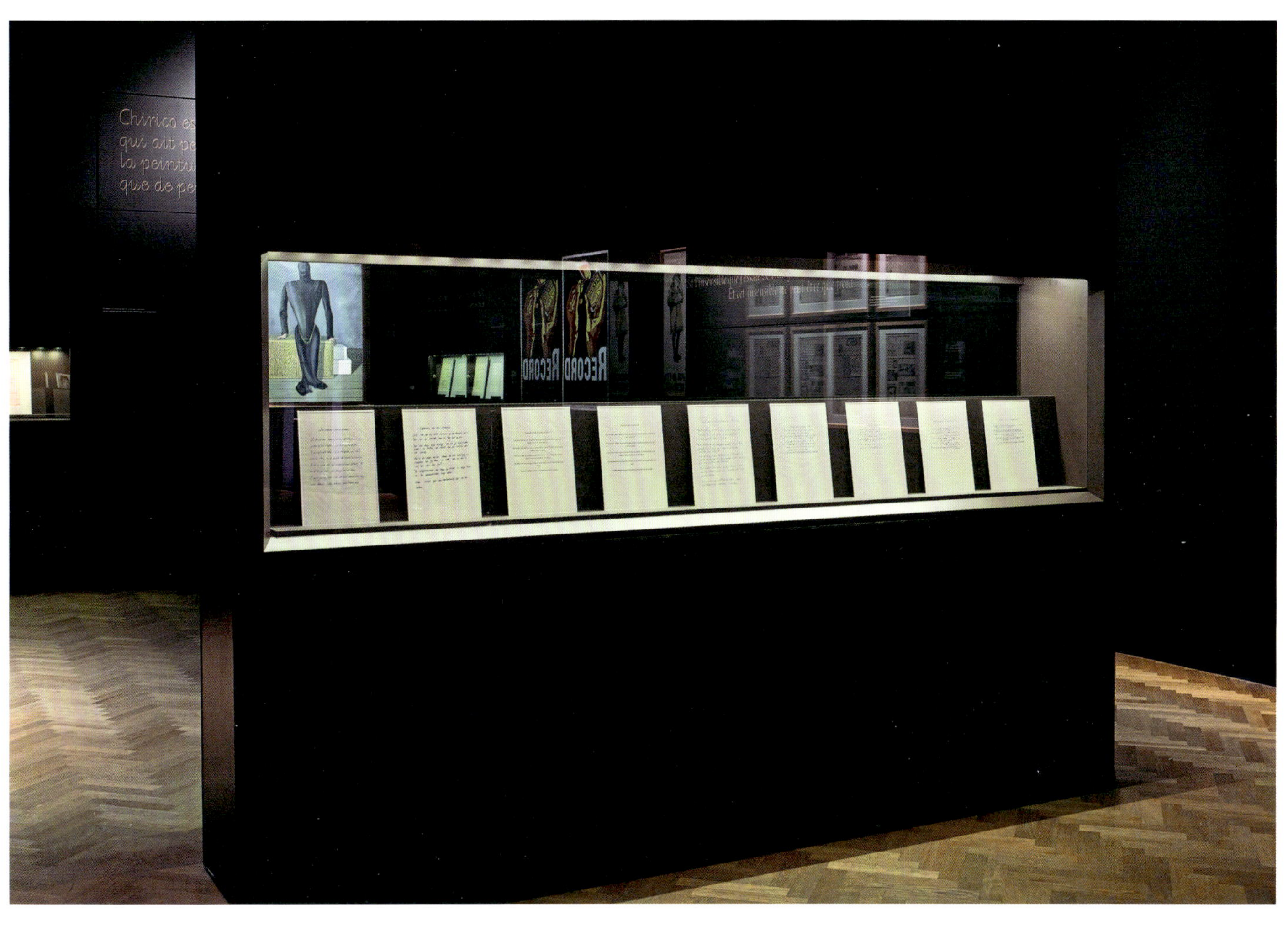

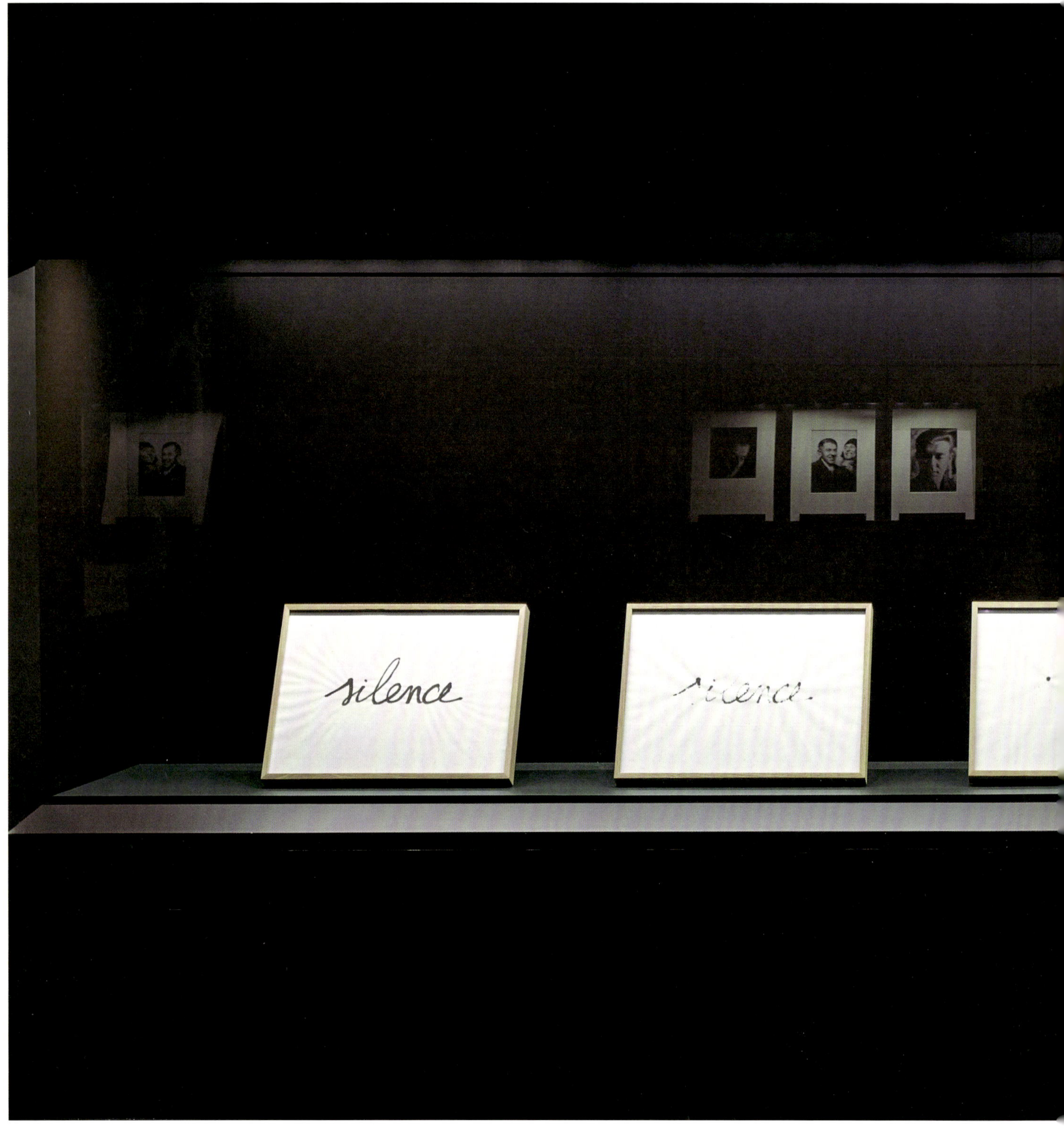

 Speech Act Calligraphy: Silence (2014)

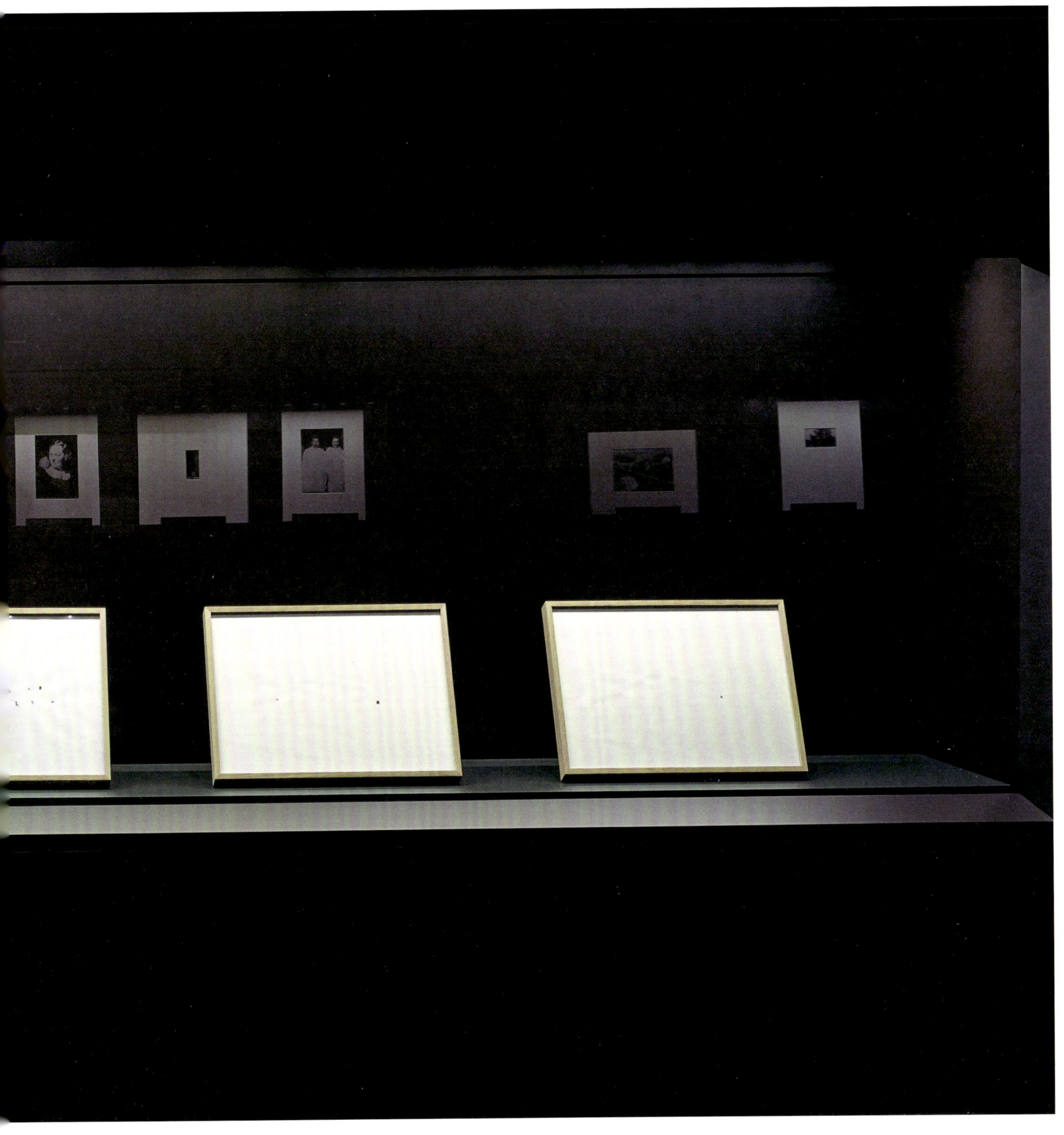

Silence

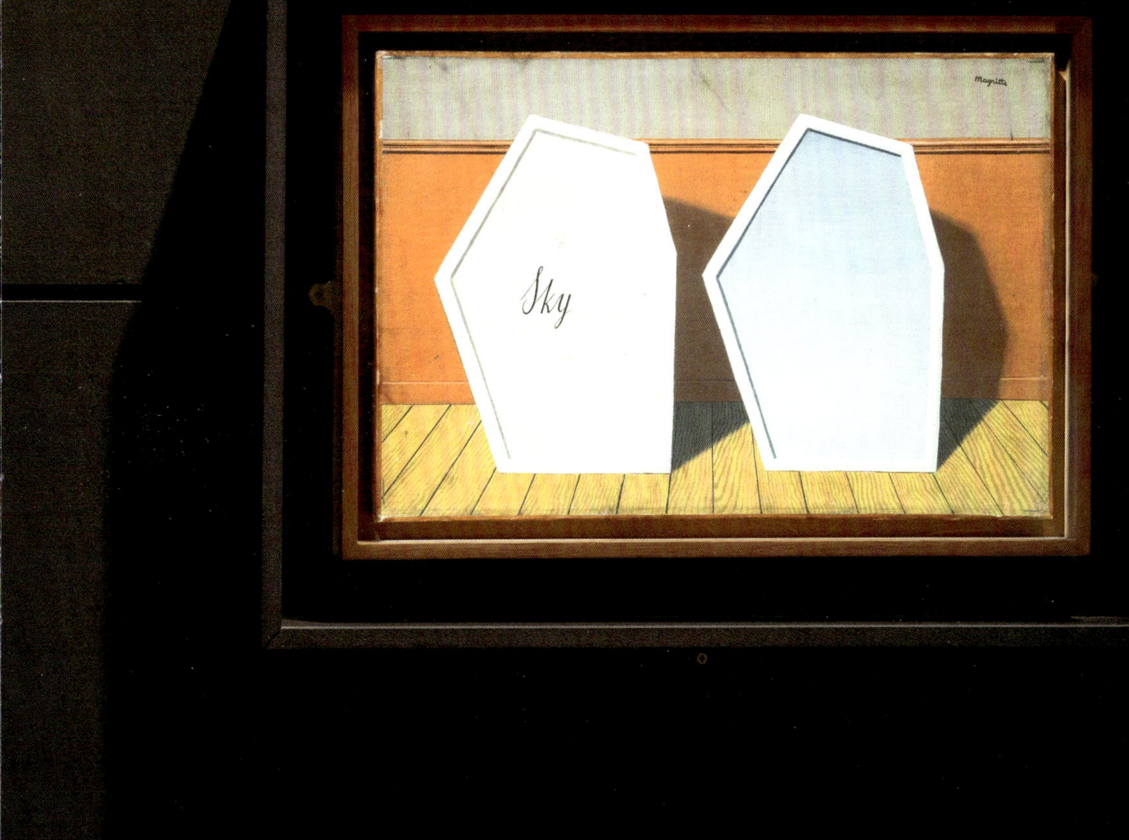

Sky
Magritte

← <u>Untitled</u>, from the "Silence" series (2020) / René Magritte <u>The Palace of Curtains</u> (1935)

LIST OF WORKS

cat. 1 (p. 19)
All the Time We Are, 2010
Silvered handblown glass mounted on oiled oak,
45 × 23 cm
Private collection

cat. 2 (p. 20)
Still Flow, 2018
Silver jewel and glass hourglass,
7.5 × 1.3 × 1.3 cm
Courtesy of the artist

cat. 3 (pp. 21, 27)
Timelessness, 2018
Oil on canvas, 70 × 60 cm
Meessen De Clercq, Brussels

cat. 4 (pp. 22, 75)
*Is Looking in the Mirror
Always Looking Back?,* 2011
Oil on canvas, 120 × 80 cm
Private collection, Europe

cat. 5 (p. 9)
Narcissus?, 2014
Egg tempera and oil on canvas,
30 × 24 cm
Private collection

cat. 6 (p. 23)
Untitled, 2011
Oil on canvas, 18 × 12 cm
Private collection

cat. 7 (p. 23)
Untitled *(Sage),* 2009
Oil on canvas, 30 × 24 cm
Private collection

cat. 8 (p. 23)
Untitled, 2006
Oil on canvas, 30 × 24 cm
Private collection

cat. 9 (pp. 22–23)
Untitled, from the *Seen Breath* series, 2019
Oil on canvas, 42 × 28 cm
Private collection

cat. 10 (p. 23)
Untitled, 2009
Oil on canvas, 30 × 24 cm
Private collection

cat. 11 (p. 23)
Untitled, 2009
Oil on canvas, 45 × 38 cm
Courtesy Olivier Meessen

cat. 12 (p. 23)
Untitled, 2009
Oil on canvas, 18 × 12 cm
Private collection

cat. 13 (fpp. 23, 83)
Untitled *(Philip),* 2009
Oil on canvas, 30 × 24 cm
Private collection

cat. 14 (pp. 23, 91)
Blinder, 2009
Locally devarnished antique painting,
63 × 50 cm
Private collection

cat. 15 (p. 23)
Untitled, 2009
Oil on canvas, 30 × 24 cm
Private collection

cat. 16 (p. 23)
History – Prehistory, 2006
Oil on canvas, 30 × 24 cm
Collection Sophie Thonon

cat. 17 (pp. 23, 80)
Narcisso, 2009
Oil on canvas, 45 × 38 cm
Private collection

cat. 18 (p. 23)
Adorned, 2009
Locally devarnished antique painting,
46.5 × 38.5 cm
Private collection, Europe

cat. 19 (p. 23)
Untitled, 2009
Oil on canvas, 27 × 19 cm
Private collection, Brussels

cat. 20 (p. 23)
Untitled, 2009
Oil on canvas, 24 × 18 cm
Private collection

cat. 21 (pp. 14, 23)
From Matter, 2010
Egg tempera and oil on canvas,
30 × 24 cm
Private collection

cat. 22 (pp. 25, 27)
Threshold, 2018
Oil on canvas, 120 × 80 cm
Private collection, Tielt

cat. 23 (pp. 26, 28, 29)
*Mourning Through the Day
(or The Covered Mirror),* 2015
Oil on canvas, 120 × 80 cm (each frame)
Private collection, Brussels

cat. 24 (p. 27)
The Observer (Study), 2018
Oil on canvas, 50 × 40 cm
Private collection

cat. 25 (pp. 27, 76)
Listen, 2013
Oil on canvas, 50 × 40 cm
Private collection

cat. 26 (pp. 27, 77)
The Mask of your Image, 2013
Oil on canvas, 80 × 60 cm
Private collection

cat. 27 (p. 33)
From Pain to Compassion, 2018
Antique brass eyeglass frame and glass drops
(1.5 × 3.5 cm) in a box (4 × 12.5 × 17 cm)
Courtesy of the artist

cat. 28 (p. 35)
Untitled, from the *Color of Time* series, 2014
Solid glass, 39 × 16 cm
Collection Tom Jonckers

cat. 29 (pp. 40, 41)
Endogenous / Exogenous, 2018
Gold leaf on agave flowers, 336 × 364 cm
Courtesy of the artist

cat. 30 (p. 43)
Eve & Adam, 2018
Oil on canvas, 70 × 50 cm
Private collection

cat. 31 (pp. 12, 44, 45)
The Fallen Tree of Knowledge, 2020
Wood and gold leaf, 232 × 287 × 480 cm
Courtesy of the artist

cat. 32 (p. 47)
Lucas Cranach's Studio, 2007
Oil on canvas, 50 × 50 cm
Private collection

cat. 33 (pp. 52, 53)
Untitled, from the *Looking from
the Black Hole* series, 2015
Ink on paper, 49.5 × 65.5 cm (day)
Courtesy of the artist

cat. 34 (p. 57)

Untitled, from the *Threshold* series, 2016

Wood, paint, 226 × 80 cm
Courtesy of the artist

cat. 35 (pp. 58, 89)

Saint Sebastien Tended by Irene, Musée du Louvre, Paris / Saint Sebastien Tended by Irene, Staatliche Museen, Gemäldegalerie, Berlin, 2007

Oil on canvas, 180 × 120 cm (each frame)
Private collection, Europe

cat. 36 (pp. 59 left, 61)

The Dream of Saint Joseph, Musée des Beaux-Arts de Nantes, 2011

Oil on canvas, 180 × 120 cm
Private collection

cat. 37 (pp. 59 center)

The Penitent Magdalen, Metropolitan Museum of Art, New York City, 2011

Oil on canvas, 180 × 120 cm
Private collection, Belgium

cat. 38 (pp. 59 right, 62)

The Education of the Virgin, Frick Collection, New York, 2012

Oil on canvas, 180 × 120 cm
Private collection

cat. 39 (p. 63)

Payment of Taxes, Art Gallery, Lviv, Ukraine, 2011

Oil on canvas, 180 × 120 cm
Private collection, Brussels

cat. 40 (p. 65)

Job Mocked by his Wife, Musée Départe-mental des Vosges, Épinal, 2011

Oil on canvas, 180 × 120 cm
Private collection

cat. 41 (p. 67)

Saint Joseph in the Carpenter's Shop, Musée du Louvre, Paris, 2009

Oil on canvas, 180 × 120 cm
Private collection

cat. 42 (pp.68, 69)

Untitled #3, from the *Twilight's Gaze* series, 2021

Oil on canvas, 180 × 120 cm
Courtesy of the artist

cat. 43 (pp. 68, 70)

Untitled #2, from the *Twilight's Gaze* series, 2021

Oil on canvas, 180 × 120 cm
Courtesy of the artist

cat. 44 (pp. 68, 71)

Untitled #1, from the *Twilight's Gaze* series, 2021

Oil on canvas, 180 × 120 cm
Courtesy of the artist

cat. 45 (p. 72)

Untitled, from the *Black is Virgin* series, 2016

Burned wood and pine resin, 23 × 10 × 9 cm
Courtesy of the artist

cat. 46 (p. 79)

The Cardinal Lioness or The Withdrawn Spine, 2014

Oil on canvas, 150 × 100 cm
Private collection

cat. 47 (p. 96)

Still Night, 2014

Oil on canvas, 65 × 55 cm
Collection Francis De Beir

cat. 48 (p. 97)

Forget Me Not, from the *When Are You More You?* series, 1987–2014

Child's tempera painting, paper (50 × 40.2 cm), clay and acrylic pot (12 × 5 × 5 cm), egg tempera and oil painting on canvas (50 × 40.2 cm)
Private collection

cat. 49 (p. 99)

Untitled *(Fountain #4),* 2010

Oil on canvas, 120 × 80 cm
Private collection

cat. 50 (p. 101)

Untitled *(Fountain #8),* 2010

Oil on canvas, 120 × 80 cm
Private collection

cat. 51 (pp. 102–103)

Untitled, from the *Color of Time* series, 2016

Solid glass, 35 × 20 cm (each globe)
Courtesy of the artist

cat. 52 (p. 107)

In Between Between, 2013

Oil and gold leaf on wood (12 antique wooden frames from different time periods), variable dimensions
Courtesy of the artist

cat. 53 (p. 105)

Brussels Said Silence, 2012

Site-specific installation, wood and inkjet print paper, Reproductions of "Silence" panels from the Belgium Royal Library
Courtesy of the artist

cat. 54 (p. 107)

Our Veil, 2018

Oil on canvas, 120 × 80 cm
Private collection

cat. 55 (p. 109)

Marianne Berenhaut & Fabrice Samyn
À nous deux, 2021

Mixed media, 168,5 × 49 × 49 cm
Courtesy Dvir Gallery

cat. 56 (p. 110)

Depth of Sky, 2019

Painted wood and aragonite, 183 × 106 × 99 cm
Courtesy of the artist

cat. 57 (pp. 112–113)

The Hatching of the Cloud, 2021

Marble, 51 × 47 × 93 cm
Courtesy of the artist

cat. 58 (p. 114)

The Temptation of the Image, 2020

Stone and wood, 13 × 40 × 27 cm
Courtesy of the artist

cat. 59 (p. 115)

Untitled #6, from the *Burning Chalice* series, 2012

Cyanotype, 24 × 20 cm
Private collection

cat. 60 (pp. 116, 117)

Naked Sight (Cumulus 1), 2021

Marble, glass, porcelain, 200 × 55 × 55 cm
Brussels, RMFAB,
donation Frédéric de Goldschmidt

cat. 61 (pp. 118, 119)

Correspondence Piece IV: Letter to Space – Activation I: Love Letter to an Unknown Person, 2014

Series of 18 letters. Paper, ink, glass, wood, 31 × 23.3 × 5 cm (each frame)
Private collection

cat. 62 (pp. 120–121)

Speech Act Calligraphy: Silence, 2014

Series of 5 drawings, ink drawing on super-imposed sheets of paper, done in one breath, 31.6 × 47 cm (each frame)
Collection Galila, Belgium

cat. 63 (p. 122)

Untitled, from the *Silence series,* 2020

Oil and ink on canvas, 24 × 18 cm
Courtesy of the artist

cat. 64 (p. 11)

Please Respect What Breaks When Spoken, 2013

Marble, 20 × 40 × 2 cm
Private collection

cat. 65 (p. 13)

*The Portrait of Time (or Twenty Years of
Instants)*, from the *When Are You More You?*
series, 2015

Pencil on paper, 54.5 × 36.5 cm (day),
59.5 × 41.5 cm (each frame)
Courtesy of the artist

cat. 66 (p. 14)

Untitled, from the *Toward Total Eclipse* series,
2014

Chinese antique bronze mirror partially polished,
ø 13.5 cm
Collection Delphine Dupont

cat. 67 (p. 86)

Untitled #4, from the *Feu la vie* series, 2010

Moulded from a funerary flame and cast in crystal,
13 × 40 × 40 cm
Courtesy of the artist

cat. 68 (p. 92)

Beyond Eros and Thanatos, 1625–2012

Locally devarnished antique painting, 118 × 89 cm
Private collection

cat. 69 (p. 93)

Je m'appelle, 2014

Steel, wood, ink on paper, 75 × 110 × 80 cm
Courtesy of the artist

cat. 70 (p. 94)

Once Androgynous, 2014

Medal, 7 × 12 × 18 cm
Courtesy of the artist

cat. 71 (not illustrated)

Blind Piece 1: Invisible but Tangible, 2016

Plaster (sculpture, 26 × 26 × 18 cm), inkjet print
on paper (protocol, 31.5 × 21.5 × 4 cm)
Courtesy of the artist

cat. 72 (not illustrated)

Untitled, from the *Stigmata* series, 2011

Ink on paper, 25,8 × 18 cm
Courtesy of the artist

cat. 73 (not illustrated)

Ellipse #1, 2011

Oil on canvas, 40 × 60 cm
Private collection

cat. 74 (not illustrated)

Ellipse #2, 2011

Oil on canvas, 40 × 60 cm
Private collection

cat. 75 (not illustrated)

Withered Painting, 2014

Oil on canvas, 65 × 54 cm
Private collection

cat. 76 (not illustrated)

Eye Does Not See Itself, 2016

Mirror and paper, 30 × 21 cm
Courtesy of the artist

cat. 77 (not illustrated)

In the Glimpse of an I, 2016

7 partially polished antique Chinese bronze mirrors,
60 × 175 × 5 cm
Private collection

cat. 78 (not illustrated)

Stairs of Time, 2018

Fossilized ammonite, rose gold plated, leather strap,
22 × 4 × 1.5 cm
Courtesy of the artist

cat. 79 (not illustrated)

The Flight, 2016

Edition of 9/9
Jesmonite and iridescent paint, 16 × 11 × 5 cm
Courtesy of the artist

cat. 80 (not illustrated)

Atlas, from the *Metacosmos* series, 2009

Oil on canvas, 120 × 80 cm
Private collection

The works illustrated on pages 10, 13, 15, 16,
31, 37, 38–39, 48–51, 54–55, 56, 73, 85, 87,
88, 90, 93 (left), and 100 are not shown in
the exhibition *To See with Ellipse*.

<u>Works of other artists
illustrated in this catalogue</u>

p. 32

Bernard van Orley (ca. 1488–1541)
Haneton Triptych, early 1520s,
detail of the central panel

Oil on oak panel, 87.4 × 108 cm (central panel),
87 × 48 cm (each wing)
Brussels, RMFAB, inv. 358

p. 34

Rogier van der Weyden (1399/1400–1464)
La Lamentation, ca. 1441

Oil on oak panel, 32.5 × 47.2 cm
Brussels, RMFAB, inv. 3515

p. 42

Jan Gossaert, also called Mabuse (c. 1478–1532)
Adam and Eve, [n.d.]

Oil on oak panel. 170 × 114.5 cm
Brussels, RMFAB, inv. 3383

p. 46

Lucas Cranach the Elder (1472–1553)
Eve, [n.d.], detail

Oil on wood panel, 177 × 69 cm
Brussels, RMFAB, inv. 2627

p. 57

René Magritte (1898–1967)
The Imp of the Perverse, 1928

Oil on canvas, 81.3 × 116 cm
Brussels, RMFAB, inv. 7418

p. 78

Jan Provoost (ca. 1465–1529)
The Penance of Saint Jerome, [n.d.]

Oil on oak panel, 68.5 × 52.5 cm
Brussels, RMFAB, inv. 10817

p. 89

Georges de La Tour (1593–1652)
Saint Sebastien Tended by Irene, ca. 1649

Oil on canvas, 167 × 131 cm
Paris, Musée du Louvre

p. 92

Giovanni Gerolamo Savoldo
(ca. 1480–after 1548)
Selfportrait, ca. 1529

Oil on canvas, 91 × 123 cm
Paris, Musée du Louvre

p. 104

René Magritte (1898–1967)
Golconde, [1953]

Gouache on cardboard, 158 × 184 mm
Brussels, RMFAB, inv. 11719

p. 106

René Magritte (1898–1967)
Black Magic, [1945]

Oil on canvas, 79 × 59 cm
Brussels, RMFAB, inv. 10706

pp. 108, 117

René Magritte (1898–1967)
The Domain of Arnheim, [1962]

Oil on canvas, 146 × 114 cm
Brussels, RMFAB, inv. 10707

p. 111

René Magritte (1898–1967)
The Empire of Lights, [1954]

Oil on canvas, 146 × 114 cm
Brussels, RMFAB, inv. 6715

p. 114

Bonifazio de' Pitati, also called Veronese
(1487–1553)
Jesus with Simon the Pharisee, [n.d.], detail

Canvas, 195 × 260 cm
Brussels, RMFAB, inv. 280

p. 123

René Magritte (1898–1967)
The Palace of Curtains, [1935]

Oil on canvas mounted on board, 27 × 41 cm
Collection Pierre Alechinsky,
on loan to the Magritte Museum

This catalogue is published
in conjunction with the exhibition

Fabrice Samyn: To See with Ellipse
Royal Museums of Fine Arts of Belgium,
Brussels
October 15, 2021 – February 13, 2022

General Director
Michel Draguet
Secretaries to the director:
Patricia Robeets, Marleen Madou

Exhibition Service
Director and Project Coordinator:
Sophie Van Vliet

Conservation
Managing Director: Inga Rossi-Schrimpf
Secretary: Charles Fumunjere
Curator Contemporary Art: Pierre-Yves
Desaive
Collection Keepers: Ludovic Godfrin,
Cédric Gérard, Laurent Médart

Support Services
Director: Colette Janssen
Secretary: Dries van Wielendaele
Human Ressources: Kristof Sneyers and
his team
Financial Management: Sarra Chebrek and
her team
IT: Benoît Lécailler and Miloud El Moussaoui
Security and Facility Management:
Maarten Lousbergh
Hard Facilities: Yves Vandeven and his team
Soft Facilities and Scenography:
Thu-Maï Dang and her team
Security: Joachim Meert, dispatching and
security staff
Technical and Security Expert: Ives Breels
Electricity and Lighting: Rudy Cloetens and
his team
Translation: Lieve Coene

Public Services
Director: Isabelle Vanhoonacker
Secretary: Dilovan Dogan
Communication, Press and Public Relations:
Amélie Jennequin, Samir Al-Haddad
Graphic Design: Piet Bodyn, Vladimir Tanghe
Cultural Mediation & Made to Measure:
Isabelle Vanhoonacker and her team
Publications: Fabrice Biasino
Patronage and Partnerships: Christine Ayoub
Late-night Openings and Events: Halima
El Ouardi
Front Office: Thomas Vanden Dorpe and
his team

External Collaborators
Transport: Mobull
Insurance: Eeckman Art & Insurance

Publication
General Coordination and Editing:
Fabrice Biasino, RMFAB
Project Management: Richard Viktor
Hagemann, Hatje Cantz
Translations: Michael Abbott (Michel Draguet,
Laurent Dubreuil), Peter Behrman de Sinety
(Donatien Grau)
Copyediting: Aaron Bogart
Graphic Design: Jurgen Persijn (N.N.)
Reproductions: Les Caméléons, Paris
Production: Thomas Lemaître, Hatje Cantz
Printed by Printer Trento s.r.l.
on Magno Volume, 150 g

All rights reserved. No part of this publication
may be reproduced or transmitted in any
form or by any other means, electronic or
mechanical, including photography, recording
or any other information storage and retrieval
system, without prior written permission from
the publisher.

Every effort has been made to trace copyright
holders. If, however, you feel that you have
inadvertently been overlooked, please contact
the publishers.

© 2022 Fabrice Samyn, the RMFAB,
Hatje Cantz Verlag, Berlin, and the authors
© Fabrice Samyn / SABAM Belgium 2022,
for the reproduction of his works
© Succession René Magritte / SABAM
Belgium 2022 – for he works of René Magritte

Published by
Hatje Cantz Verlag GmbH
Mommsenstraße 27
10629 Berlin
www.hatjecantz.com

A Ganske Publishing Group Company

Royal Museum of Fine Arts of Belgium
Rue du Musée, 9
1000 Brussels
Tel. +32 (0)2 508 32 11
www.fine-arts-museum.be

ISBN 978-3-7757-5144-5 (ENG)
ISBN 978-3-7757-5145-2 (FR)
ISBN 978-3-7757-5146-9 (NL)

Printed in Italy

Cover:
Untitled, from the series *Looking from
the Black Hole*, 2015, ink on Rives paper.
Courtesy of the artist

Endpapers:
Je m'appelle, 2021, ink on paper.
Courtesy of the artist

IMAGE CREDITS

Achim Kukulies, courtesy Sies + Höke,
Düsseldorf: pp. 9, 10, 11, 16, 77, 86b, 92a, 97.
Alamy Stock Photo: pp. 89a, 92b.
Hugard & Vanoverschelde Studio: pp. 12, 22,
23, 26, 27, 28, 29, 31, 34–35, 44, 45, 46, 47, 57,
58–59, 68, 102–103, 112–113, 114, 116, 122–123.
Kristien Daem: pp. 19, 105, 109, 110, 111, 117, 119,
120–121.
Luc Vander Plaetse: pp. 33, 79.
Nadia Agmir: p. 20.
Nicolas Dewitte: p. 107.
Philippe de Gobert, Brussels: pp. 13, 14, 15, 21,
25, 37, 38, 39, 40, 41, 43, 48–49, 50, 51, 52, 53,
54–55, 56, 61, 62, 63, 65, 66, 67, 69, 70, 71, 72,
73, 75, 76, 80, 81, 83, 85, 86a, 87, 88ab, 89bc,
90, 91, 93ab, 94, 96, 98, 99, 100, 101, 115.
Royal Museums of Fine Arts of Belgium/
photo: Freya Maes: pp. 32, 42.
Royal Museums of Fine Arts of Belgium/
photo: J. Geleyns – Art Photography: pp. 78,
106, 108.
Vincent Everarts: p. 118.

ACKNOWLEDGMENTS

"Thank you to all the anonymous taxpayers
for continuing to make this museum possible,
as well as to its team who fight to make it a
democratic project beyond the opportunities
for indulgence that art represents for some.
Thank you also to all the lenders who have
made possible the richness and generosity of
the hanging of this exhibition." – F. Samyn

Fabrice Samyn also thanks for their contri-
bution to the exhibition and this publication:
Nadia Agmir, Samir Al-Haddad, Catherine
André-Dumont, Géraldine Barbery, Pierre-Yves
Desaive, Michel Draguet, Laurent Dubreuil,
Frédéric de Goldschmidt, Helena Gomes,
Donatien Grau, Nina Hoeke, Benjamin Hugard,
Barbara Kandiyoti, Elaine Lévy, Cédric and
Cookie Liénart de Jeude, Sylvain Peeters,
Jurgen Persijn, Béatrice Ralet, Amandine
Samyn, Renaud Samyn, Virginie Samyn,
Alexander Sies, Ibrahim Tamditi, Jean-Philippe
Theyskens, Marie-Anne Truffino, Sophie
Van Vliet, and Antoine Vanoverschelde.

Fabrice Samyn and the RMFAB dedicate
this exhibition in memory of Cédric Liénart,
and to his wife Cookie. Cédric was at the
origin of this project and we wish to express
our thanks.

The exhibition *Fabrice Samyn: To See with
Ellipse* is supported by

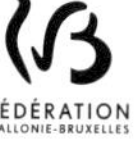

Je m'appelle, Je m'appelle, Je m'appelle, Je m'appelle
Je m'appelle, Je m'appelle, Je m'appelle, Je m'appelle
Je m'appelle, Je m'appelle, Je m'appelle, Je m'appelle
Je m'appelle, Je m'appelle, Je m'appelle, Je m'appelle
Je m'appelle, Je m'appelle, Je m'appelle, Je m'appelle
Je m'appelle, Je m'appelle, Je m'appelle, Je m'appelle
Je m'appelle, Je m'appelle, Je m'appelle, Je m'appelle
Je m'appelle, Je m'appelle, Je m'appelle, Je m'appelle
Je m'appelle, Je m'appelle, Je m'appelle, Je m'appelle
Je m'appelle, Je m'appelle, Je m'appelle, Je m'appelle
Je m'appelle, Je m'appelle, Je m'appelle, Je m'appelle
Je m'appelle, Je m'appelle, Je m'appelle, Je m'appelle
Je m'appelle, Je m'appelle, Je m'appelle, Je m'appelle
Je m'appelle, Je m'appelle, Je m'appelle, Je m'appelle